The Immense Ocean
Al-Baḥr al-Madīd

A Thirteenth/Eighteenth Century Quranic Commentary
on the Chapters of *The All-Merciful, The Event*, and *Iron*
from

The Immense Ocean

Al-Baḥr al-Madīd

by

Aḥmad ibn ʻAjība (d. 1224/1809)

Translated and Annotated by

Mohamed Fouad Aresmouk and
Michael Abdurrahman Fitzgerald

2009

FONS VITAE

First published in 2009 by
Fons Vitae
49 Mockingbird Valley Drive
Louisville, KY 40207
http://www.fonsvitae.com

Library of Congress Control Number: 2008942941

ISBN 9781891785283

This book was typeset by Neville Blakemore, Jr.

Printed in Canada

Ornamental Eastern Kufic border from Qur'an written by
Ahmad Ibn Muhammad Ibn Kamal Al-Ansari Al-Mutatabbib,
734/1334, Cairo, National Library, Egypt.
With gratitude to the Thesaurus Islamicus Foundation.

Dedicated to the memory of Ḥājj Muḥammād Belḥājj Aresmouk of Marrakesh and Mulay ‘Abdessalām al-Darqāwī of Sale who spent their lives patiently teaching the Book of God to countless grateful students, and to our beloved teacher, Mulay Hāchim al-Belghītī al-Maknāsī.

Contents

The first page of the manuscript version of *al-Baḥr al-Madīd* completed in 1221/1806 by the scribe ʿAbd al-Ghafūr al-Tuhāmī and corrected by Ibn ʿAjība himself. From the collection of *Dār al-kutub al-miṣriyya*, ref. 26246.

Foreword

> Within any given revealed or scripture-oriented religion there will be three marked tendencies: "the people of the text," or the literalists; then the rationalists, who will try to understand the text with their rational faculty (*al-'aql*); and [finally] the "people of the spirit," those who seek to understand and actualize the essential meaning of the 'word' within their own innermost beings, these are the mystics (*rabbāniyūn*).
>
> Shaykh 'Abdal Ḥalīm Maḥmūd

Aḥmad ibn 'Ajība's commentary on the chapters of *The All-Merciful, The Event,* and *Iron* taken from his Quranic commentary, *al-Baḥr al-Madīd* (*The Immense Ocean*) is an eloquent example of the manner in which the outward and inward facets of Islamic intellectual discourse contextualize the mystical/ethical norms that have traditionally defined Islamic social and religious life. This wedding of traditional linguistic commentary with teachings of the Sufi *ishārī* traditions (mystical allusion) provides the modern reader with clear insights into the role that Quranic commentary has played in the formation and transmission of the normative ethical teachings of Islam. This translation specifically portrays the multifaceted manner in which Quranic commentary actively reintegrates the Qur'ān, Islam's foundational source of knowledge, into the on-going discourse on what constitutes the Islamic worldview, its values and ethical norms, while in a more general sense affirming the Qur'ān's importance as a source within the ethical discourse of today's larger world community.

Ethics has been the central thread of traditional scholarly discourse in the Muslim world for over fourteen centuries, but it is not centuries of scholarly discourse that make ethics an important issue today. We live in a time when the ethical values that have traditionally been the foundation stones of our societies have come under question and are, in the eyes of many, in need of re-evaluation. Globalization, political activism and radical religious ideologies have forced upon many people today a view of the world in which the only ethical options offered are a choice between secular humanism or a pragmatic ethics of survival. The rhetoric of the 'Clash of Civilizations' has marked our communities today until the spiritual roots that have traditionally defined the moral basis of social interaction seem unrealistic and childish. Many people question whether any religious tradition meets the needs of today's diverse and changing world. This dilemma is not unique to one faith tradition over another. Yet given the current crisis the Muslim community faces today and the clear-cut nature of the framework from which Muslims have traditionally drawn their ethical inspiration—the Qur'ān and the traditions of the Prophet Muḥammad—that such a dilemma should be afflicting the Muslim community at all is most disquieting.

Traditional normative Islam has always included both the exoteric and esoteric dimensions, the latter being Sufism, the inherently ethical teaching methodology that constitutes the process of spiritual transformation or a path on which the journeyer passes through various states, stages or domains of knowledge of God as he or she encounters more and more subtle states of intimacy with the Divine. The commentary being presented here was written by a renowned master of both the exoteric and esoteric domains. Ibn 'Ajība is however, best known as a Sufi. His *Īqāẓ al-himam* (The Awakening of Aspiration), an esoteric commentary on the *Kitāb al-ḥikm* (The Book of Wisdom), Ibn 'Aṭā' Allāh's collection of Sufi aphorisms is one of the most widely read in the Islamic world. Ibn 'Ajība saw Sufism as a process of reorientation of an individual's ego-self until it awakens to its true nature and perceives the phenomenal world, not as a discrete entity separate from God, but as a continuum of divine presences, or centers of divine manifestation. This process gave rise to Sufi pedagogic methods that from the earliest times were portrayed as the result of the complimentary interplay between outward conduct, inner spiritual states, and divine grace. The most basic characteristic of this educational process was and is compliance with the legal foundations of Islamic society, the Qur'ān and the Sunna. These two were the keys to the direct and intimate knowledge of God. Sufism was for Ibn 'Ajība, a direct function of these two keys as much as it was a process of transformation or reorientation of the ego-self. In his commentary on the *sūras* presented here, Ibn 'Ajība communicates with his reader on multiple levels. For from his broad perspective of what constitutes Islamic spirituality, the degree to which a person was participating in the process of transformation actively or passively was the degree to which one was participating in Islamic spirituality itself. To Ibn 'Ajība this included everyone: scholars, jurists, Sufis and the generality of believing Muslims alike. He knew that even those who were not actively part of a Sufi order or those believers that had neither the time nor means to pursue traditional studies always had the opportunity to gain exposure to these teachings as they filtered through Friday sermons, public lessons and exhortatory lectures in mosques, and through the everyday, inherited wisdom and shared collective understanding of the *umma*.

The appearance of this work at the present time is heartening. Sufism is rarely mentioned today as a foundational element of Islamic intellectual discourse. The fact that the spiritual heirs and exemplars of the highest ideals and values of the Muslim community, the mentors of the Sufi path, have almost been forgotten is indicative of the acute nature of the dilemma Muslims face today. This well researched and meticulously worded work refocuses attention upon Sufism as an important source of our knowledge of the Qur'ān, the sacred text of Islam. It is worth mentioning here as well that the interest in Sufi commentary has seen an increase in the Muslim world and that over the last few years, two new editions of *al-Baḥr al-Madīd* have been published and both have become among the best-selling Quranic commentaries (*tafāsīr*) in many Arabic-speaking lands along with a greatly increased interest in traditional Sufi works in general. It is also heartening to hear of the project to translate the entirety of this commentary into French. We therefore owe *Fons Vitae* a debt of gratitude for this initial publication from *al-Baḥr al-Madīd* in English and hope to see more in the near future.

Let me add that this work is relevant for the Muslim and non-Muslim, the specialist and non-specialist alike. This work would be a welcome addition to any university level course dealing with Quranic exegesis or Islamic thought. Anyone drawn to the domains of human spirituality and psychology will find in this work a wealth of Sufi teachings and technical terminology, on the one hand, and an intimate discourse on multiple levels with the soul or human psyche, on the other. Finally, this work offers anyone seeking a deeper understanding of the human spirit a testimony to humanity's timeless spiritual quest and textual sources it is drawn from.

Kenneth L. Honerkamp
University of Georgia
December, 2008

Acknowledgements

We would like to thank the following people who helped make this work possible: Virginia Gray Henry, of *Fons Vitae*, for her on-going encouragement and enthusiasm; Dr. Kenneth Honerkamp for his support, suggestions, and for taking time from an already very full academic schedule to write the foreword to this work; our dear friends Brahim Zoubairi and Hamza Weinman for their help with certain points of translation and style; Eli H. Brown V for his excellent proofreading; and Nora and Mariam Fitzgerald for reading and editing the final manuscript. Lastly, none of this work would have been possible without the love and patience of our spouses.

Mohammed Fouad Aresmouk
Michael Abdurrahman Fitzgerald
Marrakesh, Morocco
25 Ramadan, 1428 (October, 2007)

Introduction

Thus does God explain His signs in order that you might reflect.

Qur'ān, Chapter of the Cow, Verse 219

The Beginnings of *Tafsīr*

From the perspective of traditional Islam, the first commentary (*tafsīr*) of the Qur'ān is to be found in the Qur'ān itself, and so the first commentator (*mufassir*) is the One who revealed it. God's *tafsīr* may be direct: one verse may explain another, or a given incident may be told and then retold in a different context. In some cases, a verse may even ask the one to whom it was first revealed, the Prophet Muḥammad, and by extension all who will ever read it, *And what will convey to you what* this *is?* and then provide a definition.[1] In a more general sense, however, God's *tafsīr* of His Book is the gradual unveiling of its meanings to the one who reads it with faith and tries to live according to it. This process, summed up by the words, *Observe your duty to God and God will teach you,* [2:282][2] is what al-Ghazālī was referring to when he quoted one of the saints as having said, "There is a reading of the entire Qur'ān I complete once a week, another I complete once a month, another once a year, and there is a reading that I have been trying to complete for the past thirty years but have not been able to do so."[3] It is also what the Prophet's wife 'Ā'isha meant when she was asked after his death, "What was his character like?" and she answered, "It was the Qur'ān."[4]

Inseparable, then, from an understanding of the Sacred Book is an understanding of the *sunna*, the words and deeds of the Prophet Muḥammad. In this case, too, *tafsīr* may be explicit or implicit. All traditional *ḥadīth* collections include chapters recounting what the Prophet said about particular verses, sometimes in answer to direct questions posed to him by the Companions, and other times in the midst of certain situations when he would recite a given verse and say in so many words, 'This that we are now living is what these words of God mean.' In addition to this, however, are the narratives of how he put into practice what had been revealed. The ritual ablution and canonic prayer, for example, are ordained in the Qur'ān and described in general terms, but the actual method by which they are accomplished can only be understood from the *sunna*.

After the Prophetic *tafsīr*, the next means by which to understand the verses are the sayings of the Companions, those who were in direct contact with the Prophet and witnesses to the revelation as it unfolded. Jalāl al-Dīn al-Suyūṭī, in his classic work *al-Itqān fī 'ulūm al-Qur'ān*, identified ten of these in particular: the first four caliphs, Abū Bakr, 'Umar, 'Uthmān, and 'Alī, followed by Ibn Mas'ūd, Ibn 'Abbās, Ibn Ka'b, Zayd ibn Thābit, Abū Mūsā al-Ash'arī, and 'Abd Allāh ibn al-Zubayr.[5] Of them, Ibn 'Abbās, who was still a boy when the Prophet died but who then devoted the rest of his life to collecting and memorizing *tafsīr* gathered from the older Companions, would become known as *tarjumān al-Qur'ān*, the Interpreter of the Qur'ān, and is probably the single most cited of the Companions in all *tafsīr* literature.[6]

In the generation that followed the Companions, the Followers *(al-tābi'ūn)*, Ibn 'Abbas' commentary was preserved and conveyed principally by two people, 'Ikrima, his freed slave, and Mujāhid ibn Jabr al-Makkī. 'Ikrima is reported to have said, "Ibn 'Abbās would shackle my foot and teach me the *ḥadīth* and *sunna*," and also, "Everything I have spoken of concerning the Qur'ān is from (him)." As for Mujāhid, he said, "I went over the written text of the Qur'ān with Ibn 'Abbās three times, stopping at every verse and asking him about the circumstances and manner of its revelation."[7]

It should be remembered, however, that while the Qur'ān itself had been put into writing during the life of the Prophet, recopied and collated into a single document during the caliphate of Abū Bakr, and recopied once again during the caliphate of 'Uthmān,[8] the predominant mode of transmitting the teachings related to it was oral. This was due both to the extreme reluctance towards doing something that had not been done by the Prophet, as well as concern that the revelation itself remain pristine. As al-Ghazālī mentions in the Eighth Book of *al-Iḥya'*, there was strong opposition on the part of some of the Followers even to the addition of diacritical marks or divisions to the written text of the Qur'ān. "It may be supposed," he writes, "that...they wished to keep this door closed out of their great desire to guard the text from anything that might alter it."[9] Thus, *tafsīr* remained largely oral.

By the end of the second/eighth century, however, there were enough external factors in place to make written, systematic expositions of all facets of Islamic knowledge inevitable. These factors included the spread of the religion to more and more non-Arabic speaking peoples, the confrontation of opposing points of view from both within and without the Muslim *umma*, and the need to codify knowledge that was being lost or misunderstood. Thus, following the great written compilations of *ḥadīth* --- Imām Mālik's *Muwaṭṭa'* was completed by his death in 179/796, while the Bukhārī and Muslim collections date to around 235/850 --- the collection and writing of *tafsīr* into a single book became both the obvious and necessary next step.[10]

Books of Commentary

The first formal works of *tafsīr* consisted of the verses of the Qur'ān arranged in order, each followed by usually lengthy chains of transmission (*asānid*) leading back to what the Prophet or one or more of the Companions and Followers had said concerning it or concerning a particular phrase it contained. Although it is known that there were numerous such narrative commentaries (*tafāsir bi al-riwāyā*) set down during the third/ninth century, the one work which has survived and is unquestioned in its authenticity would be Ibn Jarīr al-Ṭabarī's *Jāmi' al-Bayān fī ta'wīl al-Qur'ān*, probably completed around the year 280/893. Comparing this monumental thirty-volume work to other commentaries near it in time, al-Suyūṭī says:

> All of them relate the sayings of the Companions, Followers, and those who followed them, and there is naught but this in any of them, except in Ibn Jarīr's, for he also compares what some said (about a verse) to what others said, and indicates which of them was strongest. He also mentions the vocalization [of certain words] and what can be derived from them, so in this respect, his *tafsīr* exceeded others [commentaries of the time].[11]

For al-Suyūṭī, Quranic commentary after al-Ṭabarī began to show certain deficiencies. Their authors "abbreviated the chains of transmission, and conveyed comments without citing their sources. Thus did the extraneous enter and the sound become mixed with what was weak." At this same time specialized commentaries began to appear: those which did nothing but address the grammar of verses (*tafsīr naḥwī*), or those which concentrated on legal applications (*tafsīr fiqhī*), those which made copious use of sayings and stories (*tafsīr akhbārī*); and those which included philosophic expositions. Of this latter sort, al-Suyūṭī singles out in particular the commentary of Fakhr al-Dīn al-Rāzī (d. 606/1209), referred to variously as *al-Mafātīḥ al-ghayb*, *Tafsīr al-Rāzī* or *al-Tafsīr al-kabīr*. About this remarkable work, which like al-Ṭabarī's spans thirty volumes, al-Suyūṭī says:

> He filled his commentary with sayings from sages, philosophers and the like, moving from one thing to the other, until one is astonished by how little [of what is being said] has to do with the verse itself. Thus did Abū Ḥayyān say… "Imām al-Rāzī collected in his *tafsīr* so many and lengthy things unneeded in the science of *tafsīr* that a certain scholar went so far as to say, 'It contains everything but *tafsīr*!'"

Whether one agrees with this view or not, it could be said the thirty volumes of al-Ṭabarī and the thirty volumes of al-Rāzī to some extent mark the two poles of narrative commentary (*riwāya*) and intellectual commentary (*dirāya*), both of which are to be found in Ibn 'Ajība's *al-Baḥr al-Madīd*.

Sufic Commentary

Although it is beyond the scope of this introduction to go any further than this into the principles and varieties of Quranic exegesis, because the commentary translated in the pages to follow was written by a Sufi and contains a Sufic element, something needs to be said concerning *tafsīr ishārī* (commentary by spiritual allusion).

From the third/ninth century on, those who would later be referred to as Sufis, the mystics of Islam, began to put into writing their reflections on certain of the verses of the Holy Book. Among the earliest extant examples of these are the commentary of Sahl al-Tustarī (d. 283/896), *Ḥaqā'iq al-tafsīr* (*Inner Truths*) by 'Abd al-Raḥmān al-Sulamī (d. 412/1021) and *Laṭā'if al-ishāra* (*Subtleties of Spiritual Allusion*) by 'Abd al-Karīm al-Qushayrī (d. 465/1072). In such works the mystic attempted to express either a personal insight into a given verse, how the verse might relate to the microcosm of the soul, or what special significance it held for those on the mystic path of Islam.

The difficulty that some scholars had with such works was in trying to reconcile them with the well-known saying of the Prophet, "Whoever says what is in the Qur'ān based on his own opinion has prepared his place in Hellfire."[12] In other words, where does one draw the line between trying to explain the Qur'ān based on subjective opinion, which has always been considered unlawful, and talking about the inner meaning of its verses that someone in the mystic path might have personally experienced? This is a question that al-Ghazālī addressed in detail in Book Eight of *al-Iḥyā'*[13] and will be addressed in the section that follows by Ibn 'Ajība himself, but one of the simplest and most succinct answers is again provided by al-Suyūṭī in *al-Itqān* where he begins by saying, "The words of the Sufis about the Qur'ān are not *tafsīr*" and then quotes the renowned exegete al-Nasafī from his work on the tenets of theology: "The texts [of Qur'ān and *ḥadīth*] are according to their outward meanings, and to equate these to the meanings which the esoterists claim is heretical." Al-Suyūṭī then continues:

> In his explanation [of al-Nasafī's comment] al-Taftāzānī says: "They are considered heretical if they claim that texts do not mean what they literally say but rather have meanings that only the learned know, intending thereby the total negation of the Revealed Law. But as for what certain of the people of realization have said—that the (sacred) texts should be taken according to their literal meaning but that besides this, they contain subtle allusions to spiritual truths which are uncovered to people following the mystic path and that there is a possible correspondance between them and the outward intended sense—this is perfect faith and pure gnosis.[14]

Such is precisely the perspective of Ibn 'Ajība, whose explanation of this point is quoted in full in the pages that follow.

The Life of Aḥmad ibn 'Ajība[15]

Sīdī Bin 'Ajība, as he is affectionately referred to in Morocco, was born in the village of al-Khamīs, about 20 kilometers northwest of Tetouan, in the year 1160 or 1161 H. (1747 or 48). As was normal for a boy belonging to an erudite Sharifian[16] family and showing an aptitude for learning, the young Aḥmad's education from its earliest days centered upon religious knowledge. This would consist first in the memorization of the Qur'ān, which he completed at an early age, followed by study of the essential texts (*mutūn*) which constituted a traditional Islamic education in Morocco until fairly recently. This included such shorter works as the *Ajrūmiyya* and *Alfiyya*, both of which treat Arabic grammar, Ibn 'Ashir's *al-Murshid al-Mu'īn* on the fundamentals of the religion, and the *Ḥirz al-Amānī* , a long *qaṣīda* by al-Shāṭibī (d. 540/1194) based on 'Amr al-Dānī's (444/1053) famous treatise concerning the seven Quranic recitations.

By the age of eighteen, Ibn 'Ajība was ready to pursue higher studies of religious sciences (*al-'ulūm*) in Qaṣr al-Kabīr and Fes. Even discounting the almost deranged fervor with which he undertook these studies, "jumping into them so totally that [he] neglected any of [his] personal affairs,"[17] it appears that by the time he reached his late twenties, Ibn 'Ajība was well on the road to becoming the traditional Moroccan *'ālim*, living a life of books and teaching, respectable and respected by all around him.

This situation would begin to change, however, after he was given a copy of the famous compendium of practical mysticism, *Kitāb al-Ḥikam* by Ibn 'Aṭā' Allāh, along with its best known commentary, *al-Muwāhib al-ghaythiyya fī sharḥ al-ḥikam al-'aṭā'iyya* written by the man most responsible for making known the fundamental teachings of the Shādhilī Sufic path in Morocco, Ibn 'Abbād al-Rundī (d. 792/1390). According to his own account,

> After this reading, I abandoned exoteric knowledge and dedicated myself to devotional practice, to the remembrance of God, and to the invocation of blessings upon God's Messenger. Then I felt a desire to practice retreat and I began to detest the world and its denizens: when someone approached me, I fled... [18]

So strong was this state that he finally resolved to sell all his books and retire to nearby Jebal 'Alam to take up a life of reclusion and invocation near the tomb of Ibn Mashīsh.[19] It was a vision at the tomb of Sīdī Ṭalḥa, one of the local saints of Tetouan, which convinced him to persevere a little longer with outward knowledge. Nonetheless, in his own words, "...my mind was already oriented in its Master's direction, and my entire heart was with God. I took my place in the circle of students out of consideration for the Shaykh who had ordered me to study, but I did not know what the teacher was speaking about, so occupied was I with the invocation of God."[20]

It would be another ten years, however, at the age of about forty-seven, before Ibn 'Ajība, by this time a married man with children and one of the most respected scholars of Tetouan, was to meet the master who would formally initiate him into a *ṭarīqah*, or Sufic order. According to his own account, this took place in 1208/1793-94 on a trip back from Fes during which he stopped at a well-known *zāwiya* in Benī Zarwāl. There he met not only the most famous Moroccan spiritual master of the day, Mūlay al-'Arabī al-Darqāwī, but also one of his foremost disciples, Sīdī Muḥammad al-Buzīdī. This latter, at the behest of Mūlay al-'Arabī, would become Ibn 'Ajība's mentor in the sufic path and begin to guide him through the type of training of the lower self characteristic of Moroccan Sufism at the time. This training began with a series of ever more demeaning tasks aimed at 'slaying the *nafs,*' or breaking the strong sense of self and pride that might characterize someone of Ibn 'Ajība's status. For example, instead of being given a daily *wird*, or litany, to recite, the respected and honored scholar was told to don a patched cloak (*al-khirqa*), to beg at the entrance to the mosque, and sweep the marketplace. In a matter of weeks, his former colleagues among of the religious scholars (*'ulamā'*) of Tetuoan could scarcely look at him when they passed him in the street or while leaving the mosque on Friday.

The next phase of Ibn 'Ajība's education, at the behest of his shaykh, involved traveling on foot with other Darqāwī *fuqarā'* [21] from village to village along the rugged mountain paths of the Anjara region. Often barefoot and wearing the characteristic large-beaded rosary (*subḥāt*) around their necks, the group would walk for miles through the mountains, chanting the *shahādah* or other formula of praise, and upon coming to a village would call the locals to renew their faith through the invocation of God and the company of the pious. In many instances, they would be met with scorn and even volleys of stones. At other times, however, they would be welcomed, and nearly a whole village, women included, would join the *ṭarīqah.*

It was inevitable that Ibn 'Ajība and his spiritual companions would find themselves coming into conflict with local authorities, part of whose job in Morocco has always been to be on guard against movements that could possibly undermine the general order. In 1209/1794, Ibn 'Ajība and a number of *fuqarā'* were jailed for a short time. The accusation raised against them was that they were encouraging "dangerous innovations," among which was the wearing of the patched cloak and their practice of allowing women to attend (in a separate room) the gatherings of *dhikr*.

Although Ibn 'Ajība, thanks to his family's noble rank, was quickly cleared and released, it seems that Shaykh al-Buzīdi deemed it best for him and some companions to travel out of the area completely, towards Sale and Rabat. It was during this time that his master bade him to write esoteric commentaries on works such as the *Ḥikam* of Ibn 'Aṭā' Allāh, the *Khamriyya* of Ibn al-Fāriḍ, and the *Taṣliyya* of Ibn Mashīsh.

This period of spiritual travel (*siyāḥa*) lasted about five years. In around 1214/1799, the Shaykh returned to the north of Morocco to the village of Djimmīj in the hills about 30 kilometers from Tangier where he built a house and spent the last years of his life.

By the time of his death in 1224/1809, Ibn 'Ajība was recognized as a spiritual master in his own right, testified to by the letters of advice and spiritual instruction he was writing to various *fuqarā'*.[22] Besides a prolific body of writings surpassing thirty works, Ibn 'Ajība's legacy includes the branch of the Shādhiliyya-Darqāwiyya sufic line that to this day bears his name, *al-Ṭarīqah al-Darqāwiyya al-'Ajībiyya*. His tomb in the village of Djimmīj continues to be the site of a yearly spiritual gathering (*mawsim*) every August which attracts hundreds of *fuqarā'* of this *ṭarīqah* and others from all over Morocco.

The Composition of *al-Baḥr al-Madīd*

Date of Composition

According to Michon's chronology, Ibn 'Ajība began work on his commentary in or around the year 1214/1799.[23] It appears that during the seven years that followed, he worked simultaneously on a number of treatises, but it may be supposed from the voluminous references he cites that most of the *tafsīr* was set down after his return to Djimmīj where his library was. When one considers that he wrote much of *al-Baḥr al-Madīd* during a time when an outbreak of the plague was claiming hundreds of lives a day throughout the north of Morocco, including most of his children,[24] both the sheer quantity of his work as well as the spiritual station from which he viewed the world are all the more amazing.

The date of completing the final correction, recorded by the Shaykh himself at the end of the last volume, was Sunday, the sixth of Rabīʻa al-Nubūwa (= al-awwal), 1221 Hijrī (13 May, 1806), a little more than three years before his death on 22 Shawwal, 1224/30 November, 1809. *Raḥimahu Allāh.*

The Style

As the Shaykh himself writes in the introduction to *al-Baḥr al-Madīd*, his goal was to compose a work containing exoteric commentary and spiritual allusion—*tafsīr* and *ishāra*—for the entire Qur'ān which would be of medium length.[25] Thus the chains of transmission (*asānid*) for any *ḥadīth* mentioned are usually abbreviated to the primary narrator and quotations from earlier works are often indicated simply by the word *qīl* ("and it has been said"). As for the references he cites by name, of these he appears to favor the commentaries of al-Nasafī (d. 537/1142), Ibn ʻAṭiyya (d. 542/1148) and especially al-Qushayrī (d. 465/1072), from which he quotes extensively both in the sections of commentary as well as in sections of spiritual allusion.[26] A fourth source Ibn ʻAjība cites frequently in his spiritual allusions is al-Wartajibī. This source, whom the editors of the published Arabic editions of *al-Baḥr al-Madīd* have left unreferenced, has been recently identified as the Persian Sufi and scholar, Ruzbihān al-Baqlī (d. 606/1209), the author of the remarkable mystical commentary *ʻArā'is al-bayān*.[27] It may be supposed that the name Ibn ʻAjība cites as the commentator was actually that of either a scribe or the original owner of the manuscript of *al-ʻArā'is* that Ibn ʻAjība had in his library.

Lastly, it should be pointed out that although Ibn ʻAjība goes to some length to separate the *ishārī* (or Sufic) commentary from the traditional commentary, the former nonetheless permeates the latter in many places. By the time Ibn ʻAjība wrote this commentary, having spent thirteen years in total dedication to the *Ṭarīqah Darqawiyya*, he was undoubtedly a Sufi first and an exoteric scholar second.

Arabic Editions

For nearly 150 years after his death, Ibn ʻAjība's commentary existed in manuscripts only and was known principally within Sufic circles of North Africa and the Middle East. It was not until 1373/1953 that a printed edition was published by Dar al-Thanā' in Egypt containing the commentary from the beginning of the Qur'ān until verse 3:190. It would take another forty-five years, in 1999, for the first authoritative and complete printed edition of *al-Baḥr al-Madīd*, based on the best existing manuscripts and edited by Aḥmad 'Abd Allāh al-Qurshī Rislān, to see the light of day. The first four volumes of this six-volume work appeared in 1999, the fifth in 2000, and the sixth and last in 2001. It is from this sixth volume that the excerpt translated in the pages to follow was taken.

About this Translation

Our goal in translation has been to render into English a representative sample of what traditional Quranic commentary, whether exoteric or esoteric, has been for centuries. We have sought to produce a text that is both readable and useful while maintaining as closely as possible the meaning and tone of the original. To achieve these ends, we have made the following modifications and additions to the actual work:

1. Ibn 'Ajība's brief grammatical explanations at the beginning of each section of commentary, usually quite technical in nature, have been omitted except in cases where they explain a variation of meaning that is comprehensible in English. In this latter case, they have sometimes been partially included or else added as an endnote in a summarized form.
2. Where Ibn 'Ajība supplies an Arabic synonym for a given word that is already self-evident in the translation of the Quranic verses themselves, this synonym has been omitted, marked by three points (…).
3. In the Arabic editions of *al-Baḥr al-Madīd*, only the sections on spiritual allusion (*ishāra*) are indicated by a separate heading. We have chosen, however, to add the heading *Commentary* at the beginning of each section of more exoterically oriented *tafsīr* in order to clearly distinguish it from the *ishāra*, which is under the heading *Spiritual Allusion*.
4. The group of verses being commented upon have been placed in a vertical column which includes their numbers at the head of each section of commentary. These follow Ibn 'Ajība's divisions in the Arabic text. In addition to this, for the sake of clarity and ease of use, we have also set off individual verses immediately above the paragraph which explains them.
5. For the basic translation of the Qur'ān, we have relied mainly on the Pickthall version, but have replaced the older English forms (thou, thy, ye) that Pickthall used with their modern

forms. If Ibn 'Ajība's commentary defines a word differently from Pickthall's translation, we have modified the translation to be consistent with Ibn 'Ajība's usage. All Quranic quotations appear in italics, and citations of verses other than those being commented on are followed by the number of the *sūra* and verse in brackets.

6. We have sought to include sources for all the *ḥadīth* Ibn 'Ajība quotes and, in some cases, have added additional comments on particular verses from other traditional commentaries. All these are included in the endnotes.

   In annotating *ḥadīth*, we have used the following abbreviations:

Bukhārī :	*Ṣaḥīḥ al-Bukhārī*
Muslim:	*Ṣaḥīḥ Muslim*
Tirmidhī :	*Sunan al-Tirmidhī*
Nasā'ī:	*Sunan al-Nasā'ī*
Abū Dāwūd:	*Sunan Abī Dāwūd*
Mālik:	*al-Muwaṭṭa'*
Ibn Māja:	*Sunan Ibn Māja*
Aḥmad:	*Musnad Imām Aḥmad ibn Ḥanbal*
Bayhaqī:	*Shu'ab al-īmān*,
Ṭabarānī,	*al-Awsaṭ*: *Mu'jam al-awsaṭ*
	al-Kabīr: *Mu'jam al-kabīr*
Ḥākim:	*al-Mustadrak 'alā ṣaḥīḥayn*
Ibn Ḥibbān:	*Saḥīḥ ibn Ḥibbān*

   Other *ḥadīth* sources are cited by complete title.

   In addition to *ḥadīth*, because of Ibn 'Ajība's numerous direct or indirect references to the *Kitāb al-Ḥikam* in the *ishāra* sections, we have noted the numbers of the particular aphorism to which he refers following the system used in the Victor Danner translation (see bibliography). We have also generally depended on this translation for the wording of the aphorisms themselves.

7. We have supplied three indices to the text: one of Quranic verses, another of *ḥadīth*, and a third general index. In addition, we have indexed the names of all historical figures mentioned in the body of the commentary (apart from Prophets) in a biographical appendix.

8. In certain cases, the formulas of blessing which Islamic spiritual courtesy requires be mentioned or written following the names of Prophets, *may peace be upon them*, and the saintly,

may God be well-pleased with them, have been left for the reader who wishes to benefit from this practice to supply.

9. References to God in Arabic religious writing, either by the noun *Allāh* or by a pronoun, are usually followed by a formula or adjective of praise such as *be He glorified and exalted!* or *the Exalted!* In many cases, we have omitted these expressions and let capitalization of He, Him, or His suffice. It should be mentioned, however, that use of the masculine pronoun is a convention of the Arabic language and by no means a sign of gender, nor is *Allāh* in any way conceived of as having gender.
10. Related to this same question, we have striven to render Ibn ʻAjība's text as gender neutral as possible. The use of the masculine forms of pronouns, verbs, and adjective to indicate the indefinite was and is simply a convention of the Arabic language. But there is no doubt that Ibn ʻAjība undertook this work for the benefit of all, regardless of gender, who were seeking to deepen their understanding of the Qur'ān and their relation to God.

The Fifty-Fourth *Ḥizb*

A final comment is perhaps in order about why we chose to translate the Fifty-Fourth portion (*ḥizb*) of the Qur'ān, known in Morocco as *Ḥizb al-Raḥmān* after the *sūra* with which it begins. There are a number of reasons for this choice. Firstly, we felt that the theme of Divine Mercy, which dominates *Sūrat al-Raḥmān* and continues to reverberate throughout the *ḥizb*, is something anyone living in our times could benefit from remembering. There was also the purely logistical wish to choose a portion that began and ended with the beginning and ending of a *sūra*. In addition, the three *sūras* contained in this *ḥizb* are among the most frequently recited, widely known, and best-loved throughout in the Muslim world. Every school child in Morocco is still required to memorize this *ḥizb* along with some simple explanation by the time he or she completes grammar school. Therefore, the *sūras* it contains are often recited—aloud and in chorus following the Moroccan tradition—at spiritual gatherings or on other occasions. Indeed, in traditional Moroccan families—more so in years past than today—most children would begin memorizing the Qur'ān from the end, where the shorter *sūras* are, and upon reaching *al-Raḥmān*, would be given a small party to celebrate during which the child would recite before all those present and be given gifts and sweets.

The individual *sūras* contained in this *ḥizb* also have their special qualities. *Al-Raḥmān*, according to a *ḥadīth*, is called "the Bride of the Qur'ān"[28] and from a purely phonetic standpoint, because of its repeated refrain and the sound which ends each verse (an extended *ān*), it is one of the most beautiful sounding of all the *sūras* of the Qur'ān. *Al-Wāqi'a,* besides its special virtues described in the *ḥadīths* quoted in the body of the commentary, is also regularly recited in the group litanies of many Sufic fraternities, notably the Ṭarīqa 'Alawiyya. *Al-Ḥadīd*, for its part, is among the *musabbiḥāt*, the *sūras* that begin with the verb of glorification (*sabbaḥa/ yusabbiḥu*), which the Prophet, upon whom be peace, is said to have recited before sleep and about which he said, "In them is a verse more excellent than a thousand verses."[29] According to Bayhaqī, in *Dalā'il al-Nubūwa*, it was after reading the beginning of *al-Ḥadīd* (rather than *Ṭā Ha*, as reported in Ibn Hishām) that 'Umar ibn al-Khaṭṭāb embraced Islām.[30]

Apart from these qualities, all three of these *sūras* are among those which the late and revered scholar and teacher, Abū Bakr Sirāj al-Dīn (Martin Lings), used to call "the golden *sūras*," those in which the beauty of sound, theme, and meaning combine in perfect and sublime equilibrium.

The Tomb of Sidi Aḥmad ibn ʿAjība in Djimmīj.
The Mediterranean Sea is just beyond the hills on the horizon.

Notes on the Introduction

1. As in [97:1-4]: *Verily, We have revealed it on the Night of Power. And what will convey to you what the Night of Power is? The Night of Power is better than a thousand months. The angels and the Spirit descend therein.* This same formula occurs in twelve other places in the Qur'ān.

2. This phrase ends the single longest verse in the Qur'ān, [2:282].

3. Ghazālī, *Iḥyā' 'ulūm al-dīn*, Book Eight of the First Quarter, Chapter 3.

4. Muslim, *Ṣalāt al-Musāfir*, 139.

5. Suyūṭī's *al-Itqān fī 'ulūm al-Qur'ān*, v. 4, p. 189. In these introductory remarks, we have relied heavily upon this work, possibly the most widely recognized and comprehensive traditional source on the Quranic sciences.

6. Because of his descent from the Prophet's uncle, Ibn 'Abbās is recognized as an authority by both Sunni and Shi'a Muslims.

7. Suyūṭī, op. cit. p. 194-195.

8. In the first volume of *al-Itqān*, al-Suyūṭī relates how the Qur'ān was collected three times. The first was when the Prophet instructed his scribe, Zayd ibn Thābit, to collect the verses of the Qur'ān which had been previously written down on scraps of leather, flat stones, and pieces of palm bark, and to place them into *sūrahs*. The second was following the battle of al-Yamāma, during the time of the first Caliph, Abū Bakr, when many of those who had memorized the Qur'ān (*al-ḥuffāẓ*) were killed. At the prompting of 'Umar ibn al-Khaṭṭāb, Abū Bakr ordered Zayd to write all the parts of the Qur'ān into a single document and established the order of the *sūrahs*. This parchment was kept in the possession of Abū Bakr, then handed down to 'Umar when he became Caliph, who left it in the keeping of his daughter and widow of the Prophet, Ḥafṣah. During the Caliphate of 'Uthmān, the parchment was borrowed from Ḥafṣah and copied four separate times. These four copies 'Uthmān then had sent to Mecca, Kufa, Damascus, and Basra. *Al-Itqān* vol. 1, pp. 171 *ff.*

9. Ghazālī, op. cit.

10. This was with the notable exception of Hanbalite scholars, who continued to oppose the writing of books of *tafsīr* into the fourth/ninth centuries.

11. Suyūṭī, op. cit. p. 196.

12. Tirmidhī, *Tafsīr*, 4093. The complete wording is "Beware of relating to me anything except that of which you have knowledge, for whosoever lies about me intentionally has prepared his place in Hellfire. And whosoever asserts what is in the Qur'ān based on his own opinion has prepared his place in Hellfire."

13. Ghazālī, op. cit.

14. Suyūṭī, op. cit. p. 181.

15. The main source for the biographical information in this section is Jean-Louis Michon's translation of Ibn 'Ajība's autobiography *al-Fahrasa*. An English translation of this work, published by Fons Vitae press in 1999, referenced in the pages to follow as "Michon."

16. A *Sharīf* is literally a noble. In Morocco, this term is applied to one descended from the Prophet Muḥammad. The 'Alawī dynasty which has ruled the country since the mid-17th century, is *Ḥasanī sharīf*, their descent traced through the Prophet's grandson, Ḥasan.

17. Michon, p. 53.

18. Michon, p. 70.

19. Jebal 'Alam (altitude 6000 ft) is a mountain located in the Rīf mountains in a valley not far from Ketama. Its summit, which had been Mulay 'Abd al-Salām ibn Mashīsh's retreat throughout much of his adult life and where he was finally buried, has been the object of spiritual pilgrimages for centuries.

20. Michon, p. 73.

21. *Fuqarā'*, the plural of *faqīr*: those who are poor, needy. "Sufis, in general, do not refer to themselves as Sufis; rather they call themselves *fuqarā'*. [To quote Titus Burckhardt's *Introduction to Sufi Doctrine*], 'This *faqr* or spiritual poverty is nothing other than a *vacare Deo*, emptiness for God; it begins with the rejection of passions and its crown is effacement of the *I* before the Divinity…'" As quoted in Honerkamp, *Three Early Sufi Texts*, Fons Vitae, Louisville KY, 2003, p. 165.

22. Michon, 172 ff.

23. Op. cit., 183.

24. Jackson, p. 172.

25. See page 4.

26. In the translation which follows, al-Qushayrī is cited approximately 30 times.

27. We are grateful to Dr. Alan Godlas of the University of Georgia, who has spent several years working with Baqlī's commentary, for this information.

28. See p. 37, n. 1.

29. Abū Dāwūd, *Adab*, 4398; Tirmidhī, *Faḍā'il al-Qur'ān*, 2845; Aḥmad, *Musnad*, 16534.

30. Bayhaqī, *Dalā'il al-Nubūwa, Dhikr islāmī 'Umar ibn al-Khaṭṭāb*, 518. See the Biographical Index for the details of this story.

Ibn 'Ajība's Introduction to *al-Baḥr al-Madīd*

In the Name of God, the All-Merciful and Compassionate

May God bless our beloved master Muḥammad and his People and Companions and give them salutations of peace[1]

You we praise Who unveils Himself to His devotees by way of His Speech[2] in the perfection of His beauty and splendor, Who loosens the tongues of sages to bring forth therefrom Its pearls and gifts, Who lets flow from their hearts the springs of Its wisdom, strengthened by Its principles and design, and Who allows them to gather the benefits of Its singularities and repetitions[3] when they dive into its currents, that by Its dazzling signs and verses and Its evident proofs they might refute what is false. It is both a fathomless ocean and a verdant garden from which no blossom is lacking. And how could it be otherwise, when It is the Word of our Lord, the Knower of all that is hidden, all that was, all that is, and all that shall ever be.

May blessings and salutations be upon our master Muḥammad, the manifestation of all-mercifulness brought forth with miracles and light, and upon his People and Companions, the fountains of clemency and magnanimity and the unshakeable mountains of certitude when crises and distress loom large.

Of all the religious sciences, the science of *tafsīr* is the greatest and the most excellent object of thought and understanding. None, however, should approach this vast undertaking other than an accomplished scholar who has achieved a profound knowledge of the exoteric sciences of the religion and has then directed thought and meditation towards the Qur'ān's beautiful meanings. In other words, to explain the Qur'ān, one must first have mastered, under the tutelage of the learned, the Arabic language, its morphology, semantics, and rhetoric, then jurisprudence (*fiqh*) and *ḥadīth*. If one then becomes immersed in the science of Sufism and attains therein a genuine spiritual taste (*dhawq*), then state, and then station through companionship with experienced people of the Way,[4] [it is permissible to mention as well the Qur'ān's inner meanings], but if not, then it is better to remain silent concerning them and limit oneself to the exoteric dimension.

For the immense Qur'ān has an outward dimension for the people of the outward and an inward dimension for the people of the inward, and commentary by these latter cannot be [fully] understood or experienced except by people of the inward, nor is its mention even permissible except after having affirmed [the Qur'ān's] literal and outward meaning. Only then [is it permissible] to indicate the esoteric by means of subtle references and allusions. And if one's understanding has not reached the level of being able to grasp such mysteries, then one should at least acknowledge they exist and not hastily deny them. For the science of gnosis lies beyond the limits of discursive thought and is not to be reached by mere repetition of texts.

[In *Laṭā'if al-Minan*] Ibn 'Aṭā'Allāh wrote:

> Know that commentaries by the [Sufis] upon the Word of God and the words of His Prophets through meanings which are rare and strange in no way alter the literal meaning of the text. The literal meaning is what is understood from context and usage, while the inward meanings of either a [Quranic] verse or prophetic saying are those which are understood by someone whose heart God has opened. Even so, did the Prophet say, "Every verse has an outer aspect and an inner, a limit and a vantage point."[5] Do not, then, let yourself be turned away from these spiritual commentaries by inveterate polemicists who say to you, "This will detract you from the literal meaning of the Word of God Most High and the word of His Messenger, upon whom be peace!" Such would be the case if the mystics said that a given verse had no other meaning except an esoteric one, but they do not say this. Rather, they take the literal meaning in its literal sense, purpose, and context, and then realize from God whatever else He allows them to realize...

In his commentary on al-Nasafī's *'Aqā'id*, Sa'ad al-Dīn said after the refutation of atheism:

> But as for what certain of the people of realization have said—that the [sacred] texts should be taken according to their literal meaning but that besides this, they contain subtle allusions to spiritual truths which are uncovered to people following the mystic path and that there is a pos-

> sible correspondence between them and the literal intended meaning—this is perfect faith and pure gnosis.

By "a possible correspondence," he means that it is possible to allude to them by the inward dimension of the discourse as long as this allusion does not totally depart from the literal sense or become so remote from it as to deviate.

Shaykh Aḥmad Zarrūq, may God be pleased with him, said, "The perspective of the Sufi is more specialized than that of the exegete or the scholar basing himself on the science of *ḥadīth*, for these latter two express rules and meanings and naught else, while the former adds to that a search for spiritual allusion. But this is only after having affirmed what the latter two have also affirmed. If not, then he is a *Bāṭinī*[6] and outside the religious law let alone Sufism. And God Most High knows best."

The Prophet's saying, "Every verse has an outer aspect and an inner, a limit and a vantage point"[7] thus means that *the outward* is for those such as the grammarians, the experts in language and declension. *The inward* is for those concerned with the meanings of words, the commandments and prohibitions, parables and narratives, the affirmation of God's oneness, and other like teachings of the Qur'ān, such being the domain of the exegetes. The *limit* is for the juridical scholars (*al-fuqahā'*) who are concerned with the derivation of rules from the verses, who come to a verse and then carry its arguments as far as possible but without addition. *The vantage point* (*al-muṭṭala'u*) is for the people of spiritual truths among the greatest of the Sufis, where, from the outward meaning of a verse, they look down, as it were, into its inward meaning. Then are unveiled to them, through reflection upon the verse, its mysteries, teachings, and mystic sense.

Literally, *muṭṭala'u* means any place from which one may look down upon something from its highest to lowest point and this word is mentioned in a sound *ḥadīth* referring to the "terror of the vantage point"[8] by which is meant a place of approach from which one will look down upon the events of the Last Day. Thus too can it be said [in Arabic], "Where is the vantage point of this question?" meaning its point of approach, which is literally an elevated point from which something may be seen from its highest to lowest limits. In a like manner do the people of spiritual truth look down from the outward meaning of a verse into the mysteries of its inward dimension and then plunge into the depths of its ocean. And God Most High knows better.

I have been requested by my Shaykh, Sīdī Muḥammad al-Būzīdī al-Ḥasanī, as well as his Shaykh, the *Quṭb*,[9] Mulay al-'Arabī al-Darqāwī al-Ḥasanī, to set down in writing a commentary that would combine both exoteric explanation and esoteric allusion, and I have responded to their request...in hopes that this work will benefit many and be a joy to the heart as well as to the ear.

For each verse, I have first treated the important grammatical and linguistic features, then the literal meaning of the phrases, and finally the spiritual allusions, while trying to keep to a moderate length—all this in hopes that the treasures of God, Most Generous and Forgiving, might be opened to me thereby—and I have named it *The Immense Ocean of Commentary on the Glorious Qur'ān*. I ask God to clothe it in the raiment of His acceptance, and bring about its desired purpose. He is the One Who is Able to Accomplish whatsoever He wills and the best from whom to hope for an answer. There is neither strength nor power except through All-Mighty God. May God bless our master Muḥammad and his People and Companions and give them salutations of peace.

Notes on Author's Introduction

1. Here follows ibn 'Ajība's introduction to *al-Baḥr al-Madīd* found at the beginning of the first volume.

2. By which he means the Qur'ān.

3. *Farā'idihi wa mathānīhi.* This is a reference to [15:87], *And We have given you the seven oft-repeated verses* (sūrat al-Fātiḥa) *and the Immense Qur'ān*, as well as [39:23], *God has revealed the fairest of discourse: a book [containing] that which is repeated and which has inner resemblance.* That is, there are some verses which are unique and others which reappear, as it were, throughout the Qur'ān but in slightly different forms.

4. "The Way" (capitalized) refers throughout the translation to *al-ṭarīqa*, or methodical spiritual journey.

5. Ṭabarānī, *al-Kabīr*, 8587.

6. A heretical *shi'i* sect which believed in an esotoric interpretation of the Qur'ān to the exclusion of its literal meaning. See Ghazālī, *Iḥyā 'ulūm al-dīn*, Book 1 (*al-'ilm*), section 3.

7. Ṭabarānī, *al-Awṣat,* 777; Tirmidhī, *Manāqib*, 3255; Ibn Mājah, *Faḍā'il al-aṣḥāb*, 93.

8. Aḥmad, 14037; Bayhaqī, 10193. The complete wording of the *ḥadīth* is "Do not wish for death, for verily the terror of the vantage point is mighty, and a part of happiness is for God to prolong the life of a servant and provide him with the means of turning back to Him (*al-ināba*)."

9. The *Quṭb*, literally, "axis" or "pole," is a term applied to the greatest spiritual master in a given time or place.

The Chapter of the All-Merciful
(*Sūrat al-Raḥmān*)

This *sūra* was revealed in Mecca and comprises seventy-six verses. It is connected to what precedes it [the Chapter of The Moon] by the words which end that *sūra*: *In the presence of a Mighty Sovereign* [54:55], Who is the *All-Merciful and Compassionate*, as both the title and opening words of this *sūra* affirm.[1]

In the Name of God, the All-Merciful and Compassionate

1. *The All-Merciful*
2. *Taught the Qur'ān*
3. *Created the human being.*
4. *Taught him speech.*
5. *The Sun and the Moon follow a measured path*
6. *And the herbs and trees prostrate*
7. *And the sky He raised up, and He established the balance,*
8. *That you not transgress the balance.*
9. *Maintain, then, the balance justly, and do not fall short in the measure.*
10. *And the earth He set down for creatures*
11. *In it are fruits, and the date palm with its spathes*
12. *And the grain with its straw and its fragrance*
13. *Which, then, of the favors of your Lord will you two deny?*

Commentary

The All-Merciful taught the Qur'ān

In this noble *sūra*, God Most High enumerates the myriad blessings —those of religion and of this worldly life, those in the human soul and those in nature—which He has bestowed upon creatures, and following the mention of each, He reminds them of the necessity for gratitude and reproves their lack thereof.

Of all these blessings, He begins with the teaching of the Qur'ān, mentioned first because it is the greatest and most sublime of His gifts, and the source of happiness in this world and the Next. That the verb expressing this act, '*allama*, comes directly after His Name *al-Raḥmān* signifies that the teaching of the Qur'ān is both an effect and rule of God's All-Encompassing Mercy.[2]

[He] Created the human being [and] taught him speech.

The word 'human being' (*al-insān*) in this context has been said to refer to humankind in general, or to Adam, or to Muḥammad (upon whom be peace and blessings). That this creation is mentioned directly following the teaching of the Qur'ān signifies that human beings were made in order that they might come to know God's revelations and sacred books.[3] For this reason, too, did God endow them with that faculty which distinguishes them from all other animals, namely, speech, by which they may not only articulate what is within but also comprehend what is expressed by others...[4] These four verses taken together, then, speak of the gift of faith.

The Sun and the Moon follow a measured path.

Here God begins to mention those of His blessings which can be seen in the natural world. *The Sun and the moon follow a measured path* means they move through their positions in the sky in determined cycles. These cycles, which produce the differences in the seasons and times of day, and by which is known *the number of years and the reckoning*[5], are what give order to all terrestrial life. Indeed, if time were eternally day or night, it would negate this wisdom, there would be no way to reckon anything, and the entire order of the world would be destroyed.

According to Mujāhid, the *measured paths* are "cycles like the turning of a millstone." This supports [the views of] the astronomers, one of whom has said, "The sun is a hundred and twenty times larger than the earth and thus it is that you may see it before you wherever you are." And in the *al-Waghlīsiyya*[6] it is written, "The sun is over one hundred and sixty-one times larger than the earth, while the moon is eight times larger and yet human eyesight which is smaller in proportion than a sesame seed can encompass them both. And God is greater, mightier, and more exalted!"[7]

It has also been said that upon the face of the sun is written: "There is no god but God and Muḥammad is the Prophet of God. God is the One Who created the sun by His decree and set it in motion by His command," and upon the face of the moon is written, "There is no god but God, Muḥammad is the Prophet of God. God is the One Who created good and evil by His decree and tests thereby whomsoever of His creatures He so wills. Blessed be the one by whose hand He brings about good, and woe be to the one by whose hand He brings about evil."[8]

And the herbs and trees prostrate

The word *herbs* (*al-najm*, which can also mean *star*) designates all soft-stemmed plants, including the grasses, while *trees* (*al-shajr*) designates all woody-stemmed plants. Their 'prostration' is their acceptance and submission to what has been willed for them, likened to the physical prostration of men and jinn.[9]

Both this verse and the one before it also refer back to God's Name *the All-Merciful*...and so they are saying, '*The sun and the moon follow* the *measured paths* of the All-Merciful, *and the herbs and trees prostrate* to the All-Merciful.' Also, whereas the conjunction "and" is absent between the verbs [in verses 2 to 4] giving a tone of enumeration..., here [in verse 5] it is repeated several times to express a correspondance between the sun and the moon following their paths through the heavens and the herbs and trees prostrating upon the earth.

And the sky He raised up and He established the balance

God fashioned the sky as a lofty ceiling structured according to His laws and placed therein the angels who descend with revelation to His Prophets, that creatures might know His majesty and grandeur. Then did He *establish the balance*, by which is meant all means of measurement and weighing, including scales fine and gross and measuring rods, placed upon earth that human beings might be fair and equitible in what they give and what they take. It has also been said, however, that by *the balance* is meant justice; that is, God has made justice to be a law and has commanded thereto in order that our dealings in this world may be regulated and upright and "that each who has a right [to something] be given his right."[10] Even thus did the Prophet say, "The heavens and earth are founded upon justice."[11] [In human dealings,] this justice means governance based on the Muḥammadan Law (*al-sharīʿat al-Muḥammadiyya*) derived from the Qur'ān, the prophetic example (*sunna*), the consensus of the learned (*ijmāʿ*), and the application of legal precedents (*qiyās*).

That you not transgress the balance. Maintain, then,
the balance justly, and do not fall short in the measure.

In this verse God enjoins that after having established justice, you not transgress the balance...[12] by excess... nor fall short by stinting. In practice these verses forbid both tyranny and fraud, for the former is to take by force what one has no right to, while the latter is to promise to another what is not given. That the word balance is thrice repeated emphasizes the importance of this counsel and this commandment.

And the earth He set down for creatures. In it are fruits, and the date palm with its spathes, and the grain with its straw and its nourishing kernel.

Having mentioned the gift of [faith, which is] spiritual sustenance, God now mentions the gift of physical sustenance: the earth *He set down*, spread like a pallet upon the waters for all the animal life—or, according to al-Ḥasan, the humans and jinn—which dwells upon its surface. …*In it are fruits*…to delight the taste...*and the date palm with its spathes*…bearing dates which are both a delight to the taste and a food, *and the grain with its straw… and its nourishing kernel*[13]…which provides food for both humans and their beasts....[14]

Which, then, of the favors of your Lord will you two deny?

...This is addressed to the two heavy ones, human beings and jinn.[15] Their denial may be either their refusal to acknowledge that something such as the teaching of the Qur'ān or faith is a favor or else their refusal to acknowledge that something they admit to be a favor is from God. Rather, they attribute it, either partly or wholly, implicitly or explicitly, to someone or something other than God, and for this reason worship others….[16]

Thus, the verse asks: "If the matter is as it has been described, then which aspect of God's blessings do you reject, even while each and every one of them articulates the truth?" And God Most High knows better.

Spiritual Allusion

Know that *The All-Merciful* (*al-Raḥmān*) is one of the Divine Names which can only be applied to God. No one else may be described using it, either literally or figuratively, for it is the Name by which the blessing of existence itself (*al-ījād*) is realized, a blessing which may not be attributed to anyone except God. It thus differs from the Name *The Compassionate* (*al-Raḥīm*), by which the blessing of sustenance (*al-imdād*) is realized, for this may be figuratively applied to others. A human being, then, may be described as *raḥīm* but never *Raḥmān*.[17]

The mercy thus comprised by the Name *al-Raḥmān* has two aspects. One is Essential, inseparable from the Divine Essence, and the other Attributive, by which the sustenance of creation comes about and God shows mercy to those He will.

The Essential Mercy is called *al-Raḥmāniya* (All-Mercifulness) and inasmuch as It is inseparable from the Essence, it is this which is referred to by the Quranic verses of Assuming Dominion (*al-istiwā*) such as *The Most Merciful assumed the Throne* [20:5], or *Then God assumed the Throne of the All-Merciful* [25:56][18], and by the words of the *Ḥikam*, "O You Who, in His All-Mercifulness, assumed the Throne such that the Throne vanished in His All-Mercifulness!"[19]

Attributive Mercy, through which [existence] is sustained, varies in mode according to the Beautiful Names of God, which number ninety-nine. In the Names of Beauty, this Mercy is evident and direct, while in the Names of Rigor, it is expressed through the inseparability of God's Kindness from His Determinative Power (*qadrihi*).

Essential Mercy, then, completes the hundred, even as the Prophet, may God bless him, said, "God Most High apportioned His Mercy into one hundred portions. Ninety-nine He kept with Himself and one He placed in creation, and it is by this one portion that creatures have mercy upon one another." This, or words close to it, is what was related in the *ḥadīth*.[20]

Since the Qur'ān is among God's greatest gifts, He relates the act of its teaching to His very Essence. Indeed, the Qur'ān is itself a theophany of the Attributes of the Divine Essence, of Its mysteries and Its Acts, and it unveils these spiritual realities to anyone whose inner vision God Most High has opened.

He created the human being by bringing him forth from being a secret in the Subtle Realm to a formal manifestation in the material world, yet in his physical nature this human was ignorant of God. Then *He taught him what is clear* (*al-bayān*),[21] that is, God made the journey towards knowing Him clear and comprehensible by placing within all humans an intelligence capable of discernment, making for them landmarks and signs by which they might find the way, and bringing to them a guide to guide them and teach them the mysteries of God's Divinity and the correct behavior (*adab*) of the servant in respect to it.[22] And God continues to show them the path and be with them in their journeys until the moon of Divine Oneness appears and the sun of gnosis (*shams al-ma'rifa*)[23] rises, alluded to by

His words, *And the Sun and the Moon follow a measured path.* This is to say that they follow a course which is known, increasing and decreasing in the light of Oneness according to the disposition and orientation of the servant.[24]

About this verse al-Qushayrī said, "Such are the suns of gnosis and the moons of religious teachings when they arise in the apogee of the heart and innermost soul: by God's Eternal Wisdom and Determination, they are bound to a known and measured course."

And the star and the trees prostrate.[25] *The star* alludes to the light of natural reason, and *the trees* to discursive thought, both of which are eclipsed and effaced when the Sun of gnosis dawns. As for the divinely-endowed Intellect and intuitive thought, however, these envelop all existence, for their light partakes of the Universal Intellect, which is the First Divine Outpouring from the Ocean of the *Jabarūt*[26] and the Heaven of Souls, exalted far above the stains of the formal world. This is the locus at which the mysteries of the Essence and the Lights of the Divine Qualities may be perceived. Here, too, takes place the unveiling (*tajallī*) of the Prophets, and because the place of their unveiling is one, neither their souls nor individualities are hidden from the one who ascends to it.[27]

And He set down the balance for souls in darkness *that you exceed not the balance* by spiritual practices which entail excessive self-mortification, but *rather that you establish* them *in just measure, and you do not fall short in the balance* by giving up all effort [in the Way] and abandoning yourself totally to your appetites and whims. *And the earth* of the human state *He set down* in order that it might become the locus of regular devotional practice which God has placed in a certain order *for creatures* so that while in this [human state], when purified, they may discover the *fruits* of God-given spiritual teaching, *and the date,* which alludes to the formal religious sciences, *with its spathes*, that is, the methodical proofs by which questions of religious law are resolved. Thus may it be said that a follower of tradition (*muqallid*) is someone who has stopped at the husk, while the skilled *mujtahid*[28] is someone who has reached the kernel.

Al-Qushayrī said, "*And the date with its spathes* [are] the fruits of oneness, veiled from the alterities of the world as well as from those who are not apt to receive them.[29] ... *And the grain with its straw*, [is] the grain of love (*ḥabb al-maḥabbah*) of the Divine Essence, unalterable and unchanging, and bearing within it the nourishment of gnosis, spiritual truths, and wisdom." *Its fragrance* (*rayḥān*) is the certitude which nourishes souls (*al-arwāḥ*), or the cooling breeze of spiritual experiences and moments of ecstasy.

Which, then, of the favors of your Lord will you two deny? O you two creatures of weight, or you, the individual soul and you, the spirit. For each of you shall win by the grace of God, each of you shall arrive at the desired goal if you only act [with gratitude] for what has been described and listen with the ear of your heart to the favors We shall enumerate. And in God is all success.

14. *He created the human being from sounding clay like unto pottery*
15. *And He created jinn from smokeless fire.*
16. *Which, then, of the favors of your Lord will you two deny?*
17. *Lord of the two easts and Lord of the two wests.*
18. *Which, then, of the favors of your Lord will you two deny?*
19. *He has let free the two seas and they meet one another.*
20. *Between them is an isthmus which they do not transgress.*
21. *Which, then, of the favors of your Lord will you two deny?*
22. *There comes forth from them both pearls and coral.*
23. *Which, then, of the favors of your Lord will you two deny?*
24. *And His are the vessels rising up like mountains.*
25. *Which, then, of the favors of your Lord will you two deny?*
26. *Everything on earth is passing away,*
27. *And the Face of your Lord remains full of Majesty and Generosity.*
28. *Which, then, of the favors of your Lord will you two deny?*

Commentary

He created the human being from sounding clay like pottery, and jinn from smokeless fire. Which, then, of the favors of your Lord will you two deny?

God created the human being, Adam, from dried clay that makes a sound when struck (*ṣalṣāl*),[30] fired *like pottery*. Although elsewhere, God says that Adam was created *from mud molded into shape* [15:26], and *from sticky clay* [36:11], these terms do not contradict one another, but rather describe the stages in his creation: his origin was earth, then was he fashioned of sticky clay, then molded mud, and finally sounding clay. *And [God] created jinn*, either all jinn or the father of the jinn, Iblīs, *from smokeless fire*.[31] *Al-mārij* can mean both "a pure flame without smoke" and "something into which soot has been mixed,"... and so the verse means that the jinn were created from pure fire, or a substance mixed with fire, or from a unique sort of fire.

Which, then, of the myriad *favors* of God contained in your creation... *will you two deny*? Said al-Qushayrī, "God, be He glorified, repeats this verse many times [throughout the *sūra*] according to the particular element of His blessings, blessing after blessing, that is being affirmed. Here it is the fact that after creating Adam from the lowliness of clay, He raised him up to [a high] degree..." And while Adam was raised to the degree of the spirit and vicegerency, the jinn, *from smokeless fire*, were raised to the degree of being able to inwardly affect human beings and other creatures.

Lord of the two easts and Lord of the two wests.
Which, then, of the favors of your Lord, will you two deny?

The two easts and two wests are the points at which the sun rises and sets in summer and winter. Said Ibn al-Ḥashā, "The east and west of winter are the points on the horizon at which the sun rises and sets on the day of the winter solstice in mid-December, the shortest day of the year, and the east and west of summer are the points of its rising and setting in mid-June, the longest day of the year. These points are different from where it rises and sets during the rest of the year." [Mid-December and mid-June], however, were in his time, whereas in our time, [the summer solstice and vernal equinox] occur approximately eight days after the middle of the month... [32] Said Ibn 'Aṭiyya:

> When "the east and the west" (*al-mashriq wa al-maghrib*) are mentioned in the Qur'ān, they refer to the two directions, irrespective of season. "The places of sunrise and sunset" (*al-mashāriq wa al-maghārib*) refer to the succession of points on the horizon throughout the year. "The two easts and the two wests" refer to the limits of these points, but to mention the limits of something is to mention its totality.[33]

Which, then, of the favors of your Lord will you two deny? Here al-Qushayrī says, "The favor in this case is the marvelous order which the sun follows in its risings and settings, and through which its benefit to creation is completed."

He has let free the two seas, and they meet one another.
Between them is an isthmus which they do not transgress.
Which, then, of the favors of your Lord, will you two deny?

The two seas are those of salt water and fresh which *meet one another* with no visible distinction in the density of their waters. It is written in the *Ḥāshiyya*,[34] "Something like this can be observed viewing the ocean from the Rīf Mountains [35]—so take it as a lesson!—and the same [phenomenon] can be seen in the white and yolk of an egg." Others have said that this verse refers to the waters of the Mediterranean Sea and the Persian Sea which meet in the ocean and are actually two gulfs which branch off from it.[36]

Between them is an isthmus, or barrier, *which* by God's decree *they do not transgress* by passing beyond its limit, or intermingling their distinct natures, or drowning what is between them.

Which, then, of the favors of your Lord will you two deny? In reality, not one of them can be denied.

There comes forth from them both pearls and coral.
Which, then, of the favors of your Lord, will you two deny?

Coral is a tree which grows in the middle of the sea. It is found in the sea of Morocco between Tangier and Sebta. Al-Ṭarṭūshī says, "It is a red root which rises in the sea like the fingers of a hand. We have seen it many times while in the land of Morocco." It has also been said that the word *lu'lu'* actually means the larger-sized pearls, while *marjān* [37] means the smaller ones. If it be asked why the dual form, *from them both*, is used, even while it is known [that pearls and coral are found] only in salt water, one answer would be that when these two seas meet, they can be referred to grammatically as a single entity. However, al-Akhfash relates that according to certain people, coral and pearls are brought forth from both salt and fresh waters, and since "the one who affirms is given precedence over the one who negates," [38] and those who refute him can bring no conclusive proof, [his claim should be accepted.] [39] *Which, then of the favors of your Lord*, when they are made apparent to you, *will you two deny?*

And His are the vessels, rising up like mountains.
Which, then, of the favors of your Lord, will you two deny?

The vessels are the sailing ships, which, when their sails are raised high or when they rise up upon the waves resemble *mountains in the sea. Which, then, of the favors of your Lord will you two deny*? For it is God Who placed in creation the materials for building these ships, Who guided humankind to where these materials may be found, and Who endowed them with the science of shipbuilding and the understanding of the laws by which a vessel may move across the face of the waters. All these are blessings which none but God has placed in creation.

Everything on earth is passing away, and the Face of your Lord remains full of Majesty and Generosity.
Which, then, of the favors of your Lord, will you two deny?

The Face of your Lord is the Divine Essence. About this verse, al-Qushayrī said, "In God's remaining, every loss is restored. Such is the best consolation for one of faith who undergoes hardship or from whom any of God's gifts are taken away."

Full of Majesty (*al-jalāl*) refers to God's Power and Might *and Generosity* (*al-ikrām*) to His gift of perfect forbearance and complete generosity. These two together are among the greatest of the Divine attributes, and thus did the Prophet (upon whom be God's blessings) say, "Be steady and abundant in [the supplication] 'O You full of Majesty and Generosity (*yā dha al-Jalāli wa al-ikrām*).'"[40]... It has also been related that he once passed a man supplicating God [by these Names] and said to him, "Your prayer has been answered."[41] *Which, then of the favors of your Lord will you two deny?* For to pass away from the narrowness of this worldly abode and be raised again to dwell in the everlasting abode of Eternal Grace is surely among God's supreme gifts.

Spiritual Allusion

The human state is distinguished from all others by its inherent balance of the subtle and gross, meaning and form, spiritual and physical. It is due to this balance that if human beings be granted gnosis (*ma'rifa*), it elevates them above all other creatures. If, however, one of the jinn or angels were to be granted such knowledge, because of the predominance of the subtle element in their natures, the resulting intoxication would consume them.[42]

As for the human beings, if their spiritual dimensions come to dominate their earthly natures... they become as angels or more excellent, while if their earthly dimensions come to dominate their spirits, they become like beasts, only more lost.

Lord of the two easts and the two wests... These are where the sun of gnosis and the moon of faith rise and where they set when clouded over by lights or by vicissitudes.[43] Al-Qushayrī said, "'The east' alludes to the spirit and the heart and 'the west' to the lower self and its desires. When the light of the heart and soul arises, the darkness of the lower self and its desires is dispelled, whereas if this darkness comes to dominate the heart and soul, those suns set."

Which, then of the favors of your Lord in their myriad subtleties *will you two deny* by either letting your heart and spirit become solely fixed upon manifestations of Divine beauty or by letting your lower soul and its desires become solely fixed upon manifestations of the Divine rigor? For the perfected ones of this Way are those who witness God's beauty in His rigor and His rigor in His beauty and do not reside with either.

He has set forth the two seas, one of formal religious knowledge (*'ilm al-sharī'a*) and the other of gnosis (*ma'rifa*) *which meet* in the complete human being. *Between them is an isthmus*, the intelligence, which keeps either type of knowledge from exceeding its respective abode, the abode of the religious law being the outward and the abode of the esoteric truth (*al-ḥaqīqa*) being the inward... In someone whose intelligence is deficient, one or the other of these will dominate. If it be the religious law, he will become dry and frozen, and will be unable to rid himself of vice.[44] If it be the esoteric truth, then he may become intoxicated and even heretical. *Which, then, of the favors of your Lord*, Who guides His servants to maintain each in proportion and in its proper domain, *will you two deny*?

There comes forth from them both pearls and coral. From the sea of esoteric truths come jewels of wisdom and pearls of spiritual teachings, and from the sea of the formal religious law comes the coral of recorded narratives and the confirmation of their sources.[45]... *Which, then, of the favors of your Lord do you two deny*, when He has allowed you to plumb the depths of the ocean of esoteric truth to bring forth its mysteries, and the depths of the ocean of the religious law to reveal its lights. *And His are the vessels* of meditative reflection which sail the Red Sea of the Essence and the currents of the Divine Attributes, *rising up* in the Sea of the Essence with the deep-rootedness of the intellect like a principial mountain. The vessels of gnostics' meditations float across the sea of the *Jabarūt* and through the lights of the *Malakūt*, and then are moored in the harbor of servanthood (*al-'ubudiyya*) to maintain right comportment before

God, the Lord. *Which, then, of the favors of your Lord will you two deny*, for even if they are pounded by the waves of the Sea of the Divine Essence and could be drowned in heresy or madness, once He has made them the companions of a true spiritual master, God so willing, they need not fear.

All that is upon this Kingdom's outstretched carpet *is passing away* into extinction, *and the Face of your Lord*, His Most Sacred Essence, *remains*, for in reality, there is nothing in existence alongside Him, even as the poet said:

> All else but God, were you to truly see it,
> Is nothingness pure and simple.

This is something known to people of spiritual experience (*adhwāq*) and confirmed by the people of effacement and subsistence in God, and none but the ignorant would dispute it. Thus does God again ask, *Which, then, of the favors of your Lord will you two deny*?

29. *All who are in the heavens and upon earth ask of Him Every day He is in some task.*
30. *Which, then, of the favors of your Lord will you two deny*?
31. *We shall attend to you, O you two dependents.*
32. *Which, then, of the favors of your Lord will you two deny*?
33. *O you assembly of jinn and human beings, if you can pierce the boundaries of the heavens and earth, then pierce them. Yet you shall not pierce them save by authority.*
34. *Which, then, of the favors of your Lord will you two deny?*
35. *There will be sent upon you both flames of fire and flash of brass which you shall not escape.*
36 *Which, then, of the favors of your Lord will you two deny?*
37. *Then, when the sky is split asunder and becomes rosy like ointment.*
38. *Which, then, of the favors of your Lord, will you two deny?*
39. *On that Day, neither human nor jinn shall be asked about his sin*
40. *Which, then, of the favors of your Lord, will you two deny?*

Commentary

All who are in the heavens and upon earth ask of Him.
Every day He is in some task.

All who are in the heavens and upon earth—be they angels, humans, jinn, or others—*ask of Him* their needs, either in words or by the tongue of their state.[46] Those who dwell in the heavens ask Him for the sustenance of their spirits; those who dwell upon earth ask Him for the sustenance of both their bodies and spirits. About this, Abū al-Sa'ūd said:

> They are all one in respect to what is truly possible for them, equally undeserving of [the gift] of being, and indistinguishable in the totality of their subjugation. Were it not for their attachment to Divine Providence, they would not smell the least whiff of the perfume of existence. So in every sense, their support is through supplication and prayer.

...*Every day*, at every moment, *He is in a [new] task* in respect to His creation, which means [in this context] giving to creatures what they ask of Him. Thus is God ceaselessly bringing forth some and effacing others, ceaselessly bringing about certain conditions and removing others, when and howsoever He wills and in accordance with His Eternal Wisdom.

Concerning this verse, I heard our Shaykh, Sīdī al-Tāwudī Ben Sūda, may God have mercy upon him, say, "Among His *tasks* is to make ready, every day, three multitudes [of souls]: those which enter the wombs, those which are born into the world, and those which enter the graves."[47] According to Ibn 'Ayīna, "For God, all time is but two days. One of them is today—the duration of this world—in which His *task* is to command and prohibit, to bring about life and death, and to give and withhold. The other is tomorrow—the Day of Resurrection—in when His *task* is to reckon and recompense." It is narrated that the Prophet (upon whom be God's blessings and peace) recited this verse and was asked, "What is this *task*?" He said, "Among God's tasks is to forgive sin, to dispel sorrow, to raise up one people and bring low another."[48] It has also been said that this verse was revealed in response to the Jews' saying that God does not accomplish any task on the Sabbath.

By His *being in a task* is meant not that He is originating it—for "the pen has dried" from writing all that will ever exist[49]—but rather that He is bringing it into manifestation. So when it is said [in a *ḥadīth*] that a child's destiny and whether he shall be among the blessed or the damned is all decreed for him in the womb, it does not mean that this destiny is brought into being at that moment, but rather that what has been inscribed on the Guarded Tablet (*al-Lawḥ*) is revealed to the angels. Thus, [in one version of this *ḥadīth*] it is said to the angel, "Return to the Mother of the Book," and he does so and finds there the story of that embryo.[50]

It has also been said, "His *task* is to conduct all that has been determined to the times for which it has been determined." To quote al-Nasafī:

> They say that 'Abd Allāh ibn Ṭāhir once called for al-Ḥusayn ibn al-Faḍl to come to him and then said, "Three verses in the Qur'ān puzzle me and I have called for you in hopes that you can explain them to me. The first [said of Cain after he had slain his brother] is *He became full of remorse* [5:31], for the *ḥadīth* affirms that 'Remorse is repentance.'[51] The second is *Every day He is in a task* [55:29] for the *ḥadīth* affirms that 'the Pen has dried from writing all that shall exist until the Day of Resurrection.'[52] The last is *A human being shall have nothing except that for which he strives* [53:39], for what of God's promise to multiply the recompense of every good act we accomplish?"
>
> To this, al-Ḥusayn answered, "[In the first verse] *remorse* may be understood as being other than repentance, for the commentators have said that Cain's regret was not for having killed his brother but for the hardship of having to carry his corpse [until a crow showed him how to bury him]. The verse *A human being shall have nothing but that for which he strives* is particular for the people of Abraham and Moses, upon whom be peace. In the verse *Every day He is in some task*, this task is to manifest [what is destined] not to originate it (*yubdī hā, lā yabtadī hā*).

Which, then, of the favors of your Lord will you two deny when you see what He has mentioned concerning the generosity of these tasks.

We shall attend to you, O you two dependents.

[This verse means] 'We shall attend to your reckoning and recompense…' It may also be understood to mean that this world will be brought to its end and the Next World brought forth, so that God's task in respect to creation, referred to by the words *Every day He is in some task*, will end and there will remain but one single task: your recompense. All this He refers to by analogy as *being attended to*.[53] The *two dependents* (*al-thaqulān*: literally, *the two heavy ones*) are jinn and human beings, called *heavy* because of the weight they bear upon the earth, or because of the gravity of their appearance, or because both of them bear the weight of responsibility for their deeds.

Which, then, of the favors of your Lord, will you two deny? For it is a favor from God to be warned of what awaits us on the Day of Ressurection so that we may avoid the words and deeds that will lead to an ill reckoning.

O you assembly of jinn and human beings, if you can pierce the boundaries of the heavens and earth, then pierce them. Yet you shall not pierce them save by authority. Which, then, of the favors of your Lord, will you two deny?

To the *assembly of jinn and men*, who are *the two heavy ones* just mentioned, God says, *If you can pierce the boundaries of the heavens and earth* to escape My decree and My dominions, beyond the limits of My earth and My heavens, *then pierce them* and deliver yourselves from My chastisement. *You shall not pierce them except by authority*, which is strength and power to compel, both of which you are far from possessing.

[According to some commentaries] these words will be said to humans and jinn on the Day of Reckoning when the angels surround them. When they try to flee, in every direction they find encircling angels.[54]

Which, then, of the favors of your Lord, which include being apprised of the frightful calamities of the Last Day in order that you might make ready for them, *will you two deny?*

There will be sent upon you both flames of fire and flash of brass which you shall not escape.

When they are brought forth from their graves, there will be sent upon them flame and smoke which will drive them towards the Place of Gathering from which they will not escape. *Which, then, of the favors of your Lord will you two deny*, for to be told of these events is both a kindness and a grace to any who would take heed.

When the sky is split asunder and becomes rosy like ointment. Which, then, of the favors of your Lord, will you two deny?

The [indefinite adverb] *idhā* ("when")[55] at the beginning of this verse gives the sense of something too terrifying to mention directly. On that Day, the sky will turn the color of reddish unguent, or, as it is stated elsewhere, become like *al-muhl* [70:8] which means "the sediment left from pressed oil." Then, after the people have been brought to the Place of Gathering, it will be split asunder, the sun will be drawn near, and fear and woe will wax mightily except for those mentioned in the *ḥadīth* of "the seven."[56] It has also been said—in *al-Budūr al-Sāfirah*,[57] for example—that these events will take place before the Day of Resurrection, and God Most High knows best which is true. *Which, then, of the favors of your Lord,* when you know their mighty import, *will you two deny?*

On that Day, neither man nor jinn shall be asked about his sin.
Which, then, of the favors of your Lord, will you two deny?

They shall not be asked because from the moment they are brought forth from the graves and gathered, wave upon wave, to the Standing-place, they shall be known by their marks. As for the words of God, *By your Lord, they shall all be asked* [15:92] and other verses like it, these refer to the Station of Disputation and Reckoning. Indeed, the Day of Resurrection is a long day with many stages. At some they shall be questioned, at others not. Qatāda said, "There will the questioning and then their mouths will be sealed." It has also been said that [this verse means] they shall not be questioned in order to know, but rather in order to be reproved…

Which, then, of the favors of your Lord do you two deny. The benefits of knowing what these verses speak, of that you might stay clear of the evil that leads to it, are beyond reckoning.

Spiritual Allusion

All who are in the heavens and the earth ask of him. Those in *the heavens* of the spiritual realm ask Him for what pertains to their spiritual natures—the unveiling of mysteries and radiance of lights—but they nonetheless remain supplicants in need. Their utter need for God never ceases, nor do they find an abode of rest anywhere [but in God]. Rather, with the tongue of their states or in words they ceaselessly supplicate. And those in *the earth* of their human natures, those who have not ascended to the heavens of the spirit, ask God for what pertains to the frailty of that nature: physical nourishment, the fulfillment of human needs, or the outward virtues which will be their means of salvation and grace on the Day of Resurrection.

God's words *Every day He is in some task* allude to the diversity of His theophany at every instant. For at any one time, He reveals

Himself through the contracted state (*qabḍ*) of some and the expanded state (*basṭ*) of others,[58] the exaltation of some and the abasement of others, His giving to some and withholding from others, the ascent of some and the descent of others.

Thus when differing states come to the gnostics (*al-'ārifīn*), you will not find them trying to abide with any one of them, nor depend upon any one of them. Rather, they behold what comes forth to them from the spring of Divine Determination and go with it. "When they arise in the morning, they look to what God will do with them," and when they reach the evening, they look to what God will do with them.[59] Gnosis has razed the pillars of their self-determined goals and loosed the knots of their worldly resolve. Most of the time, they neither will, nor choose, nor plan, for they know that it is all in the Hand of Another and that, in an absolute sense, they have no real control over what will come to pass.[60]

Concerning God's words *We shall attend to you, both you heavy ones*, al-Qushayrī explained the *two heavy ones* as the soul with its virtues and the lower self (*al-nafs*) with its faults. Thus, what is being said is '*We shall attend to you*, O you assembly of purified souls, by ennobling you and raising you in degree, for I shall manifest Myself to you and you shall be conscious of Me at every time and place. *And We shall attend to you*, O you assembly of lower selves in darkness, by all means of trials and tribulations, for you shall not enter My Heaven until you have been purified from the taints of wordliness, nor shall I manifest Myself to you except in times of utter need.'

All this, then, pertains to what is done in this world. For the one who purifies himself here, [the Next World] shall be pure, and for the one who is tainted here, [the Next World] shall be tainted.

Then to the lower selves in darkness it is said, *O you assembly of jinn and human beings! If you can pierce the boundaries of the heavens and earth* by means of your mental faculty [alone], *then pierce them.* But you have no power to do so for your souls are imprisoned within your physical forms and you are totally surrounded by the spheres of this world. *You shall not penetrate them except through* the strength of your souls' *authority* over your lower selves, which will draw them towards the realm of the spirit through companionship with a skilled physician.[61] Then shall your inner visions pass beyond the spheres of this created world into the vast space of direct perception, just as when the Day of Resurrection dawns, your souls and individual forms shall pass beyond the confines of this world and into the vastness of Paradisiacal Gardens: *And the gardens shall be brought near to the righteous* [26:90]....[62]

There shall be sent upon them flames from a fire and smoke. Al-Qushayrī said about this verse:

> The assembly of lower selves is being told of the *flames* of remoteness and separation that come to them by way of their constant absorption in carnal appetites; and the assembly of souls (*al-rūḥ*) is being told of the *molten brass* that rains down upon them when they descend from the sublime degree of the spirit to the abased level of the self by turning back [in the Way]. Neither one of these is able to help the other.

Which, then, of the favors of your Lord will you two deny? One who torments his own soul merits suffering and one who nutures his own soul merits bliss, and so to be able to distinguish between the jinn-like nature of the sinful self and the humanity of the spirit is surely one of the greatest of God's gifts.

When the sky is split asunder alludes to the melting away and disappearance of the physical world when the Divine Name is invoked by the gnostic. *And* it *becomes rosy* when the cooling breezes of spiritual meanings from those who safeguard them waft forth; [*and it becomes*] *like ointment*, oil that has been warmed and liquefied through pure meditation...All of this means that when creation is subsumed in its spiritual meaning, it melts away and becomes a subtle substance. *Which then, of the favors of your Lord will you two deny*, when this great blessing, hidden from so many, has been shown you?

On that day neither human nor jinn shall be asked about his sin. For those who reach this exalted degree, the people of direct vision, there remains neither obedience nor sin, and so neither question nor reproach is directed towards them. This is the meaning of what has been related concerning an intimate discourse between God Most High and the Prophet Moses, upon whom be peace: "No, Moses, it is the people of the veil who obey or disobey Me. As for the ones for whom there is no longer a veil, there is neither obedience nor sin." And Shaykh Abū al-Ḥasan [al-Shādhilī] said, "It is said [to the saint], 'Do as you wish. We have made peace and security your companion and We have removed from you blame.'" This, however, comes only after the attributes of the lower self have been effaced, after both passing away and subsistence in God have been realized. And God Most High knows better.[63]

41. *The guilty shall be known by their marks and then shall they be seized by their forelocks and feet*
42. *Which, then, of the favors of your Lord, will you two deny?*
43. *This is the Hell which the guilty belie*
44. *They will go back and forth between it and the boiling water*
45. *Which, then, of the favors of your Lord, will you two deny?*

Commentary

The guilty shall be known by their marks and then shall they be seized by their forelocks and feet. Which, then, of the favors of your Lord, will you two deny?

The guilty in this context are the disbelievers, and *their marks*, the darkness in their faces and the blueness of their eyes,[64] or the sorrow and gloom which surround them. According to some, this verse is adverbial to the words *On that Day neither man nor jinn shall be asked about his sin* and thus means 'they shall not be asked because they shall be known by their marks.' *And then shall they be seized by their forelocks and feet*, bound by a chain behind their backs. It has also been said that this means the angels will drag them forth, sometimes by their forelocks, sometimes by their feet...

Which, then, of the favors of your Lord, will you two deny? To fear such calamity before it befalls so as to avoid what leads to it is one of the greatest favors imaginable.

This is the Hell which the guilty belie. They will go back and forth between it and the boiling water. Which, then, of the favors of your Lord, will you two deny?

This is the hell which the guilty belie are the words which will be said to them in reproach and chastisement. *They will go back and forth between it and the boiling water*...feeling the heat of Hell and drinking of its scalding waters. ...[65]

Spiritual Allusion

Al-Qushayrī takes *the guilty* as alluding to two groups. The first are the scholars of speculative theology who speak of the Divine Essence, Attributes and Acts without knowledge, and use argumentative logic to debate with the people of genuine spiritual insight and perception. There is no doubt that these former are being pulled by their forelocks[66] into the fire of remoteness from God and expelled from the ranks of the gnostics.

The second are ignorant Sufis who are cut off from the straight way and the path of virtue by having entered the Path through custom or tradition, and not by permission of a perfected master, one who has reached the goal and is therefore capable of helping others arrive. For such Sufis, there is no doubt that they will be taken by the crookedness of their feet out of the path of truth and into the fire of distance and separation from God.

The *marks* by which they are known may be their haughtiness, or the crassness of their natures, or the way in which they seek high rank and standing, or the wagging of their tongues as they show off their knowledge. The true and complete gnostics are very different. They are humble, easy, and supple. For them, to be hidden is more beloved than to be known, and the tongue of their states expresses much more than their words.

This is the Hell which the guilty belie, those who have just been mentioned, for they are *Those whose effort goes astray in the life of the world, and yet they reckon that they do good work* [18:104]. *They will go back and forth between the fire* of separation, and *the boiling waters* of self-direction and choice (*al-tadbīr wa al-ikhtiyār*), worry about provision, fear of men, and the tribulations of the veil [that is between them and God]. We ask God, in His generosity and grace, for protection from all that.

46. *And for the one who fears the station of his Lord there are two gardens*
47. *Which, then, of the favors of your Lord, will you two deny?*
48. *Full of branches*
49. *Which, then, of the favors of your Lord, will you two deny?*
50. *Therein are two springs flowing*
51. *Which, then, of the favors of your Lord, will you two deny?*
52. *Therein of every fruit there is a pair*
53. *Which, then, of the favors of your Lord, will you two deny?*
54. *Reclining upon couches lined with silk brocade, and the fruits of the garden hang low*
55. *Which, then, of the favors of your Lord, will you two deny?*

56. *Therein are those whose gaze is restrained. Neither human nor jinn has touched them before*
57. *Which, then, of the favors of your Lord, will you two deny?*
58. *As though they were sapphire or pearl*
59. *Which, then, of the favors of your Lord, will you two deny?*
60. *Is the reward for excellence other than excellence?*
61. *Which, then, of the favors of your Lord, will you two deny?*

Commentary

And for the one who fears the station of his Lord there are two gardens.

The station of his Lord means the moment when the servant will stand before the Lord *on the Day when people shall stand before the Lord of the Worlds* [83:6] for the Reckoning. But *station* may also be understood to refer to God's overseeing our states, for it is said of one who watches over another, "He stands over him," (*qāma 'alayhi*), and thus do the words of God elsewhere state, *Who is it that is standing over every soul in that which it earns?* [13:33]. Said Mujāhid, "*The one who fears the station of his Lord* is anyone who thinks about committing a sin, then remembers God and abandons it out of fear." And al-Suddī said, "Two things have been lost: the fear which discomforts us and the yearning which spurs us on."....

[For such a one] *there are two gardens*, one of red coral and one of green emerald, each of which would take a hundred years to traverse on foot. The Prophet (upon whom be peace) asked, "Do you know what these two gardens are? They are two orchards within two orchards. Their roots are eternal, their branches firm, and their trees ever blossoming."[67] By these two gardens will the believers be honored, and their joy will be completed by being taken from one to the other.

It is also said that one of the gardens is recompense for their fear of God, while the other is recompense for their having abandoned lusts; or that one is recompense for faith, the other for deeds; or that one is for having accomplished the good and the other for having avoided sin; or that one is given as recompense and the other by grace; or that one is spiritual and the other physical; or that one is for the Foremost and the other for the Companions of the Right Hand;[68] or that one is for humankind and the other for jinn, since these verses are addressed to both. But the first explanation is the most widely recognized....[69] *Which, then, of the favors of your Lord do you two deny?*

Full of branches. Which, then, of the favors of your Lord do you two deny?

Here begins the description of the two gardens. The word *afnān* is the plural of *fanan* which means "branches," particularly those which give forth leaves, bear fruit, and form a canopy of shade. It is also the plural of the word *fanna*, meaning "sort" or "variety," and taken in this latter sense, it refers to the many types of trees and fruit that fill these gardens—*all that souls desire and brings delight to the eyes* [43:71]—and none of which should be denied.

Therein are two springs flowing.

In those two gardens are two springs flowing upstream or down as [the blessed] so desire. According to al-Ḥasan, they flow with limpid waters, one from *Tasnīm* and the other *Salsabīl*.[70] It has also been said that one flows with water and the other with wine.[71]...

Therein of every fruit there is a pair.

Here the word *pair* (*zawj*) means "variety," and of these varieties, it has been said that one is known and the other strange or rare, or that one is moist and the other dry. ...

Reclining upon couches lined with silk brocade, and the fruits of the garden hang low...

Those who fear their Lord are described with praise as *Reclining upon couches* which are lined with a kind of finely embroidered cloth known as *istabraq*. And if such is the cloth which covers the inside of these couches, what do you imagine covers the outside? Some commentators have said it is *sundus*, an even more densely embroidered cloth; others have said it is pure light; and others have said only God knows. *And the fruit* borne by the trees hangs within reach of the dwellers whether they are standing, sitting, or reclining on their sides. About this, Ibn 'Abbās said, "The trees incline so that the friends of God may reach them whether standing, sitting, or reclining."

Al-Qushayrī said, "It has been related that for anyone who says 'Glory be to God, Praise be to God, There is no god but God, and God is greater,' a thousand trees are planted in Heaven, with roots of gold, branches of pearl, and fruit like maidens' breasts—softer than butter, sweeter than honey—and each time a fruit is picked from them they return to how they had been.[72] And *the fruits of the two gardens hang low,* so that if the blessed desire to eat of them, they are near at hand and may be reached without effort." *Which, then, of the favors of your Lord do you two deny?*

Therein are those whose gaze is restrained.
Neither human nor jinn has touched them before.

The word *therein* (*fī hinna*) can be read as meaning 'within the two gardens,' but the pronoun is in the feminine plural [rather than the feminine dual] because it refers not only to the gardens but to all the dwellings, palaces, and gathering places of Heaven. It may also be understood as referring back to the *favors of your Lord,* meaning that of God's many favors [to the inhabitants of Heaven]—the two gardens, the two springs, the fruit and the greenery—there are also those *whose gaze is restrained.* These are maidens who look only upon their spouses and no one else. *Neither human nor jinn has touched them before,* and the verb *tamatha* means literally "to deflower" which indicates that this is an act done by jinn as well as humans...

As though they were sapphire or pearls

The beauty of these maidens is likened to sapphire and white pearls, if the word *marjān* be understood to mean "tiny pearls."[73] If it be understood to mean "coral-stone," then it refers to the clearness and rosy color of their faces. It has also been related that the maidens of Heaven are clothed in seventy robes, yet the marrow of their limbs is visible from beneath, like red wine in a glass.[74]...

Is the reward of excellence other than excellence?
Which, then, of the favors of your Lord will you two deny?

This question refers back to all that has been so far mentioned [concerning the blessings of Heaven] and means that there is no recompense for the excellence (*al-iḥsān*) of deeds [in this world] except the excellence [of the Next World]. According to Anas, the Prophet (upon whom be blessings and salutations of peace) once recited this verse and said, "Do you know what your Lord says? He says, 'Is the reward for those to whom I have given the grace of monotheism (*tawḥīd*) other than Heaven?'"[75] And in another version, "Is the reward for those whom I have blessed with belief in My unity and direct knowledge of Me other than that, by My Mercy, I will cause them to dwell in My Heaven in the precincts of My Holiness?"[76] Or in yet another version, "Is the reward for one who says 'There is no god but God (*lā ilāha illa Llāh*)' other than Heaven?"[77] According to al-Suddī this verse means, "Is the reward for those who live a life of obedience in this world other than generosity in the Next?" And Ja'far al-Ṣādiq said, "[God says]: 'Is the reward for those to whom I have shown My excellence before creation (*al-azal*) anything other than that I shall continue to show My excellence to them after creation (*al-abad*) ?" Al-Ḥasan said, "[This verse] applies both to the reprobate and the faithful: to the reprobate in this life and the faithful in their Final Destination..."[78]

Spiritual Allusion

For the one who fears the station of his Lord, who is vigilant for God and then perceives [Him],[79] *there are two gardens*: a garden of gnosis in this world and a garden of adornment in the Next; or a garden of gnosis for their souls and a garden of adornment for their physical forms. Said al-Qushayrī,

> The *two gardens* are the garden of this world, which is the sweetness obeying God and the repose and peace of being near Him, and the garden of the Hereafter, which is the garden of recompense. The spiritual degrees of those who inhabit the garden of this world vary, just as the paradisiacal stations of those who will inhabit the garden of the Hereafter will vary.

We could also say that the garden of sweetness which comes from obeying God is for the Companions of the Right Hand, while the garden of repose and comfort in God's nearness is for the Foremost. Al-Wartajibī says of the two gardens:

> One is of direct perception and the other of intimate discourse; one is of love and the other of unveiling; one is of gnosis (*ma'rifa*) and the other of oneness (*tawḥīd*); one is of stations and the other of states; one is of the heart and the other of the soul; one is of miracles (*karāmāt*) and the other of approach (*mudānā*).

And we might add: one is of arrival and the other of perfection; one is of making efforts towards perfect virtue and the other of perfect virtue itself; one is of effacement and the other of subsistence; one is of subsistence in God and the other of infinite ascent.

As for God's words *Full of spreading branches*, these allude to the many types of knowledge, tastes, mysteries, and lights to be found in those two gardens, as well as to the differing spiritual insights which arise from the ocean of mysteries.[80] *Therein*, for each one, *are two springs flowing forth*, one with the teachings of the Revealed Law, ethics, and comportment befitting servanthood, and the other with the teachings of the esoteric truth, the Way, and the monotheism of the elect (*al-tawḥīd al-khāṣṣ*).[81] *Therein of every fruit* of spiritual experience (*adhwāq*) *there is a pair*, that is, two kinds: one which is constant and unchanging and the other which is renewed at each instant. We might also say there is a kind which pertains to the world of Divine Wisdom and another which pertains to the world of Divine Power;[82] or one which pertains to the Essence and one which pertains to the Attributes; or one which arises from the sweetness of direct perception and one which arises from correct comportment.

They are *reclining upon* the *couches* of their intimacy [with God], which are *lined with* the *silk brocade* of repose, joy and ebullience. *And the fruits of the garden* of gnosis, containing the sweetness of vision and intimacy, come willingly to their hands. Thus their percepton of the Divine is constant and their nearness to the Beloved perpetual. Wheresoever their meditations turn, they plunge into the Ocean of Unicity (*baḥr al-aḥadiyya*) and emerge with pearls and gems beyond imagination.

Such is not the case, however, for those not yet granted stability in their vision of the Divine. For such, the delight of the spiritual vision is diminished by the fatigue found in contemplation. As al-Qushayrī explained, "There is no delight when the first visions of the Divine appear, and to this did the Prophet allude in his supplication, 'O God! Grant me the delight of gazing upon Your Face, and a longing for the meeting with You, without tribulation or harm.'"[83]

Therein are ones who restrain their gaze, the virginal esoteric truths (*al-ḥaqā'iq*) which *neither human nor jinn has touched before*, for they are only unveiled to the people of spiritual 'taste' and none other. Each of them "touch" esoteric truths, like *sapphire or pearls* in their translucence and purity, which none other has touched, and to each is unveiled what has never been unveiled to another, according to their readiness and disposition.

Such is the recompense of the people who have reached the station of Excellence (*al-iḥsān*). *And is the reward for excellence other than excellence?* Is the recompense which comes to those of the station of Excellence other than excellence, proximity, and being chosen to receive these teachings and these inner truths? Or, is the recompense for your excellence with Us other than the excellence of Our Essence being unveiled for you? Or, is the reward of your excellence to My servants other than the excellence of being near Me and being among My saints?

Concerning this verse, Ibn Juzayy said, "The excellence mentioned in the verse may also be taken to mean that about which the angel Gabriel asked the Prophet when he answered, 'It is that you worship God as if you see Him.' [84] For this did God make these two gardens as recompense."...[85]

62. *And besides these are two other gardens*
63. *Which, then, of the favors of your Lord, will you two deny?*
64. *Of the deepest green*
65. *Which, then, of the favors of your Lord, will you two deny?*
66. *Therein are two springs bubbling*
67. *Which, then, of the favors of your Lord, will you two deny?*
68. *Therein is fruit, and the date, and the pomegranate*
69. *Which, then, of the favors of your Lord, will you two deny?*
70. *Therein are fair and beautiful ones*
71. *Which, then, of the favors of your Lord, will you two deny?*
72. *Houris restraining their glances, in fair pavillions*
73. *Which, then, of the favors of your Lord, will you two deny?*
74. *Neither man nor jinn has touched them before*
75. *Which, then, of the favors of your Lord, will you two deny?*
76. *Reclining on green cushions and fair carpets of marvelous design*
77. *Which, then, of the favors of your Lord, will you two deny?*
78. *Blessed be the Name of your Lord full of Majesty and Generosity*

Commentary

And besides these are two other gardens... of the deepest green.
Which, then, of the favors of your Lord, will you two deny?

Besides the two gardens for Those Brought Near (*al-muqarrabūn*) are two others for those who are lower in rank, the Companions of the Right Hand. Supporting this explanation is a *ḥadīth* related by Abū Mūsā concerning God's words, *For the one who fears his Lord are two gardens:* "Two golden gardens for the Foremost, and two silver gardens for the Companions of the Right Hand,"[86] for gold is of higher worth than silver, and one who had the first would scarcely glance at the second. Some say, however, that this explanation is faulty since it implies a kind of deprivation on the part of those of the higher rank. In *Nawādir al-uṣūl*, the author takes the words *And besides these* to mean "nearer to the Divine Throne,"[87] which would make them higher in degree than the first two, and writes at length concerning this. Ibn 'Aṭiyya and Ibn 'Abbās also favor this latter explanation and provide textual support, but the majority of commentators favor the first meaning. Further explanation of this will follow, God willing....

[These two gardens are] *of the deepest green*, the word *mudhāmmatān* literally meaning "a shade of green verging on black because of the density of vegetation." This signifies that in these latter two gardens, thick vegetation covering the ground predominates, whereas in the first two it is trees and fruits.

Which, then, of the favors of your Lord, will you two deny? The repetition of this verse after each mention of the gardens' blessings emphasizes the folly of those who deny them.

Therein are two springs bubbling....
Therein is fruit, and the date, and the pomegranate.

....[The date and the pomegranate] are distinguished from the general term fruit because of their particular excellence, for the first is both fruit and nourishment, while the second is both fruit and medicine.[88] According to Abū Ḥanīfa, "If someone has taken an oath not to eat fruit and then eats either a pomegranate or date, he has not broken that oath," basing his judgment on the most literal reading of the conjunctions [in the verse] which separate [dates and pomegranates from fruit]. For us, however, an oath is based on the accepted usage of a word which may vary from place to place...[89]

Therein are fair and beautiful ones...
Houris restraining their glances, in fair pavillions

Within these two gardens and their palaces and abodes dwell women of virtue and beauty, ... the *Houris.* They are described as being *in fair pavillions*, if one takes the word *maqṣūrāt* to mean "enclosed behind a veil." It may also be understood to mean "limiting their gazes to their spouses alone and dwelling in pavillions," and thus did al-Qushayrī say [concerning it], "Their souls, their hearts, and their gazes are for their spouses alone." And they say, "We are the gentle ones who are never sad; we are the eternal ones who never pass away; we are the contented ones who are never vexed." It has been narrated that 'Ā'isha (may God be pleased with her) said "To this, the faithful women [of this world] answer, 'But we are the ones who pray and you have never prayed; we are the ones who fast, and you have never fasted; we are the ones who give charity, and you have never given charity!' To which 'Ā'isha added, "So we have surpassed them!"[90]

It has also been said that the pavillions in which the Houris dwell are made of hollowed pearls...[91]

Reclining upon green cushions
and fair carpets of marvelous design.

The word *rafraf* may be understood to mean "thick brocaded fabric or cushions." What is indicated in the *ḥadīth* is that the inhabitants of Heaven recline upon couches of green which are found wheresoever they wish... The carpets are called *'Abqāriyyin*—"something from the land of *'Abqār*"—this being the name the ancient Arabs used to refer to a land of the jinn and to which they ascribed any marvelously crafted thing. According to Abū 'Ubayd, "'Abqār is a land where the finest embroidery is done and is used as a hyperbole in description," and al-Khalīl said, "Anything of magnificence, excellence, and rarity done by humans or others was called by the Arabs *'abqārī*, and thus did the Prophet say concerning 'Umar, 'I never saw a person with such genius for hard work (*'abqāriyyan*).'[92]
Which, then, of the favors of your Lord, will you two deny?...[93]

Blessed be the Name of your Lord,
Full of Majesty and generosity.

Sanctified, sublime, and bountiful [be God's Name]. This is the response of affirmation to all the gifts mentioned in this noble *sūra*. God is *Full of Majesty and generosity*, immense in His grandeur, generous with the graces He bestows upon His friends...[94]

It has also been said that God's mention of the blessings of this world end with the words *And there remains the Face of your Lord Full of Majesty and Generosity*, and thus invoke His Everlastingness compared to the ephemerality of the world. His mention of the graces of the Next World, however, end with the words *Blessed be the Name of your Lord full of Majesty and Generosity* because blessing (*al-baraka*)—which is goodness and increase—relates to the ever-increasing and eternal goodness given to the faithful in the Abode of His Generosity.

Lastly, according to Jābir, the Prophet (upon whom be peace) recited this *sūra* to some of the Companions and then asked, "Why do I see you silent? Truly the jinn are better than you in their response, for whenever I recite *Which, then, of the favors of your Lord do you two deny*? they say, 'Not one of Your favors do we deny, O Lord! To You belong all praise and thanks!'"[95]

This verse [*Which, then, of the favors...*], as al-Nasafī says, is repeated throughout the *sūra* thirty-one times. Eight follow verses which speak of the marvels of God's creation, its beginning, and its end. Seven follow verses which speak of Hellfire and its tribulations, seven being the number of the gates of Hell. Eight more follow verses which describe the first two Gardens and their dwellers—eight being the number of the gates of Heaven—and another eight follow verses which describe the second two Gardens. Thus [has it been said that for the] one who affirms the first eight [concerning creation] and acts in accordance with what that affirmation entails, the eight gates of Heaven shall be opened and the seven gates of Hell locked shut.

Spiritual Allusion

And beneath the two gardens of Those Brought Near *are two others* for the Companions of the Right Hand: a garden of the sweetness of obeying God, and another of virtue perfected; or a garden of the sweetness of virtuous conduct, and another of manifest miracles; or a garden of the sweetness of intimate discourse with God, and another of attaining His nearness; or a garden that is nearer in time to the Intermediary Realm of souls, and another that will come after the Resurrection of their individual forms. All of this is true for Those Brought Near as well.

Both these gardens are *of the deepest green*, which is the color most attractive to the eye, and in a like manner, when the people of outward devotions find sweetness therein, and reside with that sweetness, they may attract the eyes of the generality and be seen as great and noble, which may take away from the recompense of their practice. In this they differ from the people of the inward, the people of effacement and subsistence in God: all you will see of them is a faint glimmer from their distant campfire, both because of their having fled from mundane life and because their devotional practices are largely hidden and consist mainly of meditation and reflection.

Therein are two springs bubbling with the outward knowledge that is the fruit of their reverent fear of God (*taqwā*), even as His words declare: *Observe your duty to God and God will teach you* [2:282]. But while an abundance of this sort of knowledge is a virtue for the people of the outward, it is not held in great esteem by the people of the inward, whose domain is that of spiritual tastes (*adhwāq*), inward discovery, and attainment to the Supreme Vision. As the shaykh of our shaykhs, Sīdī 'Alī al-'Amrānī, says in his book, "News about the war and how the two armies are faring is for spectators. The one who is in the thick of the battle is too busy for news."[96]

Therein is fruit, and the date, and the pomegranate, which alludes to skill in the essential issues of *fiqh*, proficiency in the science of *ḥadīth*, and mastery in Quranic commentary; or the *fruit* of having mastered the science of conduct and interaction, *the date* of having mastered the science of figurative analogies, *and the pomegranate* of perseverance in the science of Sufism, which is the remedy of hearts.

Therein are fair and beautiful ones. In those gardens is the beauty of character, which is the fruit of beneficial knowledge. *Houris restraining their glances, secluded in tents*: those beautiful virtues which reside within the hearts of the people of purity and which are shown only to them. Or it may be said that in those gardens which are the hearts dwell sorts of knowledge which are both rare and unique and not revealed to any except them. *Neither man nor jinn has touched them before* inasmuch as none other has ever deciphered them. As it is written in *al-Tashīl*[97]: "If knowledge is a Divine and special gift, then it is not out of the question that something which was difficult for those of earlier times could be made easy for those in later times."

Reclining on green cushions and fair carpets of marvelous design. Such are the outspread carpets of meditative reflection by which jewels of knowledge are retrieved. The color *green*, for its part, alludes to the verdance and freshness which meditation leaves upon the knowledge that is gained through it, even as the Prophet said, "One hour spent by a learned man reflecting upon his knowledge is better than a thousand years of physical acts of devotion offered by an ignorant man," or words close to this.[98] Thus is it also said that in their excellence and perfection they are of *marvelous design.*

Blessed be the Name of your Lord, venerable in His power and *Full of Majesty and Generosity* for having graced both [Those Brought Near and Those of the Right Hand] with these immense gifts.

In God is all success and there is neither strength nor power except though God, the Mighty and Sublime. May He bless our master Muḥammad, and his family and companions, and give them salutations of peace.

Notes on the Chapter of the All-Merciful

1. Also concerning this *sūra*, a *ḥadīth* states, "For everything there is a bride (*'arūs*), and the bride of the Qur'ān is *Sūrat al-Raḥman*"(Bayhaqī, 2392) and certain commentaries mention that it was revealed in response to the pagans of Mecca, about whom [25:60] states, *When it is said to them, 'Prostrate to the All-Merciful (*al-Raḥmān*),' they say, 'What is* al-Raḥmān*?'*.... In respect to the Divine Name which begins the *sūra* and is included in the *basmala* that opens all but one of the *sūras* of the Qur'ān, a well-known *ḥadīth* identifies the connection between *al-Raḥmān* and the womb (*al-raḥim*) which stands for all family ties. The version of this *ḥadīth* in Tirmidhī, *Raḥmat al-nās*, 1847, states: "The All-Merciful has mercy upon those who are merciful. Be merciful, then, to those who dwell on earth, and those who dwell in the heavens will be merciful to you. The name of the womb (*al-raḥim*) is taken from [God's Name] *al-Raḥmān*. So whoever stays in contact with family, God stays in contact with, and whoever cuts himself off from family, God cuts off." Variations of this *ḥadīth* exist in Bukhārī and many other collections.

2. "Rule" or "obligation" (*ḥukm*) is used in the sense of the *ḥadīth* which appears in Mālik, 51:5 and elsewhere: "The Prophet, upon whom be peace and blessings, said, 'God the Blessed and Exalted said, "My love is an obligation (upon Myself) for those who love one another for My sake, those who sit with one another for My sake, those who visit one another for My sake, and those who spend generously upon one another for My sake." ' "

3. The opening words of the Qur'ān state that it is guidance for *those who believe in what is revealed to you [O Muḥammad] and what has been revealed before you.* [2:4]

4. In the Arabic the conjunction *waw* ("and") is absent between the three verbs. This, Ibn 'Ajība notes, gives a tone of enumeration to these verses.

5. *He it is Who appointed the sun a splendor and the moon a light, and measured for her stages, that you might know the number of the years, and the reckoning.* [10:5]

6. A well-known work in Mālikī *fiqh* named for its author. See biographical notes: *al-Waghlīsī.*

7. According to modern astronomy, the diameter of the sun is 109 times larger than that of the earth while the moon's is one-fourth that of the earth.

8. We could not find the source of this saying.

9. *Al-mukallafayn*, which literally means "the two creatures who are accountable for their actions." The word *jinn*, derived from the Arabic verb meaning "to be hidden," refers to what Muslims believe to be non-formal creatures which share the earth with human beings. They are referred to three times in this *sūra*, while *sūra* 72 is named after them and refers to them in detail.

10. *An yu'aṭī kulla dhi ḥaqqin ḥaqqahu.* Variations of this expression occurs in several sayings of the Prophet.

11. Abū Dawūd, *Buyū'*, 3410; Ibn Majah, *Zakah*, 1820.

12. Ibn 'Ajība notes that the verse may be taken either as subjunctive (as explained above) or as a negative imperative, with the meaning, '*So do not transgress the balance.*'

13. Ibn 'Ajība points out that the word *rayḥān* may also mean "that which is sweet-smelling." He refers to this meaning in his spiritual allusion.

14. He adds: "In the recitation of the people of Shām, the word *rayḥān* is in the subjective case which would make the verse read *and* (also upon the earth is the) *sweet-smelling herb.*

15. As they are referred to later in this *sūra* in verse 31. Both the possessive *your Lord* (*Rabbukumā*) and the predicate, *do you two deny* (*khadhdhibān*) are in the dual form.

16. He adds, "For more about this, refer to Abū al-Sa'ūd."

17. The Qur'ān, in fact, refers to the Prophet as *raḥīm* in [9:128]. Many other of the Divine Names—particularly those of beauty and mercy such as *al-Karīm* (The Generous), *al-Ḥalīm* (The Clement), or *al-Ḥafīẓ* (The Protector) may also be used to describe human beings.

18. These and other verses which mention *istiwā*, "*the action of being seated*" as related to God, were part of the theological differences between the Mu'tazilites and others in the 2nd/8th century. The comment attributed both to Imām Mālik and al-Shāfi'i concerning this is generally considered

the orthodox position: "The act of being seated (*al-istiwā*) is understood, its manner is unknown; to believe in it is obligatory; to debate about it is dangerous innovation and error."

19. *K. al-Ḥikam, Munājāt* 43

20. He is referring to a *ḥadīth* in Bukhārī, *Riqāq*, 5988, and Muslim, *Tawba*, 4943-46, of which one version states: "Verily God apportioned His mercy into one hundred portions. Ninety-nine He kept and one He sent down to earth, and by this single portion do all creatures show mercy to each other, so that even the mare will lift her hoof away from her foal so as not to step upon it." The Essential Mercy to which Ibn 'Ajība refers corresponds in this context to the Ninety-nine portions that God kept with Himself.

21. Ibn 'Ajība is taking the word *al-bayān*, generally understood as a synonym for "speech or language," in its literal sense of "that which is clear and evident."

22. By "a guide to guide him" (*dāllu yudilluhu*) he means the Prophet and by extension any legitimate spiritual teacher.

23. Here and throughout this commentary, the word "gnosis" is used to translate the Arabic *ma'rifa*, direct experiential knowledge of God, and "gnostic" is used to translate *'ārif* or *'ārif bi'llāh*. The similarity to Greek Gnosticism is purely lexical. By contrast, we have frequently used the word "teachings" to translate *'ilm* or *'ulūm*, that kind of knowledge (or religious science) that can be conveyed in books or by a teacher to a student.

24. The Moon of Divine Oneness (*tawḥīd*) is none other than the light of faith which, according to several traditional sayings, increases and decreases.

25. Here he is using the other meaning of *najm*.

26. The *Jabarūt*, in Islamic cosmology, is the realm of the archangels or the Divine Qualities. It is often referred to along with the *Malakūt*, the realm of souls and angels, and the *Mulk*, the physical universe.

27. This is probably a reference to the saying of Shakyh Abū al-'Abbās al-Mursī, the successor of the Shaykh al-Shādhilī, who is reported to have said, "By God, were the Prophet to be veiled from me for the blink of an eye, I would not reckon myself a Muslim." Ibn 'Iyyād, page 16.

28. One able interpret religious law in new ways according to new situations.

29. *'An ghayri ahlihā*. In the context, this means people who are not following the spiritual path.

30. The Arabic word *ṣalṣāl* is onomatopoeic for the sound made by the clay when it is worked.

31. Iblīs is the name of the jinn who became Satan, first mentioned in [2:34]: *When We said to the angels, Fall prostrate to Adam, and all fell*

prostrate except for Iblīs. He refused and waxed proud and was among the ungrateful.

32. Although Ibn 'Ajība would normally refer to the Muslim calendar, here he is referring to the Roman or Julian calendar that was in use in Morocco, especially in the countryside, in his day, just as the Gregorian calendar continues to be used today. The "drift of the solstices" is an astronomical fact and partly the reason for the adoption of the Gregorian calendar which inserts an extra day into the month of February every four years to adjust for this drift. Using the Roman calendar with a fixed 365 days would result in an error of 0.2422 days or almost 6 hours per year. After 100 years, this calendar would be more than 24 days ahead of the seasons. The site http://stellafane.org/misc/equinox.html calculates the actual solstice equinox dates going back to the year 1000.

33. This distinction is made because the root in Arabic for "east" and for "the rising of the sun," SHRQ, is the same, as is the root for "west" and "the setting of the sun," GHRB.

34. The annotation of *Tafsīr Jalālayn* by 'Abd al-Raḥmān al-Fāsī.

35. From places in the Rīf Mountains in Northern Morocco between Tangier and Tetouan, one can see where the waters of the Atlantic and the Mediterranean meet.

36. From the perspective of traditional Muslim geography, what is shown as south in European maps is north and Mecca is shown at the center of world. From this perspective "The Persian Sea" (now called the Persian Gulf) and the Mediterranean appear as branches of the Atlantic Ocean that meet, as it were, near Cape Horn.

37. Generally translated as "coral."

38. He is citing a basic rule of Islamic knowledge: to give affirmation precedence over negation.

39. According to the findings of modern science, true coral is found only in salt water. Pearls, however, are found in oysters, which inhabit salt water, as well as in mollusks, which inhabit fresh water.

40. Tirmidhī, *Da'wāt*, 3447, 3448; Aḥmad, 16935; Ṭabarānī, *al-Kabīr*, 4460; Ḥākim, *Du'ā'*, 1790, 1791.

41. Tirmidhī, *Da'wāt*, 3450; Aḥmad, 21044; Ṭabarānī, *al-Kabīr*, 16521, 16522.

42. Here the verb is read *inḥaraqat*; if it is read *inḥarafat*, however, it would mean, "they are led into heresy." Either is possible in the context.

43. More literally, "in the presence of a cloud of lights and vicissitudes (*ghayn al-anwār wa al-aghyār*)." Ibn 'Ajība is making a reference to Shaykh al-Shādhilī's words, "For a long time, I was puzzled by the saying of the Prophet, may God bless him, 'My heart is clouded over [each day] until I have asked God's forgiveness seventy times.' Then I heard a voice

say to me, 'O Mubārak! It is a cloud of *lights* (*anwār*), not of vicissitudes (*aghyār*)!' "

44. This is a reference to a saying attributed to Imām Mālik.

45. Coral is branching and convoluted, as is formal religious knowledge, while pearls are spherical, multi-layered, and translucent.

46. *Lisān al- ḥāl*, "the tongue of one's state or condition," is an expression found frequently in the writings of the Shādhilīya and means that God knows our needs whether we articulate them or not.

47. That is, all the souls which, on that day, enter the fetuses which are developing in the wombs, all the souls of babies born into the world that day, and all the souls of those who pass away on that same day.

48. Ibn Majah, *Muqaddima*, 198, Ṭabarānī, *al-Kabīr*, 1769, 3258, 6808; Bayhaqī, 1113.

49. Referring to a *ḥadīth* in Bukhārī, *Nikah, 4788; Qadr,* 6222.

50. He is referring to the *ḥadīth* found in both Muslim and Bukhārī that says that after forty or forty-five nights, "An angel comes into where the embryo has formed in the womb and says, 'O Lord, shall it be among the blessed or damned?' and that is written. Then the angel says, 'O Lord, shall it be male or female?' and that is written, as are its deeds, its preferences, the length of its life, and its provision. Then the pages are folded up and there is neither addition nor subtraction after that." Bukhārī, *Ḥayḍ*, 312; Muslim, *Qadr*, 2646. The version referred to in the commentary is quoted in *Fatḥ al-Bārī*, as related by al-A'mash.

51. Ibn Māja, *Tawba*, 4242; Aḥmad, 3387, 3808, 3811; Ṭabarānī, *al-Kabīr*, 118, 17567.

52. Ṭabarānī, *al-Kabīr*, 11394, Bayhaqī, 9645; and with slightly different wording in Aḥmad, 2666, 6559.

53. The phrase in the Qur'ān *sanafrughu lakum* may be translated either as above, *We shall attend to you,* or *We shall dispose of you*. The verb carries both meanings.

54. In several commentaries, including those of Ṭabarī, Qurṭubī, Tha'labī, and others, a narrative by al-Ḍaḥḥāk is quoted here. The version in Ṭabarī says:

Al-Ḍaḥḥāk ibn Mazāḥim said, "On the Day of Ressurection God will command the heaven of this world and it will split open with those who inhabit it. The angels from within it will descend and encircle the earth and those upon it twice, then thrice, then four times, then five, then six, and then seven, forming row after row. Then the supreme angel will descend and to his left will be Hellfire, and when the people of the earth behold it they will call to one another [and flee] but there will be no end of the earth they come to except that they find there seven rows of angels. So they will turn back to whence they came. Thus does God say *Verily I fear for you the Day when there will be mutual calling, a Day when you will turn back* [40:32], and also, *And your Lord comes with the angel rank upon rank. And Hell is brought near that Day* [89:22-23], ... *And the sky will be split asunder that Day for it will be frail. And the angel will be on the sides thereof.* [69:16-17]

55. This is often translated simply by the adverb "when," but a more precise rendering would be "at that time," meaning "on the Day of Resurrection."

56. He is referring to the well-known *ḥadīth* in both Muslim and Bukharī which states: "Seven [people] will be given shade by God on the Day of Resurrection when there will be no shade except His Shade: a just ruler, a young person brought up in the worship of God, a person who remembers God in solitude and whose eyes overflow with tears, someone whose heart is attached to the mosque, two people who love each other for the sake of God, a man who is invited by a beautiful lady of noble birth to commit fornication and says, 'Truly, I fear God,' and someone who gives in charity secretly so that the left hand knows not what the right has given." Bukhārī, *Adhān*, 620, *Zakah*, 1334; *Ḥudūd*, 6308; Muslim, *Zakah*, 1712.

57. *Al-Budūr al-sāfirah fī umūr al-ākhira*, a treatise by Jalāl al-Dīn al-Suyūṭī.

58. These terms refer to states of the soul.

59. *K. al-Ḥikam*, 114. "When the heedless man arises in the morning, he looks at what he will do that day; when the wise man awakes, he looks at what God will do with him that day."

60. He is alluding to words attributed to the Shaykh al-Shādhilī , "If you have to plan, plan how not to plan," and, "Do not choose for yourself anything; rather, choose not to choose, and flee from that choice, and flee from your fleeing, and from everything else, to God Most High!" These words refer not so much to the planning that is necessary to live but rather to the tendency to try to 'arrange events' to one's own advantage. Quoted by Ibn 'Aṭā Allāh in the introduction to *Isqat al-Tanwīr*. See bibliography.

61. By which he means a spiritual teacher.

62. In his spiritual commentary on this verse, Ibn 'Ajība says, "*And the gardens* of gnosis *shall be brought near to the righteous..... and* (the) *Hell of* separation *will appear plainly to the erring* followers of their own passions. And as it is stated in the *Ḥikam*, 'It is not feared that the ways leading to God be confusing to you; rather, it is feared that passion overcome you.' (*K. al-Ḥikam*, 107)."

63. This is a saying from Shaykh al-Shādhilī and appears in Ibn Ṣabbāgh, *Durrat al-asrār*, p. 93, and other traditional works of the Shādhiliyya. As

the editor of the Arabic edition of *al-Baḥr* comments, neither this nor the saying quoted before it should be understood to mean that Ibn ʻAjība or Imām al-Shādhilī believed that someone who is granted this station with God is no longer subject to the Revealed Law (*al-Sharīʻa*). However, there are a number of *ḥadīth* quoting the Prophet as having said about certain individuals that God had forgiven their sins past and present.

64. As in [20:102], *On that day, the Trumpet shall be blown and We shall gather the sinful together blue-eyed.* Blueness of the eye connoted for the Arabs either blindness or raging anger.

65. Concerning the words which end this verse, *ḥamīmin ānin,* Ibn ʻAjība notes that *ḥamīm* means hot water, while *ānin* means the very limit of heat. According to Kaʻab, *al-Ān* is the name of one of the rivers of Hell.

66. Inasmuch as "the forelock" is closest to the brain, the organ of thought.

67. Suyūṭī cites a *ḥadīth* close to this in his commentary on this verse in *Durr al-Manthūr* where he attributes it Ibn Mardawayh, from ʻIyāḍ, from Ibn Tamīm.

68. See the commentary on *Sūrat al-Wāqiʻa* which follows.

69. Ibn ʻAjība completes his commentary on this verse along with the spiritual allusion to come.

70. *Tasnīm,* mentioned in [76:18], is one of the drinks of Heaven. In Bukhārī, *K. al-Tafsīr,* Mujāhid describes it as "the most sublime of the drinks of Heaven." *Salsabīl,* mentioned in [83:27], is one of the paradisiacal springs

71. *Therein are rivers of water unpolluted, and rivers of milk whereof the flavor never changes, and rivers of wine delicious to the drinkers, and rivers of clear-run honey.* [47:15].

72. This is close in wording to a *ḥadīth* cited in Ṭabarānī, *al-Awsaṭ,* 8710. The words of praise are *Subḥān Allāh, wa al-ḥamdu li Llāh, wa lā ilāha illa Llāh, wa Llāhu akbar.*

73. See his commentary on verse 22 above.

74. Bukhārī, *Bad' al-khalq,* 3007; Tirmidhī, *Janna,* 2456; Aḥmad, 8186

75. Bayhaqī, *Shuʻab al-īmān,* 456.

76. *Nawādir al-uṣūl,* 2:266. This work, the complete title of which is *Nawādir al-uṣūl fī aḥādīth al-rasūl,* composed by al-Ḥakīm al-Tirmidhī (d. ca. 922/1516), is an esoteric commentary on 291 *ḥadīth* arranged as *uṣūl,* "fundamentals or principles"

77. Suyūtī on the authority of ʻIkrima.

78. The first of these two sayings is cited in the *Tafsīr al-Qurṭubī* while the second appears in the commentaries of Qurṭubī, Thaʻlabī, and Suyūṭī to mention just some. Al-Ḥasan's saying means that even if a reprobate

accomplishes an act of goodness towards others, it may bring him or her goodness in this life.

79. The meaning is that by *murāqabah*, "watching over the soul" for the sake of God, comes *mushāhada*, direct and on-going consciousness of God.

80. Here he is taking the word *afnān* to be the plural of *fanna*, "sort."

81. Literally, "the particular [understanding of the] unity [of God]." In his spiritual allusion concerning [2:163], *And your God is One God. There is no god but He. The All-Merciful and Compassionate*, Ibn 'Ajība says of this term:

Know that there are three levels of *tawḥīd*. The first, which is what the generality of the faithful affirm, is to reject that there are partners, other deities, spouses, children, similarities to creation, or opposites along with God. It is by testifying to this that their lives and property are secure and they are delivered from Hell.

The second is the *tawḥīd* of the elect. This is to see that all actions originate with God alone, and to perceive this by way of a spiritual unveiling, not by way of the formal proofs which are accessible to every believer. In the station of the elect, there is a certitude in the heart that arises from irrefutable knowledge and has no need for formal proofs. Its fruit is a turning towards God with one's whole being, and putting one's trust in Him alone. Those who are granted this knowledge hope only for God and fear none but Him because they see no other Doer except Him and thus dispense with all secondary causes and earthly lords.

The third level is [the *tawḥīd* of those] who see nothing else in existence except God, and perceive nothing else with Him. They pass away from their perception of created being in their vision of the Creator, this being the station of Effacement (*al-fanā'*) and if they then return by God to perception of phenomena, it is called the station of Subsistence (*al-baqā*).

82. Ibn 'Ajība uses the terms *ḥikmah* (Divine Wisdom) and *qudrah* (Divine Power) to signify, respectively, all that mercifully veils God from creation and all that mercifully unveils God to creation. *Mi'rāj al-tashawwuf ilā ḥaqīqati al-taṣawwuf*, Tetouan, 1982, p. 50. See also Michon, page 83, n. 144.

83. Nasā'ī, *Sahw*, 1288; Aḥmad, 17605, 20678; Ḥākim, 1854, 1878; Ṭabarānī, *al-Kabīr*, 4669, 4800, 4799.

84. Bukhārī, *Īmān*, 48 and Muslim, *Īmān*, 9, 10, and 11, as well as in nearly every other *ḥadīth* collection.

85. Ibn 'Ajība adds, "If it be understood that the two gardens described here are for the Foremost, the people of the highest spiritual degree, and the gardens described hereafter are for the Companions of the Right Hand, who

are of a lower spiritual degree, then Ibn Juzayy's explanation is strengthened ..."

86. Bayhaqī, 410.

87. *Nawādir al-uṣūl*, 1:124. The expression *min dūni* may mean "besides, at a lower level, or in closer proximity."

88. The medicinal properties of pomegranates are described in detail in Part Four of *Zād al-ma'ād* by Ibn Qayyim al-Jawziyya (pp. 315-16), translated by Penelope Johnstone under the title, *Medicine of the Prophet* (see bibliography). Its juice, or the extract in capsule form, is currently highly recommended as an antioxidant effective in the prevention of cancer and diabetes.

89. Ibn 'Ajība, like the overwhelming majority of Moroccans to this day, followed the Mālikī school of religious jurisprudence (*fiqh*). Imām Mālik based his judgments not only on textual evidence but also relied very strongly for his legal rulings on the actions of the people of Medina, where he was born less than 100 years after the Prophet's death. This is the principle Ibn 'Ajība is expressing here.

90. Tirmidhī, *Janna*, 2564. The word *ḥūr*, used to refer to the maidens of Heaven, literally means "someone the whites of whose eyes are extremely white, and whose pupils are extremely black." See Isfahānī, *Mufradāt alfāẓ al-Qur'ān*. They are described in *ḥadīth* as being maidens created from saffron (Ibn Abī Ḥātim, Ṭabarānī), or in other versions, from the glorifications of the angels (Mardawayh, Daylamī). In *Tafsīr al-Qurṭubī*, a narrative attributed to al-Ḥākim al-Tirmidhī describes them as being created from drops of Divine Mercy that rain down into Heaven from the Throne of God.

91. A description attributed to Ibn 'Abbās and quoted by Mundharī, *Janna* and elsewhere.

92. Bukhārī, *K. al-Munāqib*, 3361; Muslim, *Faḍā'il al-ṣaḥāba*, 4405. "I saw myself in a dream standing by a well and on it there was a bucket. I drew from the well as much water as I could (literally, as God willed). Then Ibn Abī Quhāfa (Abu Bakr) took the bucket from me and brought out one or two buckets, but there was a certain weakness in his drawing water, may God forgive him for his weakness. Then the bucket turned into a very large one and Ibn al-Khaṭṭāb took it—and I never saw a person with such genius for hard work—such that the people drank their fill and watered their camels that knelt there."

93. Here Ibn 'Ajība returns to the question of which of the pairs of gardens is higher, citing Nasafī's contention that everything described in this latter pair is shorter or more diminished than what is described about the first two.

94. Ibn 'Ajība notes that in the recitation of the people of Shām (which today includes Syria, Jordan, Palestine, and Israel), the attributes of Might and Generosity refer to God's Name.

95. Tirmidhī, *Tafsīr*, 3291; Ḥākim, *Tafsīr*, 3725 Bayhaqī, *Dalā'il al-Nubūwa*, *Islām al-jinn*, 533 and *Shu'ab al-īmān*, 2391, 4245. The exact words are: *Wa lā bi shayin min ni'amika, Rabbanā, nukadhdhibu, fa laka al-ḥamdu, wa laka al-shukr!*

96. Al-'Amrāni, p. 150. The wording in the recently printed edition of this previously rare book is slightly different from what Ibn 'Ajība quotes, but the meaning is the same: one who is deeply involved in spiritual practice has little time to spend studying formal religious knowledge. This should be understood in the context, however. No one in the orthodox Sufic tradition would recommend dispensing with the study of formal knowledge altogether. Rather, it is a question of how much is necessary. Sīdī 'Alī al-Jamal's illustrious disciple, Mulay al-'Arabī al-Darqāwī, explained this as being enough to properly accomplish the obligatory practices of the religion.

97. *Al-Tashīl fī 'ulūm al-tanzīl*, Ibn Juzayy's Quranic commentary.

98. Suyūṭī, *al-Jāmi' al-saghīr*, 4622. The wording in Suyūṭī is "An hour spent by a scholar reclining (*muttakī*) upon his pallet reflecting upon his knowledge is better than seventy years of physical acts of worship (*'ibāda*) by a devotee." This *ḥadīth* he quotes from Daylamī's *Musnad al-firdaws*. In the 1986 printing of this latter work, however, the *ḥadīth* is cited as "An hour spent by a scholar *weeping* upon his pallet reflecting upon his knowledge..." The two words, "reclining" (*muttakī*) and "weeping" (*yabkī*) appear very similar when written, but the former is more correct in the context.

The Chapter of the Event
(Sūrat al-Wāqi'a)

This *sūra* was revealed in Mecca and is ninety-six verses long. It is related to the *sūra* which precedes it in that it is a continuation and completion of it, for [in The All-Merciful] were mentioned the states in the Hereafter of the Companions of the Left Hand, the Foremost, and the Companions of the Right Hand. Here they are again mentioned as well as the time when their recompense shall appear.

In the Name of God, the All Merciful and Compassionate.

1. *When the Event befalls—*
2. *There will be no denying at the moment it befalls—*
3. *Abasing and exalting*
4. *When the earth is shaken with a shock*
5. *And the mountains are ground to powder*
6. *Then become as scattered dust*
7. *You will be of three kinds*
8. *The Companions of the Right Hand—what of the Companions of the Right Hand?*
9. *And the Companions of the Left Hand—what of the Companions of the Left Hand?*
10. *And the Foremost are the Foremost!*
11. *Those are the Ones Brought Near*
12. *In gardens of delight.*

About this *sūra*, Ibn 'Aṭiyya said,

> It is related that the Messenger of God—may God bless him and give him peace—said, "He who regularly recites *Sūrat al-Wāqi'a* shall never be in need."[1] And once, 'Uthmān asked 'Abd Allāh ibn Mas'ūd to accept a certain gift and he refused. When it was said to him, "Then take it for your family," he replied, "They regularly recite *Sūrat al-Wāqi'a*, and I heard the Prophet, may peace be upon him, say that whoever recites it shall never be in need."[2]
>
> Surely to understand what is mentioned in this *sūra* concerning the Resurrection and our ranks in the Next World is wealth beyond all poverty, for whoever understands these things will set about preparing for them.

Said Masrūq, "Whoever wishes to know the prophecies concerning the ancients, concerning the people of Heaven and the people of Hell, concerning this world and the Next should recite *Sūrat al-Wāqi'a*."

Commentary

When the Event befalls

This means 'When the Day of Judgment dawns,' at the second Trumpet-Blast.[3] The verb *waqa'a*[4], which can be used to describe the action of a falling object, expresses a sense of inevitability, as if to say, 'When what must happen happens.'... If this verse is recited followed by a stop, then the indefinite adverb *when* (*idhā*) that begins it is taken to express something too terrifying to mention directly. If the verse is recited [along with the verse that follows it and without a pause], then it is considered adverbial: *When the Event befalls* (then) *there will be no denying*. In a third possible reading, the verse may be taken as referring back to all that was mentioned in *Sūrat al-Raḥmān*. That is, all the blessings of the gardens promised to the Companions of the Right Hand and the Foremost will be given them *when the Event befalls*.

There will be no denying at the moment it befalls...[5]

At that moment no soul will continue to deny God or deny itself as it does today. At that moment, everyone will be a believer, everyone will be honest, and all will affirm the truth, while today most are lying and in denial....

Abasing and exalting.

[The Event] will be *Abasing* for certain peoples, *exalting* for others. This expresses its mighty and calamitous nature, for such is the result of catastrophic events. It has also been said, however, that the two words refer to the descent of the damned to the rungs of Hell and the ascent of the blessed to the ranks of Heaven, or to events that will take place in the physical world such as the falling of the stars and the collapse of mountain ranges, mentioned in the next verse.

When the earth is shaken with a shock.

The earth will be moved with such violence that everything upon it, both mountains and man-made structures, will be razed to the ground, as the word *abasing* signifies. At the same time, however, there will be a *raising up*, such that the lofty will be brought low and the lowly will be elevated....

And the mountains are ground to powder
and they become as scattered dust.

...The verb *bussat* means both "to be ground" and "to be moved from one place to another,"[6] similar to the words of God elsewhere, *And the hills are set in motion* [78:20]. *And they become* because of this grinding or movement *as scattered dust* (*habā'an*), literally, "motes of dust which float in the air [within a dwelling] and cannot be seen except in a ray of sunlight."

You will be of three kinds: the Companions of the Right Hand—what of the Companions of the Right Hand? And the Companions of the Left Hand—what of the Companions of the Left Hand?

You may be taken to mean all responsible beings or the assembly of peoples and communities. Of the *three kinds,* two will be in Heaven and one in Hell. Said Qatāda, "These are the ranks of people on the Day of Resurrection." The first, *the Companions of the Right Hand*, are those who will be given the record of their deeds in their right hands, and God's words, *What of the Companions of the Right Hand?* both proclaim and praise the beauty of their state. The second, the *Companions of the Left Hand*, are those who will be given the record of their deeds in their left hands, and in this case God's words, *What of the Companions of the Left Hand?* decry the ignominy of their state.[7] These verses may also refer to their stations with God, ... for [it may be said in Arabic] concerning someone you esteem, 'He is on my right,' and someone you disdain, 'He is on my left...' It has also been said that on the Day of Reckoning those who are to dwell in Heaven will be taken to the right and those who are to dwell in Hell, to the left.

Of this verse al-Qushayrī said, "The Companions of the Right Hand were those who came forth from Adam's right side at the moment when all his descendants were brought forth from his loins, and the Companions of the Left Hand were those who came forth from his left side."[8] Even thus did the Messenger of God (upon whom be peace and blessings) see them on the Night of the Ascension.[9]

And the Foremost are the Foremost!

The syntax [of this verse], in which the same word is both subject and complement, [is used in Arabic] to express something which is great and known to all, as in the words of the poet,

I am Abū al-Najmī and my poetry is my poetry!

The Foremost (*al-sābiqūn*) are thus the ones whose state and virtues are known to all. It has also been said that the verse means 'Those who are *Foremost* in accomplishing the good will be *Foremost* in entering Heaven...'

As to who, precisely, they are, the commentaries vary.[10] Some say they are the ones who were foremost to embrace the faith, the ones who, when the truth appeared to them, did not hesitate. Some say they are the people who are foremost in realizing the virtues. Some say they were the people who prayed towards both prayer directions,[11] as the words of God [elsewhere] state, *The Foremost were the first among the Emigrants and the Helpers*. [4:100]. Some say they are the ones who hasten to offer the five canonical prayers (*al-ṣalawāt al-khams*), or who hasten to accomplish acts of goodness. Above all, they are the foremost in making spiritual effort to reach the station of direct perception of God, and that is the Station of Excellence (*al-iḥsān*).

Those are the Ones Brought Near, in Gardens of bliss.

The demonstrative of distance, *those,* is used even while the ones being described are *near* to indicate how far beyond all others is their spiritual rank. In other words, the verse is saying, 'Those who are foremost in the race to God are the ones nearest to God in honor and nobility,' and the only station higher than theirs is that of the Prophets and Messengers, may peace be upon them all. They shall be *in Gardens of bliss*, of comfort and ease, in *Firdaws*, the eternal abode of Those Brought Near....[12]

Spiritual Allusion

When the Event befalls, when the Supreme Truth (*al-ḥaqīqah*) descends upon those travelling the Way, there comes to them knowledge and mysteries beyond what normal thought can comprehend, and to say it *befalls* means it appears to them, its lights dawn upon their hearts, and the created forms around them fade away. Both images and allusions are effaced, and naught remains but the Living and Eternal, alone, as He has always been.

There is no denying it will befall:[13] there is neither denial and nor doubt that it will come to pass for those who seek it, who keep company with other seekers, and lower their heads to the teachers of the Way, following the guidance they have to give.

Abasing and exalting. To anyone who seeks it, is granted its lights, and realizes its mysteries, [the Supreme Truth] is both *abasing and exalting*. Such is its over-all effect: it will abase some people even as it exalts others. Abasement comes about when *the earth* of the lower self *is shaken with a shock* by the ever-changing spiritual states which descend upon it, and from bearing both hardships and crises, from being overwhelmed by the power of invocations and disoriented by travel. For the Supreme Truth exists in the human soul like butter in milk: only when the milk is churned does the butter appear.

And the mountains of reason *are ground to powder* and *then become as scattered dust*, when the light of reason is subsumed in the Light of gnosis, just as the light of the moon is subsumed at sunrise. *You*, O seekers of God, traveling the Way, *will be of three kinds*. The first are those who set out on the journey and then stop at whatever glimmers of light appear to them, this being the case for the majority of seekers. The second are those who glimpse the Way from afar, decide that they lack the strength to bear its lights, and so turn back. These misfortunate ones we also call "those who have been deprived." The third are those who reach the Truth, who are granted a taste (*dhawq*) and then an unveiling, who are effaced in God and then returned to subsistence, who are made drunk, then returned to sobriety. They are *the Foremost, the Ones Brought Near*, dwelling *in gardens of* gnosis, in the *bliss* of Direct Perception, eternally and forever. May God make us among their ranks. Amen...[14]

13. *Many among the first*
14. *And few among the last,*
15. *[They shall be] upon embroidered couches,*
16. *Reclining, face to face.*
17. *There wait upon them immortal youths*
18. *With bowls and ewers and a cup from a pure spring*
19. *They have neither headache nor madness therefrom*
20. *And fruit that they choose*

21. *And flesh of fowls that they desire.*
22. *And [there are] fair ones with wide, lovely eyes,*
23. *Like unto hidden pearls.*
24. *Recompense for what they used to do.*
25. *They shall hear therein no vain talk nor recrimination;*
26. *Only the saying: Peace, Peace.*

Commentary

Many among the first and few among the last.

The Foremost were many when the Muhammadan community began and fewer in later days. When this community started there was abundant good, many lights and mysteries were revealed, and many scholars and saintly people appeared. In later times, however, these have been much fewer in comparison to the Companions of the Right Hand. Supporting this explanation is the saying of the Prophet (upon whom be peace) "The best generation is mine, then those who follow them, then those who follow them."[15] According to al-Tha'labī, in another *ḥadīth* the Prophet said, "Both are from my community," meaning that the Foremost, who were numerous when his community started, will continue to be part of it even while fewer in number until the Day of Reckoning.[16]

It has also been said that the words *among the first* refer to the older religions while *the last* refers to the Muhammadan community, but this explanation is considered [by most] as remote or even defective. In *Nawādir al-uṣūl* it is written that "many" means all the Prophets, ending with the Prophet Muḥammad (upon whom be peace) then after him are the saints, who are few in number in every age.[17] In al-Maḥallī however, these are mixed [and one who wishes to study this more should] refer to the *Ḥāshiyya*.[18]

On embroidered couches, reclining, face to face. There pass among them immortal youths with bowls and ewers and a cup from a pure spring. They have neither headache nor madness therefrom.

[They] recline *upon... couches embroidered* with threads of gold and soft pearl. The height of these couches, it has been said, is three hundred span but if one of the Foremost wishes to sit upon them, they descend and then rise back up.... They recline upon them in the manner of royalty *facing one another*, looking towards each other's faces such that none shall see another's back. Such is the beauty of their company, the perfection of their manners, and the purity of their love....

*There pass among them...youths...*described as *immortal* because they remain ever as children without growing old. According to some commentators, however, the word *mukhalladūn* (*immortal*) means "those who wear earrings".... or other such ornaments. It has also been said that these servants were those who died as children and so had neither good works nor sins, and a *ḥadīth* considered authentic states, "The servants of Heaven are the children of the unbelievers."[19]

[They will pass among them] *with bowls... and ewers... and a cup...* filled *from a pure spring* flowing with a wine that causes neither *headache nor madness...* In the recitation of the people of Kūfā, the last verb (*yunzafūn*) is read as *yunzifūn* [which is said about a well that has dried up]. This is the same verb which appears in the *ḥadīth*, "Zamzam will never fail nor will its waters grow scarce."...[20] [In this reading, then, the verse is saying that the wine of heaven causes no headache,] nor will it ever cease to flow....

And fruit that they choose, and flesh of fowls that they desire. And [there are] fair ones with wide, lovely eyes, like unto hidden pearls: recompense for what they used to do.

They shall have the *fruit which they choose*, the best and most excellent, which they shall pick with their own hands—for the act of picking fruit from a tree is both a blessing and joy—and they shall have *the flesh of fowl*, cooked as they desire.

The words *fair ones with wide, lovely eyes* may be read as the subject of the sentence along with *eternal youths*. This would then mean that the Foremost are served both by eternal youths and large-eyed maidens. The words may also be read as a complement, however, in which case they would mean that among the blessings of those gardens are fruit, the flesh of fowls, and wide-eyed maidens who are likened to *pearls, hidden* in their purity and beauty within shells. Of this latter verse, al-Zujāj said, "They are like pearls at the moment they are taken out of their shells, untarnished by time or from being passed from hand to hand."

All this has been made for the blessed as *Recompense for* the good and righteous actions they accomplished, for while entering Heaven is purely by the mercy of God, the many blessings and dwellings therein come by way of deeds, and the degrees therein, by certitude and gnosis. And God Most High knows better....

They shall hear therein no vain talk nor recrimination; only the saying: Peace, Peace.

This verse has been explained to mean that in Heaven they shall hear only peaceful speech...; or that they shall hear only the words (*Salām! Salām!*), for they shall greet one another, greeting upon greeting; or that each one who greets and each one who is greeted shall hear either a greeting given or a greeting returned. And God Most High knows best.

Spiritual Allusion

God Most High tells us that Those Brought Near (*al-muqarrabūn*) were greater in the beginning than in later times, but this is only in respect to quantity. In respect to quality, the Ones Brought Near who appear towards the end of time are of a higher degree and are vaster in knowledge and realization, for they are the ones who have awakened in a time of heedlessness, and made efforts in a time of lassitude. They are the ones who come at a time when few people make any spiritual effort at all and when the people of God are extremely rare. Thus, because they come to a spiritual awakening on their own, God grants them a rank not given to others.

They are the ones, in fact, to whom the Prophet referred when he said, "I long for my brethren." When the Companions then asked, "Are we not your brethren, O Messenger of God?" he answered, "You are my companions. My brethren are those who will come after me." Then, after describing some of their qualities, he said, "The deeds of one of them shall be equal to the deeds of seventy." They asked, "Seventy of them?" He answered, "No, seventy of *you.*" Then they asked, "Why is that so, O Messenger of God?" To which he answered, "Because you found help and support towards the good, but they will find no such help and support."[21]

In another *ḥadīth*, which I have seen verified as authentic, the Companions asked the Prophet, "Will there be anyone better than us?" He answered, "Yes, a people who will come after you. They will find a book between two covers.[22] They will believe in it and believe in me though they will have never seen me, and they will affirm what I have brought and act according to it. They are the ones who will be better than you."[23] This does not mean, however, that they will be better in every respect.

Those Brought Near are then described as being *upon couches* of Divine Guidance, which are *embroidered* with honor and providence, and filled with support and watchfulness. *Reclining upon them*, in their profound stability, and *facing one another* in their spiritual station and virtue, which is to say they are turned towards one another with their hearts and innermost souls and neither anger nor envy comes between them. *There passes among them* all creation at their service, for "You are with creation as long as you have not perceived the Creator, but when you have perceived the Creator, creation is with you."[24]

They are given to drink from *bowls and ewers* filled with knowledge of the Way, *and a cup* filled with the Wine of esoteric truth. *They have neither headache nor madness therefrom*, for this is not worldly wine. They do not become drunk with an intoxication that cuts them off from their reason but rather with an intoxication that is intermingled with sobriety, for the wine-pourer is a gnostic skilled in the Way. *And* [they have] *fruit*—the sweetness of perceiving God—*which they choose*, so that if they wish, they may taste this fruit in contemplation and reflection, and if they wish, in invocation and spiritual discourse (*al-mudhākarāt*). Thus one of our shaykhs used to say, "For people, the wine is in the sacred dance (*al-ḥaḍra*), while for us it is in conversation (*al-hadra*)!" by which he meant spiritual discourse. *And they shall have the flesh of fowls* from the teachings of the Way and of the Revealed Law (*'ulūm al-ṭarīqa wa'l-sharī'a*) *that they desire, and fair ones with lovely eyes*, the maidens of esoteric truths which are veiled from all others except those to whom they belong, *like unto hidden pearls*: *recompense* for the effort they make in the Way. *They shall hear* in that garden of gnosis *no vain talk nor recrimination* because the character of the ones therein has been refined. Thus does Ibn al-Fāriḍ, may God be pleased with him, say [of this Wine]:

> It refines the characters of those who drink it:
> The irresolute it guides to the path of resolve,
> The miser's hand it makes generous,
> And it gives to the one with no clemency
> Forbearance when anger strikes.

You will not hear from the Sufi anything *except the saying, Peace, peace,* for it has been said concerning the real meaning of Sufism, "It is noble character, shown by a noble folk, at a noble moment."

27. *And the Companions of the Right Hand; what of Companions of the Right Hand?*
28. *Among thornless lote-trees*
29. *And clustered plantains,*
30. *And shade extending,*
31. *And water flowing,*
32. *And fruit in plenty*
33. *Neither out of reach nor forbidden,*
34. *And raised couches.*
35. *Lo! We have created them a (new) creation*
36. *And made them virgins,*
37. *Beloved, of equal age,*
38. *For the Companions of the Right Hand;*
39. *A multitude among the first*
40. *And a multitude among the last*

Commentary

And the Companions of the Right Hand; what of Companions of the Right Hand? Among thornless lote-trees, and clustered plantains, and shade extending, and water flowing, and fruit in plenty—neither out of reach nor forbidden—and raised couches.

What of Companions of the Right Hand? is an expression of marvel at their state and degree, [and as if in response], God Most High then describes the paradisiacal blessings they will experience beginning with the words *Among thornless lote-trees.*[25] The lote-tree is the mimosa … and *makhḍūd* means that these trees, unlike the lote-trees of this world, are without thorns. It also means that their branches are so laden with fruit that they hang down almost to the ground. Concerning the fruits, Ibn Jubayr said, "They are larger than water pots, and like all the fruit of Heaven, they are without husk or peel." It has been related that the Muslims once saw a valley in Ṭā'if and marveled at its lote-trees, saying, "Would that we had something like this in Heaven!" and then this verse was revealed. Umayya ibn Abī al-Ṣalt said in verses describing Heaven:

The gardens are shaded
and therein are maidens
and lote-trees without thorns.

The *plantain* (*ṭalḥ*) is the banana tree and *manḍūd* (*"clustered"*) means that the fruit is so dense from top to bottom that the trunk is no longer visible. According to al-'Utbī's compendium,[26] [Imām Mālik] said, "It has been related to me that *the clustered plantains* mentioned in this verse are the banana tree whose fruit is like the fruit of Heaven in that its *food is unceasing* [13:35], for bananas are eaten both in winter and summer."

The *shade* therein is described as *extending* (*mamdūd*) , by which is meant spreading without decrease or end, and is similar to the light that may be seen in this world between the *fajr* prayer and sunrise.[27] *Flowing water* runs to the dwellers of Heaven wheresoever and howsoever they wish without effort on their part and the fruit is plentiful in both its varieties and shapes. It is *Never ending* in that it is always there and has no season as does the fruit of this world, nor is it *forbidden* either by being enclosed behind walls as are orchards in this world or in any other sense of the word. It has also been said that *never ending nor forbidden* means that time does not bring it to an end nor cost forbid it.

The couches [of Heaven] are described as *raised* (*marfū'*), either in degree or height, and a *ḥadīth* describes this latter as being equal to "a journey of five hundred years."[28] It has also been said that the word *couches* refers [indirectly] to the women of Heaven, as in God's words, *They and their spouses shall be in shade, reclining upon couches* [36:35] and the verse which follows supports this reading.

Lo! We have created them as a creation and made them virgins, beloved, of equal age, for the Companions of the Right Hand: a multitude among the first and a multitude among the last.

We have created them as a creation means "anew and without birth." This verse may refer either to the Houris who are created for Heaven alone, or to the women of this world, who will be created anew. ...*And We have made them maidens*, that is, virgins, such that each time their spouses come to them, they find them as virgins anew. They are also *Beloved* as companions and *of equal age* with their spouses, this being thirty-three years.

[Such are the blessings of Heaven] *for the Companions of the Right Hand* who will be *a multitude among the first and a multitude among the last*, while the Foremost were abundant only among the first...

Spiritual Allusion

The Companions of the Right Hand are the people of the veil,[29] confined within the prison of created forms and the realm of the senses. They include the devotees and ascetics (*al-'ubād wa al-zuhād*), the scholars of outward knowledge, and the generality of pious Muslims. They are among the *lote-trees* of abundant physical devotions *free of the thorns* of ostentation, vanity, indolence, and weakness, *among clustered plantains* layered with the sweetness of obeying God and reaching [ever-higher] spiritual stations, and *the extending shade* of tranquility and relief—the tranquility of one who is satisfied when God gives to him, and the relief of one who is accepting when God tries him.

[They enjoy] the *flowing water* of knowledge of God's Oneness gained either by way of logical proofs or by inspiration, *And fruit in abundance*, this being the sweetness of communing with God and witnessing the miraculous, along with the delight of having mastered the fundamental teachings of the religion, teachings which are *neither out of reach nor forbidden* to those who have truly acquired them. *And* [they are upon] *raised couches,* the levels of which vary in accordance with their practice. *We have made* for each of the types just mentioned *a special creation*, which is a particular sort of increase in the path they follow, be it in physical devotions, or learning, or asceticism, for each [path] has its own kind of ascent and increase. *And We have made them virgin*, for the increase granted is new, unfamiliar to its possessor, *beloved*, for he loves it and it is made loveable to him, and *equal in age*, inasmuch as it corresponds to his state, understanding, and spiritual experience. All of this is for the generality *of the Companions of the Right Hand* who are *abundant* among both the earlier and later peoples.

41. *And the Companions of the Left Hand: what of the Companions of the Left Hand?*
42. *In scorching wind and scalding water*
43. *And shade of black smoke*
44. *Neither cool nor generous*
45. *Lo! they had lived aforetime in luxury*

46. *And they used to persist in the awful sin*
47. *And they used to say: When we are dead and have become dust and bones shall we then be truly raised again*
48. *Along with our forefathers?*
49. *Say: Lo! those of old and those of later times*
50. *Will all be brought together to the appointed time of a well-known day*
51. *Then lo! you who are in error and denial*
52. *You will surely eat of a tree called Zaqqūm*
53. *And will fill your bellies therewith*
54. *And thereon you will drink of boiling water*
55. *Drinking as the rabid camel drinks*
56. *This will be their welcome on the Day of Judgment*

Commentary

And the Companions of the Left Hand: what of the Companions of the Left Hand? In scorching wind and scalding water, and shade of black smoke neither cool nor generous,

God's words, *What of the Companions of the Left Hand?* exclaim the ignominy of their state. ...They shall be *in scorching wind* as hot as fire that penetrates the very pores of their skin *and scalding water... and the shade of black smoke...* which is *neither cool... nor generous*. Thus, while it is called *shade*, it is a shade of heat and harm, devoid of "generosity," the coolness and relief which this world's shade gives .

Lo! they had lived..., whilst in this world, *in luxury*, enjoying all manner of bounties in their food and drink, their goodly dwellings and honored positions, engrossed in the pursuit of their desires, all of which kept them from reflecting upon the state of their souls, and this is what led them to these punishments.

And they used to persist... in the awful sin (al-ḥinth al-'aẓīm) of associating partners with God (*shirk*). The word *ḥinth* literally means "to break a solemn oath sworn to by the right hand,"[30] and here it is to abandon worship of the True Sovereign in order to ally oneself with another.[31] It may also be taken to mean denial of the Resurrection, as in God's words, *And they swear to God their mightiest oaths that God will not resurrect the one who is dead* [16:38]. This word later came to be applied to sin in general, so that when it is said of a youth, "He has reached the age of *ḥinth*," it means puberty, the earliest time at which he or she can be considered as having sinned.

And they used to say: When we are dead and have become dust and bones, shall we then be truly raised again, along with our forefathers? Say: Lo! those of old and those of later times will all be brought together to the appointed time of a well-known day.

In their obstinancy *they used to say: When we are dead and* our bodies are reduced to *dust and* particles of *bone*, *shall we then be truly raised again... along with our forefathers?...* God answers their question with His words *...Lo! those of old*, meaning all the ancient communities which include their forefathers, *and those of later times*, all the later communities which include the one to which they belong, *will be gathered to the appointed time*, the moment at which this world will pass away, *of a well-known Day*, the Day of Resurrection and Reckoning....

Then lo! you who are in error and denial, you will surely eat of a tree called Zaqqūm, and will fill your bellies therewith; and thereon you will drink of boiling water, drinking as the rabid camel drinks. This will be their welcome on the Day of Judgment...

You who are in error and denial, words considered to have been addressed [first] to the people of Mecca and their like, are those who have strayed from Divine Guidance and who live in denial of the Resurrection. [God says to them:] 'After having been brought back to life, and brought to the Gathering, and put into Hellfire, *you will surely eat from a tree called Zaqqūm...and* in the extremity of your hunger, you will *fill your stomachs therewith*, and *will drink ... of scalding water*...like the rabid camel (*al-huyām*), who drinks but cannot quench his thirst...

This will be their welcome. The word *nuzul* literally means a certain amount of food prepared to honor "one who is to arrive" (*al-nāzil*). This is what they shall find awaiting them *on the Day of Judgement,* the Day of Recompense, and if such is what first greets them, what can be said of that which will follow...?

Spiritual Allusion

The Companions of the Left Hand are the sinful and ignorant, abandoned *in the toxic fumes* of their ignorance and remoteness from God. Both their hearts and souls are cast into these fumes and into the *scalding waters* of wantonness and fatigue, restlessness and anxiety. *The shade of smoke* alludes to self-direction and choice which is *neither cool nor refreshing* like the shade of contentment and the coolness of acceptance,[32] but, rather, an inauspicious shade which veils the one who has fallen from the sun of direct perception into the depths of depravity. *Lo! they had lived* before their contact with the gnostics *in luxury,* enjoying all manner of worldly gifts and engrossed in the pursuit of their desires. *They used to persist in the awful sin*, this being the love of the world, which is the source of all error, and would deny that souls may be revived ..., saying *When we are dead and have become dust*, earthly and base in our natures, *and* dry as *bones* in the hardness of our hearts and our distance from God, *shall we then be truly raised again* from this death, back to the life of our souls by teachings and direct knowledge of the Divine*?* In other words, they used to deny that there are teachers in the Way by whom God may give new life to spirits which have died from ignorance and heedlessness.

Say: Lo! the first of you thus described *and the last*, until the Day of Judgment, *will all be brought together* into the Divine Presence if you become the companions of the people of spiritual training. Then God will open for you the way to *an appointed time of a well-known day* which is the moment determined for your spiritual opening to occur. *Lo! You who are in error and denial* that there are physicians who can revive both hearts and spirits which have died, *you surely eat of a tree called Zaqqūm*, the tree of ignorance and stream of doubts and [demonic] suggestions that flows upon your hearts. *And you fill your bellies therewith*, for there remains within you no room for the lights of certitude and gnosis, *And thereon you drink of* the *boiling water* of anger, self-direction, and choice, *drinking even as (a rabid) camel drinks*, for you do not get your fill of it day or night. Even thus do they continue to build up and tear down [what is built], and such is the essence of vanity and waste. *This is their welcome on the Day of Judgment*, on the day when God, the Truth, recompenses the seekers with arrival and the relief of union.... And God Most High knows best.

57. *We created you. Will you not then affirm it?*[33]
58. *Do you then see the [human seed] that you emit?*
59. *Is it you who create it, or are We the Creators?*

60. *We have determined amongst you Death, and We are not to be frustrated*
61. *From changing your forms and creating you (again) in (forms) that you know not*
62. *And you certainly know already the first form of creation: will you not then be reminded?*
63. *Do you see the seed that you sow?*
64. *Is it you that cause it to grow, or are We the Cause?*
65. *Were it Our Will, We could surely make it into dry chaff, and you would be left wondering*
66. *(Saying), We are indeed left with debts (for nothing)*
67. *Nay, we are truly deprived.*
68. *Do you see the water which you drink?*
69. *Do you bring it down (in rain) from the clouds or do We?*
70. *Were it Our Will, We could make it brine: then why do you not give thanks?*
71. *Do you see the Fire which you kindle?*
72. *Is it you who grew its tree, or are We the Growers?*
73. *We have made it a reminder, and a use for the nomads in the wilderness*
74. *Then glorify the Name of your Lord Supreme!*

Commentary

We created you. Will you not then affirm it?

This is an exhortation to affirm the truth either of creation—for even while they may affirm it with their words, their actions do not—or of the Resurrection, for the One Who brought about the first creation is not incapable of bringing about a second.

Do you then see the [human seed] that you emit? Is it you who create it, or are We the Creators?

God asks concerning *the seed* cast into the womb who it is who determines its existence, gives it shape, and finally fashions it into a complete human form. Of this process, al-Ṭayyibī wrote:

> It is said that the reproductive fluid arises from what is left over from the digestion of food, and then exists as minute droplets dispersed throughout all the members of the body, which is why they share in the pleasure of ejaculation. It is to gather these scattered droplets that God, be He Glorified

> and Exalted, made physical desire so strong that it takes control of the entire body.
>
> So these particles which first exist (as food) dispersed in the physical world, God brings together in the living body and there they are dispersed once again throughout its members. Then does He gather them once more into the seminal vessel, and finally cause them to be emitted as a fluid into the abode of the womb.
>
> Thus, if God is Able to gather these twice-dispersed particles and from them form a living being, when by death they are dispersed once again, there is nothing which hinders Him from gathering them and forming them anew.

Elsewhere, he says concerning the verse, *[He is created from a fluid] gushing from between the loins and the ribs* [86:6-7]: "The reproductive fluid arises from what is left over from the fourth digestive process and collects from all the parts of the body, taking from each its nature and particularity, but mostly arising from the nervous system which has the greatest effect upon it." For the rest of what he has to say, refer to *al-Ḥāshiyya.*[34]

We have determined amongst you Death, and We are not to be frustrated from changing your forms and creating you (again) in (forms) that you know not. And you certainly know already the first form of creation: will you not then be reminded?

[Here God is saying,] 'To all have We apportioned death and for all have We appointed a moment at which that portion will be delivered according to Divine Wisdom.' To quote al-Qushayrī, "[This verse means:] 'Death is at the moment We wish. Some of you die as infants, some in their youth, some in their prime, and some in old age, from various infirmities, for varied reasons, and at varied times.'" *And We are not to be frustrated* by feeble mankind *from changing your forms*. Nay, We are capable of doing this, and you will neither outrace nor prevent Us from removing you [completely] and bringing forth in your stead other creatures who are similar to you, but different in their essential identities or their attributes. [In this sense] shall We have created you anew but *in forms you know not*. And according to al-Ḥasan, "[Here God is saying] 'We can make you even into apes and swine.'"

Thus, the verse means 'We are able to do both: to create that which is like you and that which is unlike you, so how could We be unable to bring you back to life again?'.... *And you ... know already* of the primordial nature of Adam, upon whom be peace, and of the stages of development of a human being from a seed, so *will you not then be reminded* that the One Who is able to do this is able to bring forth another creation?

Do you see the seed that you sow? Is it you that cause it to grow, or are We the Cause? Were it Our Will, We could surely make it into dry chaff, and you would be left wondering. (Saying), We are indeed left with debts (for nothing): nay, we are truly deprived.

After having reminded them of the blessing of existence, God here reminds them of the blessing of subsistence, saying *Do you see the seed* that you cast upon the earth and then turn under the soil? *Is it you that cause it...* to vegetate and spring forth from the soil as a plant, *or are We the Cause?* Thus is there a *ḥadīth* which says, "Let none of you say, 'We *grew* (a crop),' but rather, 'We *sowed* it.'"[35] *Were it Our Will, We could surely make it into* straw broken before its harvest *and you would be left wondering...* at its desolation after having seen it in all its beauty; or left in regret for the wasted money and labor you had put into it, or for the sins that had brought this [loss] upon you..., saying *We are indeed left with debts* for what we spent to sow this crop; or 'If our food has perished, so have we!' ... *Nay we are truly deprived* of the fruits of our labor by the misfortune of our loss, for [in this context] "someone deprived" (*al-maḥrūm*) means "someone kept from his provision." To quote Ibn 'Abbās, "He is *muḥāraf*," someone whose provision has been turned away from him."

Do you see the water which you drink? Do you bring it down from the clouds or do We bring it down? Were it Our Will, We could make it salt. Then why do you not give thanks?

Do you see the sweet and potable *water which you drink? Do you bring it down from* the white clouds (*al-muzn*), those which bear the sweetest water? *Or do We* by Our power *bring it down,* then cause it to reside within the earth, and then bring it forth in springs and rivers? *Were it Our Will, We could make* it salty or bitter and unpalatable, all of which is included in the meaning of the word *ujāj*. *Then why do you not give thanks?* This verse, then, exhorts to gratitude for all of God's gifts ....[36]

Do you see the Fire which you kindle? Is it you who grew its tree, or are We the Grower? We have made it a reminder and a use for the nomads in the wilderness

... The Arabs used to kindle fire by rubbing two sticks together. The upper stick they called *al-zand* and the bottom one *al-zanda*, likening them to the stallion and the mare.... The [wood they used for the kindling sticks] was traditionally from the *markh* and *'afār* trees[37], about which [the verse] asks whether it was men or God who determined them and brought them into existence. Here, the action of creation is expressed by the verb *nasha'a*,[38] the same used to describe the soul's being breathed [into the body] in God's words, *Then We caused it to grow into another creation* [23:14]. This verb carries the sense of artistry in design and the perfection of Divine Power and Wisdom reflected in the unique qualities which distinguish these trees from all others, even as the proverb states: *In every tree there is fire, but the most generous in giving it are the* markh *and* 'afār.[39]

Then God elucidates the benefits of fire. One of these is that it is...*a reminder*. That is, when human beings gaze upon it, they may be reminded of the fire of Hell. It may also be called both a *reminder* and an example following the words of the Prophet, "This fire of yours which men kindle contains but a seventieth of the heat in Hell."[40] It has also been said that the *reminder* means insight into the matter of the resurrection, which is as wondrous as fire coming out of something green and moist.

It is also *a use for the nomads in the wilderness...* who are mentioned in particular since they are the ones most in need of it, whereas settled peoples or those near their dwellings are not forced to use kindling sticks.

It has been said that the word *muqwīn* ("nomads in the wilderness") may also mean "those whose stomachs are empty and whose provision of food has run out"...but the first definition is the more widely accepted one.

Thus after having mentioned the gift of existence, God mentions here the three means by which we are nourished: the blessing of food [itself] which sustains us; the blessing of the water which we drink and mix with food; and the blessing of fire with which we cook it.

Then glorify the Name of your Lord Supreme!

...When the mind comes to know there is a Creator, it is drawn higher towards knowledge of His Nature and may fall into the errors of comparability, corporealism, or contingency. And so it is that God says *Glorify the Name of your Lord.* In other words, 'O you who are hearing [these verses] and seeking direction, affirm your Lord's transcendence beyond all not meet to His Divinity!'

And by *the Name* is meant the Named, as the presence of the connective participle *ba'* (in *bi'smi*) signifies. The verse may also be understood to mean: 'Glorify your Lord by immersing yourself in the invocation of His Name,' with the adjective *Supreme* describing both the Lord and His Name... And God Most High knows better.

Spiritual Allusion

We created you, originating you from nothingness. *Do you not affirm* that your souls can be revived after their deaths by teachings and gnosis? For the One Who is able to bring into being your physical forms is able to give life to your souls as well.

Do you see, O teachers of the Way, *the seed* of aspiration that you plant in hearts of your students? *Is it you who create it* there so that it might germinate, and the tree of God's love flourish and bear the fruits of gnosis, *or are We the Creators? We have determined amongst you Death,* and while some of you undergo physical death, others experience spiritual death by turning back in the path before having reached the Goal. *And We are not to be frustrated from changing your forms* through the transformation of your natures, for your hearts are in God's Hand, *and creating you (again) in* a state which, in your ignorance and remoteness from God, *you know not.* But *you certainly know the first creation*, that state of heedlessness and vanity that you were in before you encountered people of the Way. *Will you not then be reminded* and give thanks for the bountiful blessings of having been awakened and given knowledge?

Do you see the deeds and states, the spiritual efforts and acts of self-denial that *you sow. Is it you that cause* them *to grow* so that they are accepted from you and you gather their fruits, *or are We the Cause? Were it Our Will* We could render them vain and return them to you as scattered dust, *and you would be left* regretting the efforts you made without having harvested the fruits *(Saying), We are indeed left with debts* because we spent of our possessions and we became needy in that time when the initial attraction to God was upon us. And now we are *Indeed truly deprived* of the fruits of our efforts and devotions.

Do you see the water of Life by which hearts are revived, *which you drink* from the teachers of the Way. The shaykh pours it into an aspirant's soul like a mother bird feeding her fledgling and by it your spirit is awakened and you pass away from this physical world. *Do you bring it down from the clouds* of guidance and providence *or do We? Were it Our Will, We could make it salt* so that the soul which drank from it would spit it out again—this being the case of one who sets out in the path, but whose ship flounders because the winds of destiny do not reach it—or else would be unable to drink from it at all—this being the case of those who continue seeking but are deprived of the provision of gnosis. *Then why do you not give thanks* for the bounty of God Who allowed you to first drink the wine that you continued to drink until you were made drunk and then sober and both your soul and your physical form were revived.

Do you see the Fire of human desires and appetites *which you kindle* within yourselves? *Is it you who grew its tree*, which is the natural self, *or are We the Grower? We have made it a reminder,* that is, a means of awakening to stir you towards seeking your Guardian Lord, even as it is said in the *Ḥikam*, "He stirred your soul against you so that your drawing near to Him would be permanent."[41]

And He *made* [the lower self] *a use* for those who are traveling the path to God, for by striving against it, they actualize their journey; by purifying it, they actualize the virtues; and by passing away from it, they reach union with God. Thus, when someone would complain about his lower self to the shaykh of our shaykh,[42] he would say, "As for me, I say, 'May God reward it with goodness!' Without it, I could have never progressed in the Way!"

Al-Qusharyī said concerning these verses:

> *Have you seen the fire* alludes to the fire of Love kindled by the flint of seeking in the heart of the lover who is sincere in his journey. *Its tree* is Divine Providence, even as Abū al-Ḥasan al-Manṣūr, may God sanctify his soul, said when asked about the reality of Love: "It is Divine Providence, without which *You would not have known what the Book*

> *is nor faith* [42:52]." *And We made it a reminder* for those absorbed in their lower natures to seek guidance to God's Path, *and a thing of use for those whose stomachs are empty,*[43] for by it are nourished the souls of Lovers who abstain day and night from food and drink. And it has been said that Sahl al-Tustarī would abstain from food for thirty days, and that 'Aqīl al-Maghribī did not eat for the sixty years he lived in Mecca. The same has been said about many of the travelers in the Way.

Then glorify the Name of your Lord Supreme! Al-Wartajibī said concerning this verse,

> God commands the Prophet to affirm His transcendence not by himself but by his Lord.... And inasmuch as the Name and the Named are one, [the verse means], 'Sanctify Me by Me, for I am far greater than what can be sanctified by your own self or by anything else beneath Me.' Do you not see that by His word *Supreme* is meant 'More immense than what the praises of creatures can reach or what humanity can describe?'

75. *Nay, but I do swear by the setting of the Stars—*
76. *And that is truly a tremendous oath if you only knew*
77. *That this is indeed a Noble Recitation,*
78. *In a Book kept hidden.*
79. *None shall touch it but the purified.*
80. *A Revelation from the Lord of the Worlds.*
81. *Is this the statement that you demean?*
82. *And do you make of your provision denial?*

Commentary

Nay, but I do swear by the setting of the Stars—and that is truly a tremendous oath if you but knew— that this is indeed a Noble Recitation in a Book kept hidden.

...This oath specifies *the setting of the stars* for when they set, their physical traces cease, which indicates the existence of a Cause which is Itself unceasing and unchanging. Also, [when the fixed stars are no longer visible is the time of night] when those striving to draw nearer to their Lord stand in prayer and supplication and when God's Mercy and Contentment descend.[44]...

The words *if you only knew* may be read as the condition of a clause that is understood: 'But you do not.' They may also be read as adverbial to what precedes them, in which case they mean, 'This is a [tremendous] oath, if you only knew it as such, but you do not,' or 'If you only knew this, you would affirm God's greatness,' or 'If you only knew this, you would act on what that knowledge entails.'

This is a Recitation (*Qur'ān*) which is *Noble* and *Generous*,[45] well-pleasing [to God], and of inestimable value inasmuch as it contains the fundamental teachings necessary to reach the goodness of this life and the Next. The verse may also be understood to mean that this is a recitation that is Noble and precious to God. *In a Book* that is safe-guarded from all but the highest of the angels and to which no others may ascend, this being the Guarded Tablet (*al-Lawḥ al-Maḥfūẓ*).[46]

None shall touch it but the purified.

[The pronoun] *it* may be read as referring to *a hidden Book*, that is, the Guarded Tablet, in which case *the purified* are the angels who are beyond the turbidity of the physical state and untainted by sin. It may also be read as referring to the word *Recitation* (*Qur'ān*), in which case this verse means that no one may touch the Qur'ān—that is, the written book—who is not in a state of purity. To quote Ibn Juzayy:

> If we take the *hidden Book* to mean the one with the angels, then *those who are purified* means the angels, who are pure of sin and defect. If we take it to mean the one which is with human beings, then *those who are purified* means the Muslims, who have been purified from disbelief, or cleansed from the greater impurities—from either the state of *janāba*[47] or menses, in which case purification means bathing; or from the lesser impurities (*al-ḥadath al-aṣghar*),[48] in which case purification means ablution....
>
> Based on [the differing interpretations of] this verse, the scholars of religious law differ concerning who may physically touch the Qur'ān.[49] All agree that a nonbeliever may not touch it, but apart from this, opinions vary. Imām Mālik, for example, and the scholars of his school say that it may not be touched or even carried in a sack or holder by

anyone in a state of greater or lesser impurity. They thus consider *those who are purified* to mean those who have cleansed themselves of the greater and lesser impurities. In *al-Muwaṭṭa'*, Mālik cites both this verse and also the letter sent by the Prophet (upon whom be peace) to 'Amr bin Ḥazm in which it is mentioned that the Qur'ān should not be touched by anyone who has not performed the ablution.

The second view is that of Aḥmad ibn Ḥanbal as well as of the Ẓāhirīs,[50] who take *those who are purified* to mean either the angels or human beings who are Muslim, and believe that it may be touched by the latter without the greater or lesser ablution.

The third view is that *those who are purified* means those who are free from the greater state of impurity.

Finally, Imām Mālik exceptionally allows both a teacher and children to touch the Qu'rān without the lesser ablution because of the difficulties posed [by having to repeat it].

There is also disagreement concerning whether someone in a state of *janāba* may recite the Qur'ān [without touching the Book]. For al-Shāfi'ī and Abū Ḥanīfa it is unconditionally prohibited, for the Ẓāhirīs, it is unconditionally allowed, while for Imām Mālik, it is permitted to recite a few verses, for example, in order to seek protection from the Devil. There is disagreement as well concerning whether a woman may recite it by heart during her menstrual period or during post-partum bleeding. In respect to Mālik's view, there are two narrations, and those who follow his view distinguish between reciting a short or a lengthy portion of the text.

What is most widely recognized in the case of a woman who is in either of these conditions is that it is unconditionally permissible for her to recite [by heart without touching the Book].

Finally, to quote al-Kuwāshī citing Ibn 'Aṭā, "[This verse means] that no one will understand the allusions of what they are reciting except the one who has purified his innermost soul from the created world." And at the end of Bukhārī is the comment, "*None shall touch it*, that is, none shall find its nourishment and benefits except the one who believes in it, and none shall bear it as it should be borne except the faithful, even as [God's words concerning some of the Jews] attest: *The likeness of one bearing the Torah who does not apply it is the likeness of an ass carrying books.*" [62:5][51]

A Revelation from the Lord of the Worlds.

This is the fourth attribute of the Qur'ān.[52] It is described here by the gerund *tanzīl* [literally, "a coming down from above"], because among all other heavenly books, it is the one sent down portion by portion…

Is this the statement that you demean? And do you make of your provision denial?

The first of these two verses asks whether it is this Qur'ān which *you demean?…* The word *mudhinūn* means "those who take something lightly,"…and Ibn 'Aṭiya quotes Ibn 'Abbās as saying that *mudāhana* means to be indulgent concerning something that is not lawful….[53]

[The second verse means,] 'Do you turn the gratitude you should have for your daily provision into denial?' In other words, 'Do you put denial in the place of thanks?' …. or, 'Do you turn the gratitude you should have for the blessing of the Qur'ān into denial?' It has also been said that this verse was revealed concerning the Arabs' practice of attributing rain to certain stars, in which case it means, 'Do you turn the gratitude for the rain God has sent you into denial that it is God Who sends it by saying, "We have been sent rain by such and such a star?"' What is prohibited in this respect is to believe that a star itself causes weather, but not that it is a sign of certain weather. There are those, however, who say, in order to close a door [that could lead to polytheism], that even to consider stars as a sign is prohibited. Such is the view of Ibn Rushd, for example, who in turn refers to al-Saḥnūn. But it remains a point of disagreement.

The Prophet (upon whom be peace) said, "When the stars are mentioned, desist."[54] There are some, however, who go into more detail concerning the matter and say, 'It is permissible to attribute misfortune to the stars because of Prophet's saying, "Seek refuge in God from the evil of this," indicating the moon, "for it is *the darkness when it grows intense.*"[55] As for good, both gratitude and correct comportment (*al-adab*) necessitate that it always be attributed to God. And God Most High knows best.

Spiritual Allusion

The setting places of the Stars are the innermost souls of the gnostics, oceans in which all else but God is drowned. Therein vanish the stars of both rational and conveyed knowledge and the moons of formal proofs of Divine oneness, for once the Sun of gnosis rises, no trace of starlight or moonlight remains, or as I have written in a *qaṣīda 'ayniyya*[56]:

> To us the Sun of day appeared and rose
> And naught remained of starlight once it dawned

The shaykh of our shaykhs, Sidī 'Abd al-Raḥmān al-Fāsī, said, "I used to know fourteen of the religious sciences, but when I came to know the Spiritual Truth, I tore them all up." By this he meant that he no longer depended upon them because he had reached the treasure of direct knowledge of God after which there is no longer any loss for the soul whatsoever; or, in the words of the *Ḥikam*, "One who has found You, what has he lost?"[57] It does not mean, however, that he discarded all his prior learning. In fact, if he had returned to it, he would have found it vaster and richer. Rather, what is meant is that he had discovered a treasure that rendered all preoccupation with anything else vain.

Even thus did al-Ghazālī say to Ibn al-'Arabī al-Mu'āfirī, "You were my companion during my years of vanity," by which he meant the time before he had met his spiritual master.

An oath sworn by this is *tremendous* because there is nothing vaster for God than the hearts of those who have reached Him and the innermost souls of the gnostics, made expansive by knowledge and theophanies: "Neither My earth nor My Heavens contain Me, but the heart of My faithful servant contains Me."[58] The oath is thus *tremendous*, as is the One Who swears it, and the object upon which it is sworn.

None shall touch it but the purified. Of this verse, al-Junayd said, "None shall touch it except the gnostics whose innermost souls have been purified from all else but God," which is to say that none shall touch the maidens of its spiritual realities and subtleties of its allusions except hearts which have been purified from turbidity and illusion, these being the hearts of the gnostics.

A Revelation from the Lord of the Worlds to the master of those who were sent [the Prophet], that the hearts of his successors among the gnostics might drink deeply of its mysteries.

Is this the statement that you demean? And do you make your provision denial? Al-Qushayrī said, "[It means] 'you are remiss in accepting this Discourse as truth and in wonder at these subtleties and inner truths.'" This, then, is a reproach to those who demean the science of spiritual allusion, who deny [its truth] and shun its reading. *And you make* the gratitude you should have for having been given this provision from the hearts of gnostics *into denial* and rejection of the ones who bear it.

83. *Why, then, when it reaches the throat*
84. *And you, the while, are looking on*
85. *And We are nearer to him than you, and yet you do not see*
86. *Why, if you are free from all constraint, do you not*
87. *Call back the soul, if you are truthful?*
88. *Then, if he be of Those Brought Near*
89. *There shall be for him Rest and Satisfaction, and a Garden of Delights*
90. *And if he be of the Companions of the Right Hand*
91. *Then, 'Peace be upon you,' from the Companions of the Right Hand*
92. *And if he be of those who treat (Truth) as Falsehood, who go wrong*
93. *For him will boiling water be the welcome*
94. *And burning in Hellfire*
95. *Verily, this is the Very Truth and Certainty*
96. *So Glorify the name of your Lord, Supreme.*

Commentary

Why, then, when it reaches the throat, and you, the while, are looking on—and We are nearer to him than you, and yet you do not see—why, if you are free from all constraint, do you not call back the soul, if you are truthful?

Beginning with *We created you...* [verse 57], the words of God reproach His servants for their denial [of the Resurrection], remind them that their food, drink, and other means of survival are subject to His control, and that in the face of death they are helpless: *Why, then,* at the moment of death, *when* the soul *reaches the throat* and you are present with the dying man and *looking on* as his life ebbs away... At that moment God is *nearer to him* through His knowledge, strength, and understanding *than you.* All you know of death are the final tribulations that you witness, but you remain unaware of its true nature, of how it comes to pass, and of its [real] causes, nor can you repel from yourselves the least particle of it. God controls its every stage *and yet you do not see* this nor comprehend it in your ignorance of His role. *If you are free from all constraint*, if you are truly subject to nothing and no one, *why*, then, *do you not* return the soul to the body after it has reached the throat?...

The meaning of [God's words here] is: 'For the greater part of your lives, you have been in denial. If I sent you a Book, you said, "This is sorcery and forgery!" If I sent you a truthful Messenger, you said, "Sorcerer and liar!" If I sent you life-giving rain, you said, "Such-and-such star was right!" All this arose from your rejection of God's Attributes. So now [at the moment of death], since you believe you are absolutely free of God's control, and you deny that God is the One Who Gives Life and Who Gives Death, and the One Who Originates and Begins Creation Anew, how is it that you cannot return the soul of this dying man to his body?'

Then, if he be of Those Brought Near, there shall be for him Rest and Satisfaction, and a Garden of Delights.

In these [concluding verses] God mentions the states of souls in the Intermediary Realm (*al-barzakh*) after death. *Those Drawn Near* are the ones called at the beginning of this *sūra* "the Foremost," here referred to by their highest attribute: their extreme proximity to God.... These are the gnostics who know God by experience and direct perception and are effaced in His Essence. Concerning them, the Prophet, upon whom be peace, said, "The solitary ones are foremost in the journey!" And when the Companions asked, "Who are the solitary ones, O Messenger of God?" he answered, "They are the ones madly in love with the remembrance (*dhikr*) of God!"[59] The Foremost, then, are those who are so in love with the remembrance that it has intermingled with their flesh and bones and has brought them this nearness.

There shall be for him Rest (*rawḥ*), which means relief (*raḥa*) for their souls from mundane cares and woes, from the narrowness of the physical world into the purity of the spiritual world. And even while this is something they had reached before death, its domain will be infinitely expanded thereafter. The word *rawḥ* may also be understood as referring to an aspect of the Divine mercy (*raḥmah*) particularly for them, or to a cooling breeze (*nasīm*) that will waft upon them...[60] According to what has been passed down about the Prophet's recitation, it is also possible to read this word as *rūḥ*, meaning [in this context] "life" or "sustenance," in which case the verse would mean: *His shall be the sweetest life, eternal and without death.*

And [his, too, shall be] *rayḥān*. In the Amoritic tongue, this word means "provision," and would then refer to the teachings and mysteries which nourish their souls—or their bodies—for souls progress according to the gratitude of those who possess them, and eat from the fruits of Heaven, and drink from its rivers. Such is what has been said in the *ḥadīth* about the martyrs, and for the saints (*al-ṣiddiqūn*) it is truer still.[61] *Rayḥān* can also mean Heaven itself, or the sweet-scented herb [called by this name].[62] To quote Abū al-'Āliyya, "Those Brought Near do not depart from this world until they are given some of the *rayḥān* of Heaven to smell and its perfume fills their souls."

And (his shall be) *a Garden...* which will bring delight to his soul while he is yet in the Intermediary Realm, and then to his body and soul after the Resurrection. In all of this it is understood that it is a special grace of martyrs and saints to enter Heaven before the Day of Resurrection.

And if he be of the Companions of the Right Hand, then,
'Peace be upon you,' from the Companions of the Right Hand.

If he is one of the Companions of the Right Hand, he will be greeted by his brethren from among the Companions of the Right Hand with salutations of peace....For after the soul is questioned in the grave, it mounts up therefrom to the souls of those who are like it to meet them and be greeted by them, and this eases the departure from the prison of this world. [Another meaning of this verse is] 'Peace be to you, O Muḥammad, from the Companions of the Right Hand. You shall not see in them other than peace.'[63]

And if he be of those who treat (Truth) as Falsehood, who go
wrong, for him will boiling water be the welcome and burning
in Hellfire.

This verse refers to the third of the three groups mentioned [at the beginning of the *sūra*], those to whom it was said, *Then you who are in error and denial...* [56:51]. It is cited by some as textual proof that a disbeliever may enter the fire at the very moment of death, but it has also been said to refer to the fire and smoke of the grave. Thus, it may be understood to apply to the Intermediary Realm as well as to what is beyond it.[64]

In fact, people have spoken at length about [the states] of souls in the Intermediary Realm. What we gather from the *ḥadīth* and narrations (*al-akhbār*) is that the souls of the saintly, who are Those Brought Near, will be reunited with their forms and go wheresoever they wish in the [paradiasical] gardens and elsewhere. The souls of the martyrs, which had been confined within their physical forms whilst in the world, will be confined within the bodies of green birds upon entering Heaven and as such, they too will go wheresoever they wish through its gardens...[65] Unlike them, however, are the gnostics, for just as their meditations had ranged freely through the realms of the *Malakūt* and the *Jabarūt* [in life], so shall their souls after death be set free.

As for the souls of the righteous and the generality of believers—other than those against whom the threat [of punishment] is fulfilled—their abodes in the Intermediary Realm will vary. Some will be in the shade of the Lote-Tree of the Furthest Boundary (*sidrat al-muntahā*),[66] and others in Heavens that correspond to the efforts they had made in the world, and gathered with their like—the scholars with scholars, the Qur'ān reciters with reciters, the charitable with the charitable, and the saintly with the saintly.

As for those who were totally engrossed in the world, if they are delivered from punishment, their souls [in the Intermediary Realm] will be as if in a deep sleep, unconscious of the passage of time, until they are awakened by the sound of the Trumpet on the Day of Resurrection.

And as for those against whom God's threat is fulfilled, they will be chastised as described in the *ḥadīth* in Bukhārī, in which the Prophet recounted the vision he had of the adulterer, the interest-taker, and others.[67]

Ibn Ḥajar says in his commentary on this *ḥadīth* that even while the souls of the faithful will be in *'Ilīyyīn* and those of the ungrateful in *Sijjīn*,[68] they will have a connection to their bodies, but not like the connection that exists in the physical world. Rather, it will most ressemble the connection of the soul of a sleeper [to his body], although much stronger. This reconciles what has been related about souls abiding in *'Ilīyyīn* and *Sijjīn* with the well-known narration from Ibn 'Abd al-Barr which states that they are in "the court yards of the graves." [Ibn Ḥajar says] that even with this, they are allowed to move about after which they return to their places in *'Ilīyyīn* or *Sijjīn*.[69] This connection remains even if a body be moved from one grave to another, and even after its complete dissolution.

In the Fifty-Fourth Principle of *Nawādir al-uṣūl* it is stated:

> When the faithful go forth to their Lord, they are met with *rawḥ* and *rayḥān* and good tidings from the [angelic] messengers, as in God's words: *Verily, those who say, 'Our Lord is God' and then remain upright—to them do the angels descend* [41:30]. Then it is ordered whilst they are still in the grave that they be clothed with robes and sweet-smelling herbs (*riyāḥīn*), as in God's words, *And those who do right make comfort for themselves* [30:44]. Then they are given light in their resting places, and the noble angels stay near them and comfort them until they meet their Lord on the open plain of the Resurrection when God will raise them up to the abode which He has created for them.

And in the Seventieth Principle:

> For the martyrs, God hastens the meeting, revives them before the sounding of the Trumpet, and speaks to them directly as He does to the people of Heaven. This degree is granted to none other of the dead except for the saints (*al-ṣiddīqūn*), for whom it is even more fitting, for while the martyrs gave up their souls for God at one particular time, the saints gave up their souls for God during the totality of their lives. So while it is certain that the martyrs are given life [in the Intermediary Realm] in a way others are not, it is even more certain for the saints.

Thus, some souls are in the Intermediary Realm where they range freely and are shown the state of the people in this world; some are beneath the Throne; some range through the gardens of Heaven wheresoever they wish to the measure of their efforts whilst in this world; some travel and return to their resting places; and some meet the souls of others who have died. To quote Salmān, "The souls of the faithful," that is, those who completed their faith, "are in the Intermediary Realm of the earth and go wheresoever they wish between Heaven and earth until God returns them to their bodies. When these souls are returned, they know about the condition of the living, and if one of the living is sent to them upon death, they gather about him and ask for tidings."

[We would say] that this concerns the souls of the gnostics about whom it has been said "When the gnostic dies, it is said to his soul, 'Travel wherever you wish.'" But God Most High knows better.

Verily, this is the Truth of Certainty.
So Glorify the name of your Lord, Supreme.

Verily, this—all that has been mentioned in this noble *sūra—is the Truth of Certainty*, the Truth affirmed as certitude, or the Truth of tidings which are certain, *so Glorify the name of your Lord, Supreme*. [In this context] the particle *fa* may be understood either as "then", expressing an order of actions or as "so", expressing purpose. That is, the truth which the *sūra* contains necessitates that God's transcendence be affirmed beyond all attributions of His divinity to others, beyond all rejection of His articulated signs, and beyond all that is not meet to His sublime station.

Spiritual Allusion

Then, if he be of Those Brought Near, there shall be for him the *rest and repose* of union, the *sweet-smelling herbs* of God's Beauty and the bliss of Perfection; or the rest and repose of Space, *the sweet-smelling herbs* of the Gift, and the Garden of Everlastingness; or the *rest and repose* of effacement, the *sweet-smelling herbs* of subsistence, and the Garden of Eternal and Endless ascent; or *rest and repose* for his heart in the human realm, *sweet-smelling herbs* for his spirit in the Divine realm, and the *garden* of *Firdaws* for his individual soul.

And if he be of the Companions of the Right Hand, then, 'Peace be upon you,' O Muḥammad, *from the Companions of the Right Hand,* for it is they who invoke blessings of peace upon you, who long for the moment they will meet you, and are joyful at the prospect of approaching you and being in your company. Thus, while the comfort and bliss of *Those Brought Near* is found in being united with their Lord, the *Companions of the Right Hand* long for God's Prophet, and their comfort and bliss is in his company and proximity. The Ones Brought Near, then, are effaced in God's Essence while the Companions of the Right Hand are effaced in His Prophet, the best of creation. … Thus, [it is as though God says] *if he be of Those Brought Near,* 'then he is Mine and I will recompense him with *Rest and repose and a Garden of Delights. And if he be of the Companions of the Right Hand, then* 'he is given (*musallam*) to you (O Muḥammad!).' This sums up what the shaykh of our shaykhs, 'Abd al-Raḥmān al-Fāsī, said of these verses in his *Ḥāshiyya*.[70]

And in *al-Iḥyā'*,[71] the essence of what he says is that the One Brought Near attains the beatitude of the (Divine) King, while the Companion of the Right Hand attains salvation. The latter is a traveler and the former has arrived, and for the one who turns away from God, there is Hell.

These tidings, for the one who knows God, are *the Certain Truth*, known through direct experience and perception (*mushāhadatan*). Thus, to quote *al-Qūt*:

> For the Ones Brought Near there is relief (*rawḥ*) from every calamity in their perception of the One Who is Near, and there are the sweet-smelling herbs (*riḥān*) of nearness to the Beloved in every distress, while for the People of the Right Hand there is safety....[72]

According to al-Nasafī, it is related that 'Uthmān ibn 'Afān (may God be pleased with him) came to visit Ibn Mas'ūd who was in the last throes of the illness from which he died and asked him, "Of what do you complain?" To which Ibn Mas'ūd answered, "My sins." 'Uthmān then asked him, "What do you desire?" To which he responded, "The mercy of my Lord," or according to some versions, "What my Lord has decreed." 'Uthmān then asked, "Shall I not call you a physician?" He said, "The Physician is the One Who has caused me to be ill." 'Uthmān then asked, "Can I not give you something?" to which Ibn Mas'ūd answered, "I have no need of anything." 'Uthmān then said, "So let it be for your daughters who will survive you." To which Ibn Mas'ūd replied, "They too are not in need of anything, for I have enjoined upon them the recitation of *Sūrat al-Wāqi'a* every night, and I surely heard God's Messenger say, 'Whosoever recites *Sūrat al-Wāqi'a* every evening shall never be afflicted by want.'"...[73]

In God is all accord. There is neither strength nor power except through God, the Sublime, the Tremendous, and may blessings and salutations of peace be upon the Prophet and his companions.

Notes on the Chapter of The Event

1. Bayhaqī, 2497, 2498.

2. Another rendition of this incident is cited at the end of the commentary on this *sūra*.

3. *And the Trumpet is blown, and all who are in the heavens and the earth swoon away, save him whom God wills. Then it is blown a second time, and behold them standing waiting!* [39:18]

4. The first meaning of this verb is "to fall," and then, by extension, "to befall or happen."

5. Ibn 'Ajība explains that the *lam* in *li waqa'atihā* can express either "at the moment or time of"—as in [17:78] *And establish the prayer at* (li) *sunset*—or "concerning, for the sake of." He follows the former here and the latter in the spiritual allusion below.

6. Ibn 'Ajība mentions that this word is also used to refer to the herding of sheep.

7. Ibn 'Ajība explains that the syntax of this sentence is both interrogative and exclamatory: 'How amazingly beautiful is the state of the companions of the right hand!' and 'How shockingly wretched is the state of the companions of the left hand!'

8. *When your Lord brought forth the descendants of Adam from his loins that they might bear witness against themselves and said to them, Am I not your Lord? They answered, Yes! You truly are!* [7:172]

9. He is referring to a long *ḥadīth*, describing the Prophet's Ascension, found in Bukhārī, *Ṣalāt*, 342 and *Anbiyā'*, 3164; Muslim, *Īmān*, 263.

10. The Arabic word translated as 'the Foremost,' *al-sābiqūn*, is derived from the verb *sabaqa*, which carries the meanings of going first, going ahead of someone else, or winning a race.

11. The earliest Muslims around the Prophet offered their devotions in the direction of Jerusalem until the revelation of [2:150] which contains the commandment to turn towards Mecca.

12. "[*Those Brought Near*] are mentioned last even while they merit being mentioned first in order that their mention be followed directly by the description of their paradisiacal state."

13. See note 5 above.

14. Ibn 'Ajība adds that more will be explained concerning the distinction between Those Brought Near and the Companions of the Right Hand towards the end of this *sūra*.

15. Bukhārī. *Faḍā'il al-Ṣaḥāba*, 3451; Muslim, *Faḍā'il al-Ṣaḥāba*, 212.

16. Besides Tha'labī, both Ṭabarī and Qurṭubī cite this *ḥadīth* in their exegesis of this verse with the wording "They are both totally of my community."

17. *Nawādir al-uṣūl,* 1:369.

18. By *al-Maḥallī*, he means the latter half of *Tafsīr Jalālayn*. This work was begun by Jalāl al-Dīn al-Maḥallī (791-864/1389-1459) who wrote the commentary from *Sūrat al-Kahf* (18) until the end of the Qur'ān

but died before he could complete the entire Book. This was done by Jalāl al-Dīn al-Suyūṭī (849-911/1445-1505). Both scholars were Egyptian and both named Jalāl al-Dīn, hence the title *Jalālayn* ("The two Jalāls"). For *al-Ḥashīya*, see p. 40 n. 34.

19. This is actually a saying attributed to Salmān al-Farsī, quoted in numerous commentaries on this verse, and referring to children of non-believers who die in childhood.

20. The saying is part of a dream that 'Abd al-Muṭṭalib, the Prophet's grandfather, had in which he was shown the location of the well of Zamzam which had been lost, according to Muslim history, since the time of Abraham. Bayhaqī, *Dalā'il al-nubūwa*, Part 1, p. 94; Ibn Isḥāq, *Sīrah*, v. 1, p. 257.

21. Abū Dāwūd, *al-Malāḥim*, 4341; Ibn Ḥibbān, *Ṣaḥīḥ*, *al-Birr wa'l-iḥsān*, 385; Bayhaqī, *Sunnan*, 19980; Ṭabarānī, *al-Kabīr, B. al-'ayn*. Versions of this *ḥadīth* which include the words "Because you found help and support towards the good.." are cited by al-Ghazāli, *Iḥyā' 'ulūm al-dīn, K. al-Amr bi'l-ma'rūf, Bāb al-awwal*, and by Qāḍi Abū Bakr ibn al'Arabī in *Aḥkām al-Qur'ān*, in his *tafsīr* of [5:33].

22. By which he means the Qur'ān. It should be remembered that when this is reported to have been said, the Qur'ān had not been put into the form of a book.

23. Ṭabarānī, *al-Kabīr*, 3461; Abū Nu'āym, *Ma'rifat al-Ṣaḥāba*, 1992; Ibn 'Asākir, *Tārikh al-Dimashq*, part 9, p. 100.

24. *K. al-Ḥikam*, 227

25. The lote- or lotus tree (*al-sidr*), as Ibn 'Ajība points out, is more commonly known as *al-nabq*. This is generally identified as the *Ziziphus spinichristi* (Christ's Thorn), which gives shade and edible berries ("Jujubes"). These berries are still eaten in the Moroccan countryside, especially by children.

26. One of the principle works of Mālikī jurisprudence. See the biographical index for information about its author.

27. The *fajr* prayer is offered about an hour and a half before sunrise.

28. Tirmidhī, *Tafsīr*, 3348; Aḥmad, *Musnad*, 11294; Ibn Ḥibbān, *Janna*, 7528

29. Those who, although righteous, are stilled veiled from God.

30. The "solemn oath" is the pledge referred to in note 8 above.

31. By whom he means the devil.

32. *Al-tabdīr wa al-ikhtiyār*. This pair of terms is part of the well-known answer given by Mulay 'Abd al-Salām ibn Mashīsh upon meeting his future and only disciple, Abū al-Ḥasan al-Shādhilī, quoted in *Laṭā'if al-minan* and elsewhere, "I complain of the coolness of my contentment

and acceptance just as you complain of the heat of you self-direction and choice." (pp. 85-86)

33. Although the printed edition of *al-Baḥr* groups this verse, its commentary, and allusions immediately after verse 56, we have chosen to include it with this grouping of verses because of its subject matter.

34. He is referring to the theory of reproduction described by Ibn Sina (d. 428/1037) in Book Three, Part 20, page 553 of his renown *Qānūn fī al-ṭibb*, begun around the year 400/1010. For *al-Ḥāshīya*, see p. 40 n. 39.

35. Bayhaqī, *Sunnan*, *Kitāb al-Muzāra'a*, 115311 and *Shu'ab al-īmān*, 4997; Ṭabarānī, *al-Awsaṭ*, 8255 and *al-Kabīr*, 1157.

36. Here Ibn 'Ajība points out that while in the previous verse (*Were it Our will, We could surely make it dry chaff*) there is a *lam* of emphasis attached to the verb 'make' (*laja'alnāhu*), in this verse there is not (*ja'alnāhu*) and explains that because the commandment to eat always precedes the commandment to drink (*kulū wa'shrabū*) throughout the Qur'ān, it implies that to deprive creatures of food is a more severe process.

37. The *Markh* tree, *Leptadenia pyrotechnica*, is an erect leafless shrub which grows both in the Arabian and African deserts, and is still used for kindling, fodder, and certain herbal remedies. In Morocco this plant is generally known under the name *kalkh*, or in Ḥassanīyya, *titorekt*.

38. This verb expresses particularly the methodical fashioning of something that is created.

39. *Fī kulli shajarin nār, wa'stamjada al-markhu wa' l-'afār* (*Majmu' al-amthāl*, 2752). This expression was used by the desert Arabs to refer to someone who is particularly generous or to express the superiority of one thing over another. It is recorded that in areas where *markh* trees were dense, they were known to burst into flame just from their branches rubbing against each other in the wind.

40. Bukhārī, *Bad' al-khalq*, 3092; Muslim, *Jahannam*, 2843,

41. *K. al-Ḥikam* 256.

42. By which he means Shaykh al-Darqāwī

43. See the commentary on this verse above for this second meaning of *al-muqwīn*.

44. He is referring to a well-known *ḥadīth* in which the Prophet is reported to have said, "Every night, during the last third of the night, our Lord, be He blessed and exalted, descends to the heaven of this earth and says, 'Who calls upon Me that I might answer him? Who asks of Me that I might give to him? Who seeks My forgiveness that I might forgive him?'" Bukhārī, *Du'ā'*, 1077; Muslim, *al-Targhīb fī al-du'ā'*, 1262, 1265.

In respect to the word "stars" in this context, other exegetes, including al-Ṭabarī, al-Qurṭubī, and Ibn al-Kathīr, cite the words of Ibn 'Abbās which concern the other meaning of the word *nujūm*: "portions or pieces of something." "The *stars* thus mean the portions (*nujūm*) of the Qur'ān, for it was sent down in its totality on the Night of Power from the highest heaven to the heaven of this world, then it was sent down part by part in the years that followed." Ibn 'Abbās would then recite this verse. In another narrative conveyed by Ḍaḥḥāk, he said, "The Qur'ān descended in its totality from the Guarded Tablet with God to [the angels called] the Noble Scribes (*al-kirām al-kātibīn*) in the heaven of this world. They apportioned it (*najjamathu*) to Gabriel over twenty nights, and Gabriel apportioned it to Muḥammad, upon whom be peace and blessings, over twenty years. Thus does God Most High say, *Nay, but I swear by the descent of the stars*, meaning the portions of the Qur'ān."

45. *Karīm* means both "noble" and "generous," expressing the inseparability of nobility and generosity.

46. 'The Guarded Tablet" (*al-Lawḥ al-Maḥfūẓ*) is mentioned in [85:22]. In the commentary of Ibn Abī Ḥātim on [3:29], Ibn 'Abbās is quoted as having said, "God created the Guarded Tablet like a journey of a hundred years and then said to the Pen before He created the world and God was upon the Throne, 'Write!' to which the Pen answered, 'What do I write?' And God said to it, 'Write My knowledge of My creation until the Day of Resurrection.' Then did the Pen flow with all that exists in God's knowledge until the Day of Resurrection."

47. *Janāba* refers to the state following sexual intercourse or orgasm from other causes, either in men or women, while awake or asleep. Islamic ritual law requires that someone in this state take a complete bath before offering the ritual devotions (*al-ṣalāt*), reciting or touching the Qur'ān, or accomplishing certain other devotional practices.

48. *Al-ḥadath al-aṣghar*: those occurrences which necessitate the ritual ablution before offering devotional practices. Generally, this means urination, defecation, or passing wind.

49. By which is meant the actual Arabic text.

50. The Ẓāhirite School (*al-madhhab al-ẓāhirī*) refers to the theological beliefs of those who followed the doctrine of Abū Dāwūd 'Alī al-Iṣbahānī (d. 270/833) in Baghdād. The *ẓāhirī* ("outward" or "literal") doctrine accepted a literal understanding of the Qur'ān and *ḥadīth* and rejected analogical reasoning (*al-qiyās*). It was spread in Muslim Spain through the influence of Ibn Ḥazm (d. 456/1059) and reached Morocco during Almohad times, eventually to be replaced by Ash'arite theology.

51. Bukhārī, *Tawḥīd,* 6978. The verb *ḥamala* means both to physically carry something and to be entrusted with something.

52. The first three being that it is Noble or Generous (*Karīm*), in a Protected Book, and not touched except by the pure.

53. *Mudhinūn* comes from the root *dahana*, meaning "to make something slippery with oil or unguent." It came to be used as a synonym for "hypocrite" in the sense that "to oil the face" is to give a certain outward appearance.

54. Suyūṭī, *al-Jāmi' al-ṣaghīr*, 615; Ṭabarānī, *al-Kabīr,* 1411, 10296; Bayhaqī, *Dalā'il al-nubūwa*, 542. The complete text is, "When my Companions are mentioned, desist; when the stars are mentioned, desist; when destiny (*al-qadr*) is mentioned, desist." That is, if discussion turns to these subjects, refrain from getting involved in it.

55. Ḥākim, *Tafsīr*, 3948; Tirmidhī, *Tafsīr*, 3425; Aḥmad, *Musnad*, 23187, 24619, 24807; Nasā'ī, 10137, 10139. The entire text, related by Ā'isha, is "The Messenger of God took me by the hand and said, 'Seek refuge in God from this darkness, for it is the *darkness when it grows intense*.' And he was indicating the moon." *The darkness when it grows intense* is from [113:3], *And (I seek refuge) from the evil of the darkness when it grows intense*. Traditional explanations of this *ḥadīth* say that the Prophet did not mean that evil arises from the moon, but rather that it is during the darkest part of night when criminals are most active.

56. An ode in which every line ends with the letter *'ayn*.

57. *K. al-Ḥikam*, *Munājāt* 26.

58. This is related in *al-Iḥya'* as a *ḥadīth qudsī* although its editor, al-'Irāqī, states, "I see no source for it." Imām Aḥmad relates a saying very close to it from Wahb al-Munabbih, in which God is reported to say, "The heavens and earth have not the strength to bear Me and are too narrow to contain me, but the heart of a faithful servant, scrupulous and lenient, contains Me." Aḥmad, *K. al-Zuhd*, 429.

59. Bayhaqī, 536, ending with the words, "and the remembrance has removed from them their burdens so that they shall come to the Day of Resurrection light."

60. Ibn 'Ajība notes that in the dictionary, the meanings of *rawḥ* include rest and mercy, as well as "a beneficent wind."

61. Who these are is explained below in *Sūrat al-Ḥadīd*, verse 19.

62. This is often identified as sweet basil.

63. This explanation is possible due to the fact that the pronoun *you* in the words *Peace be upon you* is singular.

64. The term *barzakh* (barrier or isthmus) in this context appears in [23: 99, 100]. *Until, when death comes to one of them, he says, 'My Lord! Send me back that I might do right in that which I have left behind!' But nay. It is but a word that he speaks, and behind them is a barrier* (barzakh) *until the day when they are raised*. It has also been referred to in commentaries as "what is between this world and the next," a period of time between death and resurrection, or the length of time in the grave.

65. This refers to a *ḥadīth* in Muslim, *Imāra*, 3500; Tirmidhī, *Faḍā'il al-jihād*; 1565; 2937. For the definitive discussion of how martyrdom was traditionally understood in contrast to its modern association with terrorism and suicide bombing, see *The Hijacked Caravan* which can be read and downloaded at http://www.ihsanic-intelligence.com/dox/The_Hijacked_Caravan.pdf.

66. This is mentioned in [53:14] as the place, during his Ascension, where the Prophet entered into the Divine Presence. Ibn 'Ajība explains in his commentary on that *sūra*, "According to the consensus of scholars, it is a tree in the seventh heaven... 'the Furthest Boundary' being the limit of the heavens, or that which no one has ever passed beyond, or that which marks the limits of what creatures can know of God." A *ḥadīth* states that a rider could travel in its shade for a thousand years and still not traverse it.

67. Bukhārī, *Janā'iz*, 1297

68. Mentioned in [83: 7, 8, 18]. *'Illīyūn*, a word related to the adjective *'alā*, "high," is according to a *ḥadīth*, a celestial abode above the seventh heaven, beneath the Throne. *Sijjīn*, related to the word meaning "prison," according to a saying attributed to Ibn 'Abbās, is an abode beneath the lowest of the earths.

69. This paraphrases what Ibn Ḥajar said in his commentary in *Fatḥ al-Bārī*, *Janā'iz*, 1290.

70. See p. 40 n.34.

71. That is, *Iḥyā' 'ulūm al-dīn* by al-Ghazālī.

72. *Qūt al-qulūb*, *Maqāmāt al-riḍā*, v. 2, p. 45

73. Ibn 'Ajība also notes here that in the three *sūras*, *al-Qamar*, *al-Raḥmān*, and *al-Wāqi'a*, the Name *Allāh* does not appear.

The Chapter of Iron
(Sūrat al-Ḥadīd)

This *sūra*, which is twenty-eight verses, was revealed in Medina and contains Meccan verses as well. It is connected to the *Chapter of the Event* which precedes it through the words which end that *sūra*, *So Glorify the name of your Lord, Supreme* and the words which open this one, *All that is in the heavens and the earth has glorified God*. [The two verses taken together] mean, 'Glorify the Name of your Lord as He has enjoined along with all those in the heavens and earth who have glorified Him.' Al-Tha'ālibī said, "The words of God Most High, *So Glorify the name of your Lord, Supreme*, mean to glorify Him by His Supreme Name. Thus does this *sūra* open with the words *He is the First and the Last, and the Outward and the Inward*." And Ibn 'Abbās said, "The Supreme Name of God (*ismu Llāhi al-a'ẓam*) is present in six of the opening verses of *Sūrat al-Ḥadīd*."[1]

In the Name of God, the All Merciful and Compassionate.

1. *All that is in the heavens and the earth has glorified God; and He is the Mighty, the Wise.*
2. *His is the Sovereignty of the heavens and the earth; He gives life and He gives death; and He is Able to do all things.*
3. *He is the First and the Last, the Outward and the Inward; and He is Knower of all things.*
4. *He it is Who created the heavens and the earth in six Days; then He mounted the Throne. He knows all that enters the earth and all that emerges therefrom and all that comes down from the sky and all that ascends therein; and He is with you wherever you may be. And God is Seer of what you do.*
5. *His is the Sovereignty of the heavens and the earth, and unto God [all] things are brought back. He causes the night to pass into the day, and He causes the day to pass into the night, and He is knower of all that is in the breasts.*

Commentary

All that is in the heavens and the earth has glorified God;
and He is the Mighty, the Wise.

The verb of Glorification (*al-tasbīḥ*) occurs in the Qur'ān in the perfect, imperfect, imperative, and gerund forms. Here, God Most High says, [*All that is in the heavens and earth*] *has glorified* [Him] and in *Sūrat al-Jumu'a*, [*All that is in the heavens and earth*] *glorifies* [Him] and [in *Sūrat al-A'lā*], *Glorify* [*the Name of your Lord*], and in *Sūrat al-Isra', Glory be to the One Who carried His servant by night*....[2] Sometimes the verb is followed by the particle *lam* [as in this verse] and sometimes not....

The basic meaning of this verb is "to be beyond," that is, beyond all evil, and it is derived from the most ancient sense of *sabaḥa*, "He went far." When the particle *lam* follows the verb, it may have virtually the same meaning as without the *lam*, or else may carry the sense of accomplishing this act of glorification purely for the sake of God alone.... All this is according to al-Nasafī.

To glorify God is to affirm His transcendence beyond beliefs, words, or deeds that are not meet to His Majesty and Honor. *All that* resides *in the heavens and earth*—angels, jinn, men, and inanimate objects—do this either in words or by the tongue of their state, inasmuch as every individual aspect of creation by its very possibility and occurrence is evidence of an Eternal Maker, of a Necessary Being, of the One Described as Perfect and Complete, beyond all deficiencies and defects, expressed as well in His words, *And there is nothing that does not hymn His praises* [17:44]. ... *And He is the Mighty* and Vengeful to those who, in their obstinance and pride, will not glorify Him, and *the Wise* in recompensing those who, in their submission, do.

His is the Sovereignty of the heavens and the earth; He gives
life and He gives death; and He is Able to do all things.

To God belongs complete control over the modes of existence, nonexistence, and other dispositions of [the heavens, earth], and all that exists therein. To quote al-Wartajibī:

> God—be He glorified—mentions His sovereignty [here] to the measure of what creatures may comprehend. Otherwise, compared to His sovereignty, what are the heavens and the earth? In the [vastness] of His dominions, all the heavens

and all the earths are less than a mustard seed! But knowing that creatures are incapable of comprehending what is beyond their vision, He says the heavens and the earth are the domain of His Power, by which, if He wishes for a thing to be, He says *Be*, and it is. [In reality, however,] His Power and Will have neither limit nor end.

The words *He gives life and He gives death* explain certain aspects of *Sovereignty*: it is He who gives life to the dead and death to the living *and He* [*who*] *over all things has power,* including the giving of life and death. Nothing is beyond His ability.

He is the First and the Last, the Outward and the Inward, and He is the Knower of all things.

God is the One Who existed eternally before all things and the One Who will continue to exist eternally after all else has passed away, the One Who is manifested by way of all things, and the One Who, after His manifestation, is hidden within all things, even as the *ḥadīth* states: "O God, You are the First, and there is nothing before You, and You are the Last, and there is nothing after You, and You are the Outward (*al-Ẓāhir*), and there is Nothing above You, and You are the Inward (*al-Bāṭin*), and there is nothing beneath You." About this, al-Ṭayyibī said, "*The Outward* according to the Prophet's explanation, is the One Who triumphs over all and is not triumphed over, Who conducts the heavens by way of ascendancy and control with none above Him to hinder Him. His Name *the Inward* [means] that there is no shelter or salvation nearer than He, and He saves whosoever seeks refuge in Him." (This will be further explained in the Spiritual Allusion to follow, God willing.) *And He is the Knower of all things* and nothing, either evident or hidden, is excluded from His knowledge.

He it is Who created the heavens and the earth in six Days; then He mounted the Throne. He knows all that enters the earth and all that emerges therefrom and all that comes down from the sky and all that ascends therein; and He is with you wherever you may be. And God is Seer of what you do.

...He *created the heavens and the earth in six* earthly *days,* and had He wished to create them in the blink of an eye, He could have done so, but He made six to be a basic cycle, and also in order to teach the value of slowness.[3] *Then He mounted*, that is, assumed authority, *upon the Throne* so that the Throne and all It contained vanished in the Immensity of the Mysteries of His Essence. *He knows* every seed, every drop of rain, and every treasure that enters the earth, as He does the angels, the dead, and the deeds of men that *emerge therefrom. And He is with you wherever you may be* through His knowledge, power, and Essential All-Encompassingness. Ibn 'Aṭiyya explains that by the consensus of scholars, this means [that God is with you] through His knowledge, and if, in saying this, he is referring to the people of outward knowledge, then it is acceptable. The people of inward [knowledge], however, would not agree, as will be explained in the Spiritual Allusion to come. *And God is the Seer of what you do* and recompenses each according to his deeds.

His is the Sovereignty of the heavens and the earth, and unto God [all] things are brought back.

[These words] are repeated for affirmation and also introduce the verses which follow. *And unto God* alone, and to no one else, either independently or in association, *are (all) things brought back.*

He causes the night to pass into the day, and He causes the day to pass into the night, and He is knower of all that is in the breasts.

He causes the night to enter into the day in summer when nights are shortened and days lengthened, and He causes the day to enter into the night in winter when the opposite occurs. *And He is knower of all* the thoughts and notions *that* are hidden *in the breasts*. This verse declares that God's knowledge encompasses not only your actions—that not only is He *the Seer of what you do*—but also the thoughts and intentions which your limbs then translate into action. It also means that He knows the truths, both salutary and corrupting, that human beings keep hidden even from their own hearts. And God Most High knows better.

Spiritual Allusion

The word "glorification" (*tasbīḥ*) is derived from the word "swimming" (*sabḥ*), that is, "floating" (*'awm*).[4] [In this there is an allusion to] how the gnostics' meditations float in the Oceans of the Essence and the currents of the Attributes, and then return to shore to maintain the rites of servanthood and devotion. They swim this Ocean even while the inhabitants of the heavens and earth are drowned therein—whether they perceive it or not—nay, even while all that exists is drowned in this Ocean, effaced in its Unicity. [About this verse] al-Qushayrī said:

> *All* the Essential Names *in the heavens* of the Essence, manifested in the theophany of the Totality, and *all* the Attributive Names *in the earth* of the Attributes, manifested in the theophany of the Particulars affirm by God's All-Inclusive Name His Transcendence beyond the Names and Attributes of both Rigor and Beauty.
>
> And know that the sphere of the Essence is "heaven" to the Attributes[5] and the sphere of the Attributes "earth" to the Essence, just as the sphere of the Attributes is "heaven" to the Names, and the sphere of the Names "earth" to the Attributes, and that these heavens and earths are but the theophany of God's Supreme Name, and He is the One Who is Glorified in the station of separation and the One Who Glorifies in the station of union.

By his words "the sphere of the Essence is heaven to the Attributes" and so forth, [al-Qushayrī] means that the mysteries of the Subtle and Primary Essence are "heaven" in relation to the Attributes through which they are manifested, just as the Attributes are "earth" in relation to those mysteries. Likewise, the Attributes are "heaven" in relation to the "earth" of the Names, and the Names are "earth" in relation to the "heaven" of the Attributes. What remains to be added to this is that the sphere of the Names is "heaven" in relation to formal manifestation (*al-āthār*),[6] which is "earth" in relation to the heaven of the Names.

Said more simply, every level of existence is "heaven" to what is beneath it and "earth" to what is above it. So the physical world is earth to the heaven of the Names, the Names are earth to the heaven of the Attributes, and the Attributes are earth to the heaven of the Essence. [Similarly, it is said in the *Ḥikam*]:

> By the existence of His created things,
> He points to the existence of His Names,
>   and by the existence of His Names,
> He points to the existence of His Qualities,
>   and by the existence of His Qualities,
> He points to the existence of His Essence.

Such is the way for those in the station of ascent, while for those in the station of descent, it is the reverse, as [the rest of this aphorism] in the *Ḥikam* describes.[7]

And He is the Mighty beyond our ability to fully comprehend His Divinity, and *the Wise* in having concealed Himself after having revealed Himself.[8]

To Him belongs the Sovereignty of the heavens of our souls *and the earth* of our bodies (*ashbāḥ*); or *to Him belongs Sovereignty of the* heavens of the Essence, Attributes, and Names, and their earths, according to what has been said above. *He gives life* to the hearts of His saints by granting them gnosis, *and He gives death* to the hearts of His foes by leaving them in ignorance of Himself; or *He gives life* to hearts through knowledge, *and death* to our lower selves through effacement. *And He—over all things*—in the giving of life, the giving of death, and all else—*has power.*

He is the First without beginning *and the Last* without end. He is *the Outward* and there is no other outward beside Him and He is *the Inward* even as He reveals Himself; or He is the Outward in His theophanies (*tajalliyyāt*), and the Inward by spreading out upon them the cloak of His Majesty;[9] or, He is the Outward in identity, the Inward in manner, Outward in His inwardness, Inward in His outwardness. In whatever manifests Him, He is the Inward, and in whatever conceals Him, He is the Outward. Through His Name *al-Ẓāhir*, the inwardness of all things is realized, and then their eventual annihilation and dissolution, for there can be no other outward beside Him. Through His Name *al-Bāṭin*, the physical nature of all things is realized, in order that He might be concealed therein. To quote the *Ḥikam*, "He manifests all things because He is the Inward, and He conceals the existence of all things because He is the Outward."[10] This will be understood, however, only by the people of "spiritual tastes" (*al-adhwāq*). Said al-Qushayrī:

> *He is the First* even in His Finality, *the Last* even in His Primacy, *the Outward* even in His Inwardness, *and the Inward* even in His outwardness, at one and the same time, from any perspective, beyond contingency and contradiction, encompassing all and independent of all. Thus, when it was asked of Abū Sa'īd al-Kharrāz, "By what have you come to know God?" he answered, "By His union of opposites." Then he recited *He is the First and the Last...* And

> the union of opposites is inconceivable except from the aspect of absolute Oneness…

He it is Who created the heavens and the earth in six Days. Concerning this verse, al-Qushayrī said, "This alludes to the order of the Six Divine Attributes: Life, Knowledge, Power, Will, Hearing, and Sight. The verse thus means that He is the One Who unveils Himself to all things by His Essence which is qualified by these six attributes…."

As for the verse, *then He mounted the Throne,* this has already been spoken of in the commentary upon *Sūrat al-A'rāf* and *Sūrat al-Sajda.*[11]

He knows all the vices *that enter into the earth* of the human state *and all* the self-purification and spiritual effort (*mujāhadah*) *that emerges therefrom.* [*He knows*] *all* the teachings and mysteries *that come down from the sky* of the unseen realms and into purified hearts *and all* the sweetness of direct perception *that ascends therein, and He is with you wheresoever you may be*, through His Essence and Attributes in a manner meet to the Majesty and Perfection of His Divinity. And inasmuch as an Attribute cannot be separate from the One it describes, if His "withness" (*ma'iyyatuhu*) is by way of Knowledge, then it must be by way of His Essence. Understand this, and if you have not tasted it, [then at least] accept it.

One of my teachers, the skilled jurist al-Janwī, once told me that the scholars of Egypt assembled to consider the question of God's "withness"[12] and ended in consensus that it was by way of the Essence in a manner fitting to God. I also heard him say, "The well-known scholar, Sidī Aḥmad bin Mubārak, met with the saintly Sidī Aḥmad al-Ṣaqallī and asked him, 'In what way do you believe *He is with you wheresoever you may be*?' He answered, 'By the Essence,' to which Sidī Ibn Mubārak replied, 'Then I bear witness that you are truly one of the gnostics!'"

The Ocean of the Essence is continuous. A discontinuity therein is inconceivable, as is any connection to time or place. "God was, and there was neither time nor place, and He is now as He ever was."[13] Said al-Wartajibī:

> Concerning this, the gnostics have two stations: the station of Eternal Oneness beyond all contingency in which all creation is perceived as subsumed in the Majesty and Honor of the Most Merciful until there remains of it not even a trace; and the station of Essential Union, in which there is a perceptible connection between the Light of the Attribute, existing in the Divine Essence, and the Light of the Intellect. [In this latter station]

> God is perceived as unveiling Himself in His Essence and Attributes to His Acts, and then by His Acts, so that every aspect of existence is seen as a mirror of His Being.
>
> He is *Outward* to everything and from everything. For the generality, this is by way of His Acts, for the elect, by way of His Names and Traits, for the elect of the elect, by way of His Attributes, and for those who are established in the consciousness of His Essence, by way of His Essence. He transcends intermediary and incarnation, separateness or junction. This is by a taste of Divine love, however, *and none will know its explanation*[14] except the lovers.

To sum up what he has said, if you perceive Oneness, there remains no "other" with whom to achieve "withness" for naught else exists but God. If you perceive union and separation, you realize that separation exists in union itself and that "withness" means union if it is with God, and separation if it is with created things. In the highest sense, however, there is really no separation. Understand this, yet none shall understand it except the people of complete love, and they are the people of effacement to which Ibn al-Fāriḍ alludes in his lines:

> *You do not truly love Me*
> *Unless you are effaced within Me*
> *And you shall not be effaced within Me*
> *Until I appear within you.*

7. *Believe in God and His messenger, and spend of that-whereof He has made you trustees; and such of you as believe and spend [aright], theirs will be a great reward What ails you that you do not believe in God, when the messenger is calling you to believe in your Lord, and He-has already made a covenant with you, if you are faithful?*
9. *He it is Who sends down clear revelations to His servant, that He may bring you forth from darkness into light; truly, for you, God is Full of Clemency and Most Merciful.*
10. *And what ails you that you do not spend in the way of God when unto God belongs the inheritance of the heavens and the earth?*
11. *Those who spent and fought before the victory are not upon a level [with the rest of you]. Such are greater in rank than those who spent and fought thereafter, but to*

each has God promised good. And God is Informed of what you do.

12. *Who is the one who will lend to God a goodly loan, that He may multiply it for him and his may be a generous recompense?*

Commentary

Believe in God and His messenger, and spend of that whereof He has made you trustees; and such of you as believe and spend [aright], theirs will be a great reward.

If these words are understood to be addressed to the faithful, then they mean, 'Maintain your faith,' and introduce the injunction which follows: to spend [in charity] out of one's wealth and possessions, for the faithful merit this elevated rank. If they are understood to be addressed to those who do not believe, then the words mean 'come to faith.' *And spend* by way of the obligatory tithe (*al-zakat*) and other forms of charity, *out of what* God has entrusted to you and put under your control. Spend of it even though, in reality, it is not yours. Rather, you are but God's caretaker or agent for it. So spend what is God's right upon it. Hence, this task is made as easy for you as it would be for someone given permission to spend the wealth of another.

This [verse] may also be understood to mean, 'Spend what God has caused you to inherit from those before you. They once had in their hands what you have inherited and which will be [eventually] taken from you totally and given to others.' Consider, then, their state and be not miserly. *And such of you as believe* in God and His Messenger, *theirs will be a great reward*, the amount of which is beyond reckoning.

What ails you that you do not believe in God, and the messenger is calling you to believe in your Lord, and He has already made a covenant with you, if you are faithful?

This verse asks [the non-believers], 'What has befallen you that has not befallen those who believe?' It both reproaches them for having abandoned faith after they had been called to it, and denies that they have any real excuse [for their non-belief]. *And the messenger is* alerting you and bringing you proofs, *to believe in your Lord, and He has already made* a covenant with you in the pre-temporal world, after having endowed you with intelligence, that you might acknowledge the Divinity and believe in the one who calls. No excuse remains for you to abandon faith. This may also be understood to mean 'He made a covenant with you' by placing in creation signs [of His existence] that you could see. So behold them, reflect, and believe *if you are faithful* to this covenant or by any other means necessary, for this is a necessity above all other necessities.

He it is Who sends down clear revelations to His servant that He may bring you forth from the darkness into the light. And truly, for you, God is Full of Clemency and Most Merciful

He sends the *clear revelations* of the Qur'ān *to His servant* Muḥammad, upon whom be peace and blessings, to *bring you forth...* [15] *from the darkness* of disbelief, sin, and heedlessness, *into the light* of faith, repentance, and vigilance. God *is Full of Clemency and Most Merciful* for having guided you to the happiness of this world and the Next by sending the Messenger and revealing the verses and placing [in creation] comprehensible proofs …

And what ails you that you do not spend in the way of God when unto God belongs the inheritance of the heavens and the earth ?

'What has befallen you that prevents you from spending what would bring you nearer to God and which, in reality, belongs to Him, while you are His vicegerents? ... Since to God and to no other will go the inheritance of all that *the heavens and earth* contain, what is it that hinders you from giving it for His sake? He is the One Who will cause you to pass away and the One Who will inherit what you possess, so to send it forth now for the sake of God is best.'

This is the strongest encouragement towards charity, and the fact that the Name of Majesty is repeated instead of a pronoun deepens its importance and significance.

Those who spent and fought before the victory are not upon a level [with the rest of you]. Such are greater in rank than those who spent and fought thereafter, but to each has God promised good. And God is Informed of what you do.

Here God elucidates how those who spend [in His way] differ in respect to time. The *one who spent and fought before the* conquest of Mecca, before Islam was strengthened and given victory, *is not on* the same *level* as the one who did so afterwards... Those who spent and fought before the conquest of Mecca were *the first and foremost among the emigrants and the helpers* [9:10] about whom the Prophet once said, "If one of you were to spend the equivalent of Mount Uḥud in gold, it would not equal what they did, or even half of what they did."[16] *They are greater in rank than those who spent and fought thereafter.* Indeed, a person who gives charity in a time of need and hardship is of a higher rank than someone who does so in a time of sufficiency and ease. *But to each... has God promised good*, which is Heaven itself, even while their abodes therein differ.... *And God is Informed of what you do* and recompenses you in accordance with your deeds.

Who is the one who will lend to God a goodly loan, that He may multiply it for him and his may be a generous recompense?

After enjoining the faithful to spend for His sake, reproaching those who do not, and elucidating the ranks of those who do, God strikes this metaphor concerning the charitable: those who spend for God's sake and in hopes of Divine recompense are making a loan to God.

The best charity is what is given purely, with a pure intention, from possessions that have value for the giver, and to people who are deserving. [If these conditions are met], then will God, by His Grace, *multiply it for him* and return to him whatever he spent many times over. *And his may be a generous recompense*: any recompense that God calls *generous* is worth striving for even if it were not multiplied, and more so seeing that it will be.

Spiritual Allusion

God Most High enjoins upon spiritual teachers and pious scholars to *believe* with a faith of vision and perception, or of confirmation and evidence, the first being for the saints and the second for the learned, *and* to *spend* of the knowledge which He has given them through inspiration or through formal study. *Such of you as believe* in this way and give from the vastness of inspired knowledge or the confines of formal knowledge, *theirs will be* the *great reward* of dwelling in the Divine Presence in the place of sincerity or at the center of Heaven among the most blessed of forms. *What ails you that you do not believe in God* and regularly revitalize your faith by way of meditation and reflection, *when the Messenger is calling to* you to do so and God *has already made a covenant with you* in the pretemporal world then renewed it with the advent of the Prophets and their successors from among the teachers of the Way who call to God, *if you are faithful* to this covenant. *He it is Who sends* the *clear revelations* of the Qur'ān *to His servant*, the Messenger of God (may peace and blessings be upon him) *that He may bring you forth from the darkness* of sin *into the light* of repentance and righteousness, from the darkness of heedlessness to the light of vigilance, from the darkness of desire and selfishness into the light of renunciation and purity, from the darkness of the sensual into the light of the spiritual, and from the darkness of ignorance into the light of knowledge by God.

And what ails you that you do not spend your hearts and souls in the Way of God, giving them freely for the pleasure of God, *when unto God belongs the inheritance of the heavens and the earth.* He will inherit both your bodies and souls, but to the one who gives them freely, He will give in return an ongoing consciousness of the Divine, while the one who tries to horde them He will chastise with the weariness of being veiled [from Him].

Not equal among you is the one who gave up his lower self and battled against it before the Way was shown to him and the one who did so after it was shown. The Foremost are those who found no help and support while the ones who came later (*al-muta'akhkhirūn*) did. *To each has God promised* the *goodness* of formal Heaven, while to the Foremost He adds the spiritual Heaven of gnosis. *And God is informed of what you do* and it is not hidden from Him who is advancing [in the Way] and who is lagging behind.

Who is the one who will lend to God a goodly loan? [Of this verse] al-Qushayrī said, "This means, 'Lend it to God and rid your heart of love for the two abodes.' And according to a tradition, 'The best charity is what is given by one who is wealthy.'"[17]

That He may multiply it for him by ascent to the limitless, *and his may be* the *generous recompense* of [a place] in *the Assembly of Truth, in the Presence of a Sovereign Omnipotent* [54:55].

12. *A day when you will see the believers, men and women, their light shining forth before them and on their right hands, [and will hear it said unto them]: Glad news for you this day: Gardens underneath which rivers flow, wherein you are immortal. That is the supreme triumph.*

13. *A day when the hypocritical men and the hypocritical women will say to those who believe: Look upon us that we may borrow from your light! it will be said: Go back and seek for light! Then there will separate them a wall wherein is a gate, the inner side whereof contains mercy, while the outer side thereof is toward the doom.*
14. *They will cry unto them [saying]: Were we not with you? They will say: Yea, verily; but you tempted one another, and lay in wait, and doubted, and vain desires beguiled you till God's command came to pass; and the deceiver deceived you concerning God.*
15. *So this day no ransom can be taken from you nor from those who disbelieved. Your home is the Fire; that is your patron, and a hapless journey's end.*

Commentary

A day when you will see the believers, men and women, their light shining forth before them and on their right hands, [and will hear it said unto them]: Glad news for you this day: Gardens underneath which rivers flow, wherein you are immortal. That is the supreme triumph.

This verse may be read independently to mean 'Remember *a day when you* [O Muḥammad] *will see*,' or it may be read as a continuation [of the verse] before it: *And his may be a generous recompense on a day when you will see the believers, men and women. Their light,* which was the light of faith in this world, will become a physical light [on that day] *shining forth before them and on their right hands*. Some have said this light is the Qur'ān. It is also related that Ibn Mas'ūd said, "They will be given their light to the measure of their deeds. For some it will be as tall as a palm tree, for some, as tall as a standing man, and for the one who has the least light, it will be just at the tip of his big toe and will sometimes shine and sometimes go out."

For some, it will be like the full moon, and for some, like the midday sun illuminating a journey of five hundred years, as is stated in another *ḥadīth*, and all this will be to the measure of their faith and gnosis. Ḥasan said, "They will be given light thereby upon the Bridge (*al-Ṣirāṭ*) and they will cross it at different speeds."[18] And Abū Naṣr al-Ḥamdānī said:

> The community of Muḥammad, upon whom be peace, will be in seven groups: the saints, the learned, the substitutes,[19] the martyrs, the pilgrims, the obedient, and the sinners. The saints will pass over the Bridge like lightning. The learned—that is, those who act on what they know —will pass over like the wind that comes with a storm. The substitutes will pass like birds in a single hour. The martyrs will pass over like running coursers in half a day. The pilgrims will pass in a single day, and the obedient ones, in a month. As for the sinful, they will place their feet upon the Bridge, with their loin clothes hiked up upon their backs, and they will cross over stumbling. Hell will seek to burn them but it will see the light of faith in their hearts and say, "Pass on, O one of faith! Your light has extinguished my flame!"

The saints themselves will be of two sorts [in their crossing]. For the ones who guided to God through imitation and method, their chambers in Heaven will approach them, they will mount up into them, and thus will they pass,[20] while the solitary ones (*al-afrād*) will fly across like lightning. And God Most High knows best. Said al-Muqātil,

> This light will signal their entering Heaven. *Before them and on their right hands* are mentioned in particular because these are the directions from which the blessed are given their scrolls, while the damned are given theirs from the left and from behind their backs. Hence, the light placed for the blessed in these two directions will be a sign that by the good they accomplished and their white scrolls, they have succeeded.[21]

The angels say to them, *Glad news for you this day: Gardens*—that is, of entering Heaven, for the tidings [of Heaven] had come to them while they were yet in their graves—*underneath which rivers flow, to dwell therein eternally. That is the supreme triumph.*

A day when the hypocritical men and the hypocritical women will say to those who believe: Look upon us that we may borrow from your light! It will be said: Go back and seek for light! Then there will separate them a wall wherein is a gate, the inner side whereof contains mercy, while the outer side thereof is toward the doom.

Look upon us (*unẓurūnā*) in this context means *wait for us* (*untaẓirūnā*).[22] This will be said by the hypocrites left behind in the darkness to the faithful as they are taken into Heaven with the swiftness of lightning. 'Stop in your journey so we can light our way with your light.' [The verb] is also said to be derived from "look" (*al-naẓr*) and would thus mean 'Turn in our direction and look upon us' *that we may borrow from* your light, for the light [of the faithful] will be in front them. *It will be said* in rejection and scorn from the direction of the faithful or from the angels, *Go back* to the Place of Standing, the place where we were given this light, *and seek* it, for it was there that it was illuminated for us. It is also said that these words mean, 'Turn back,' and the moment they do, *a wall will be struck between* the two groups, between Heaven and Hell. In this wall will be a gate near to the hypocrites through which they will be able to look into Heaven and see the faithful and the mercy and light they have been given, which will add to their sorrow. *The inner side* of that wall, on the side of the faithful, *contains mercy, while the outer side*, which is near the hypocrites, *is toward the doom,* which is to say that the outside of the wall will face hellfire or darkness and in this sense it faces *the doom*. The hypocrites are thus between the fire and the wall.

They will cry unto them [saying]: Were we not with you? They will say: Yea, verily; but you tempted one another, and lay in wait, and doubted, and vain hopes beguiled you till God's command came to pass; and the deceiver deceived you concerning God. So this day no ransom can be taken from you nor from those who disbelieved. Your final destination is the Fire; that is your patron—a hapless journey's end.

The hypocrites *will cry out* to the faithful, seeking outward affirmation: *Were we not with you* in the world? to which the faithful will respond, *Yea, verily,* outwardly you were with us *but you tempted one another,* which is to say, you brought tribulation and destruction upon yourselves by your hypocrisy and disbelief, *and you lay in wait* for disaster to strike the faithful, *you doubted* religion, *and* your *vain hopes* that Islam would perish *beguiled you.* The vain hopes may also be understood as their hopes for longer and longer lives. [This they did] *till God's command*, that is, death, *came to pass. And the deceiver* who is Satan *deceived you concerning God*, by leading you to believe that because God is forgiving and generous, He would not punish you, or that the resurrection and the reckoning do not exist. *So this day no ransom can be taken from you nor from those who disbelieved* openly.[23] *Your final destination*, the one from which you will never again journey forth, *is the Fire*. It *is your patron,* in that it has control over you like an owner has control over his possessions. The word *patron* (*mawlā*) may also be understood as 'the one who is nearest to you' (*ūlā bikum*)… . *And* Hellfire is *a hapless journey's end.*

Spiritual Allusion

On the day when you will see the believers, men and women, complete in their faith, seeking union with God. *Their light* which is the light of orientation [towards the Way] *shines forth before them and on their right hands* and by it they are guided to the Lights of Encounter, that is, Direct Perception. And it is said to them *Glad news for you this day: gardens* of gnosis, *underneath which* the *rivers* of formal teachings *flow, wherein you shall dwell eternally. That is the supreme triumph.* [Of this verse] al-Qushayrī says:

> On the Day of Judgment, they will have the selfsame light which is now in their hearts and in which they walk and are guided in all their states. About this light, the Prophet said, "The believer sees by God's light"[24] and God Most High says elsewhere, *He is upon a light from his Lord* [39:22]. It may happen that this light falls upon those who are near them and some of it may even reach their hearts. Surely, things such as this are particular to the friends of God.

Al-Wartajibī said, "The light of God which adorns the gnostic humbles before him the world and what it contains," and something similar was said by Sahl [al-Tustarī].

On the day when the hypocritical men and the hypocritical women, those who occupied themselves with beautifying the outward at the expense of the inward and so became devoid of light, *will say* in this world *wait for us* and turn in our direction *that we may borrow from your light!* And *it will be said* in ridicule, '*go back* to your world and all that your lower selves were attached to, *and* [there] *seek for light*.' *Then a wall will come between them*, and this wall is to break with the familiar (*kharq al-'awā'id*) and [be willing to] leave the outward to fall into neglect (*takhrīb al-ẓawāhir*), which they will be unable to surmount.[25] *Therein is a gate* which those who want their light may enter with them. On *the inner side* of this wall *there is the mercy* of rest, inner peace, and the splendor of gnosis, *while the outer side thereof*, facing the generality, *is toward the punishment* of cupidity, weariness, anxiety, and narrowness of soul. *They will cry unto them [saying]: Were we not with you* in the physical world, in the world of forms (*'ālam al-ashbāḥ*)? *They will say: Yes, verily; but you* attempted no ascent towards the world of the spirit, the world of souls, which is the abode of repose, tranquility, and joy. Instead, *you tempted one another* with mundane distractions, the pursuit of rank and status, and the finest of foods, drinks, and garments, *and you lay in wait* for misfortune to befall the people of the Way or for them to return to the condition which you yourselves [are in]. *You doubted* the existence of a special sort of [spiritual] training, *and* the *vain* and deceptive *hope* that you could reach the ranks of the elect without spiritual companionship or effort *beguiled you*, just as vain hopes and procrastination *beguiled you* from repenting and committing yourself wholly to following the Path. *And the deceiver deceived you* with his dreams, and made it fair-seeming to your eyes to be sedentary and left behind from the journey through the stations of the Way. *So this day* when those spiritual stations are apparent in this world and the Next *no ransom can be taken from you* to deliver you from the tribulations of being veiled from God, *nor from those who disbelieved. Your home is the fire* of separation and distance. *That is* the *patron* proven true for you, *and* [it is] *a hapless journey's end.*

16. *Is not time for the hearts of those who believe to grow humble at the Remembrance of God and to the truth which is revealed, that they not become as those who received the scripture of old but the term was prolonged for them and so their hearts were hardened, and many of them are corrupt.*
17. *Know that God gives life to the earth after its death. We have made clear Our revelations for you, that haply ye may understand.*

Commentary

Is it not the time for the hearts of those who believe to grow humble at the Remembrance of God and to the truth which is revealed

... *Is it not time for the hearts of the faithful* to find humility, submission, and peace in the remembrance of God and hasten to devotion and the keeping of God's commandments? It has been said concerning this verse that after the [first] believers had gone through trials and tribulations in Mecca, and then emigrated [to Medina] where they found provision and bounty, their initial fervor began to wane. It was then that this verse was revealed, and they were taught thereby that hardship is one with ease, Rigor is one with Beauty, and that wherever your beloved is, there too is your foe.

According to Ibn Mas'ūd, may God be pleased with him, "Between the time we entered Islam and the time this verse came to gently reproach us was only four years."[26] And according to Ibn 'Abbās, "Believers' hearts had grown tepid, then they were reproached at the beginning of the thirteenth year of the revelation."[27] It has also been related concerning Abū Bakr, may God be pleased with him, that this verse was recited before him in the presence of some people from Yemen and upon hearing it, they wept profoundly. Then he looked towards them and said, "We were thus, for our hearts had grown hard."

By "hardness" (*al-qaswah*) is meant callousness and being closed to Divine inspirations (*al-wāridāt*).[28] This happens because the heart, at the outset, is tender and so sensitive to spiritual states and inspirations that the least thing will affect it. But if lights and inspirations continue, they become familiar, the heart grows firmer and steadier until it is not as greatly affected, and it becomes the possessor of states rather than being possessed by them.... Thus, while weeping is common among the pious and the seekers, the gnostics have [generally] been relieved of it.

This verse was also the means of repentance for Fuḍayl [ibn 'Iyād]. He was climbing a wall [on his way to rob a house] when he heard someone reciting this verse and answered, "Yes! Now! Now is the time for humility and the moment of return!" and repented of the life he had been leading.

The remembrance of God here may mean either the mention of His Name in whatever context it appears, even as God's words [elsewhere] state, *The believers are those whose hearts tremble when God is mentioned* [8:2], or else the Qur'ān, in which case the words *and to the Truth that has been revealed* are *tafsīr* of the word *remembrance*... By humility (*al-khush'u*) is meant turning back and submitting to God, and keeping His injunctions.

...That they not become as those who received the scripture of old but the term was prolonged for them and so their hearts were hardened, and many of them are corrupt.

...*Those who received the scripture of old* are the Jews and Christians and *the term* that *was prolonged for them* was the time between them and their prophets when *their hearts were hardened* by their pursuit of desires. For the Children of Israel, God would come between them and their desires so that when they heard the Torah, their hearts would soften and they would turn back in humility. But when the time grew long, dryness and hardness overcame their hearts and they fell into dispute. To quote Ibn Mas'ūd:

> When the time grew long for the Children of Israel and their hearts grew hard, [a group among them] wrote a book which pleased them. [Before this] God would come between them and many of their desires, so *they placed the Book of God behind their backs as if they did not know*.[29] [Those who had written the new book] said, "Present this to the Children of Israel. If they follow you, leave them alone, but if not, slay them." Then they decided to take it to one of their most learned men, saying, "If he follows us, no one else will oppose us, and if not, slay him and no one else will oppose us." [This man, however, learned of their plan in advance] and [before they arrived], wrote the Book of God on a parchment, placed it inside a horn, hung this horn around his neck, and then donned his robes over it. When they came to him and presented him with their book, they asked him, "Do you believe in this?" He responded by patting his chest and saying, "I believe in this!" by which he meant what was hanging upon his breast. Following this, the Children of Israel split into about seventy communities.[30]

And many of them are corrupt, having left their religion and rejected what is in the [sacred] books [that were sent to them]. In other words, few of them remain faithful, and God Most High prohibits the believers from being like them. According to Ibn 'Aṭiyya,

> *Those who received the scripture* are the Children of Israel at the time of Moses (upon whom be peace) which is also why it says *of old*. Hence, God compares the people living during the time of one Prophet to the people living during the time of another. His words *The term was prolonged for them* have been said to mean either "life itself or the period of awaiting the Resurrection grew long."

Al-Muqātil says that *the term* means "their lives." When they began to expect ever longer lives, their hearts were sure to grow harder. It is also said that the Companions grew weary and said, "Relate to us something!" and the verse was revealed *We convey to you the most beautiful stories* [12:3]. Then after a period of time they said, "If only you would remind us," and this entire *sūra* was revealed.

Know that God gives life to the earth after its death. We have made clear Our revelations for you, that haply you may understand.

Here is a metaphor: the remembrance (*al-dhikr*) of God revives hearts just as a heavy rain revives the earth. It also teaches that this hardness is not removed by our own strength or ability, but rather by sincerely turning to God. He alone can do this just as He alone can revive the earth with rain. *We have made clear Our signs*, among which are these verses, *that haply you may understand* what they contain, act in accordance with what they require, and in doing so achieve the happiness of this world and the Next. And God Most High knows better.

Spiritual Allusion

For the heart *to grow humble at the invocation and remembrance of God* means for it to become lost in the radiance of One Invoked—for the invoker to vanish in the One invoked—this being what [the Sufis] call effacement (*al-fanā'*). And for the heart to *grow humble* at hearing *what is revealed of the Truth* means for it to hear the Truth from the Truth, not from people (*min al-Ḥaqq, lā min al-khalq*), such being the highest degree for Those Brought Near.

Then God Most High prohibits [the Sufis] from becoming like the people of formal articulated knowledge whose ambitions are so far reaching that they compete for rank and destroy one another trying to gain the ephemeral. Thus do their hearts grow hard, until they totally abandon the path. Said al-Qushayrī:

> Hardness of heart comes about from the pursuit of one's lusts, for lusts and purity cannot exist together. Hence the cause of this hardness is the heart being turned away from vigilance. It is also said that the first cause is a passing notion which, if not rectified, becomes a deeper thought which, if not rectified, becomes a resolution which, if not rectified becomes a violation of the law which, if not redressed, becomes hardness of heart, its second-nature and its religion.

At that point, reminders and exhortations [from people] avail it not:

> When a land goes barren, it is too late for rain.
> When a heart grows hard, it is too late for warnings.

Know that God gives life to the earth of the heart by way of [spiritual] teachings and gnosis *after its death* from heedlessness and ignorance. *We have made clear Our revelations* to anyone who reflects upon them and understands.

18. *Surely men and women who give in charity, and lend unto God a goodly loan, it will be multiplied for them, and theirs will be a generous reward.*
19. *And those who believe in God and His messengers, they are the utterly veracious and the martyrs [are] with their Lord; they have their reward and their light; while as for those who disbelieve and deny Our revelations, they are owners of Hellfire.*

Commentary

Surely men and women who give in charity, and lend unto God a goodly loan, it will be multiplied for them, and theirs will be a generous reward.

[The opening words of this verse] may be read either as men and women who give in charity (*al-muṣṣaddiqīna wa al-muṣṣaddiqāti*) or men and women who affirm the truth [of God and His Messenger] (*al-muṣaddiqīna wa al-muṣaddiqāti*).[31] *To lend to God a goodly loan* means to give in charity with a pure and wholesome heart from wealth that has been earned in a pure and wholesome manner. This is what will be multiplied for the givers many times, even seven-hundred fold. *And theirs will be a generous reward*: Heaven and all it contains.

Many *ḥadīths* have been related concerning the virtues of charity, including the fact that it wards off seventy different kinds of harm and evil[32] and increases blessings in one's life. It is also said that a young man and young woman came to the Prophet Solomon (upon whom be peace) and he joined them in marriage. But after they had left his presence, joyful with their bond, the angel of death appeared to him and said, "Do not marvel too much at their joy for I have been ordered to take the soul of that youth five days hence." And Solomon became full of worry for the young man's fate until six days had passed, and then five months, and he was amazed [to see the young man still alive]. Then the angel of death returned to him and, when Solomon asked him about this, replied, "I was commanded to take his soul as I told you, but after he left your presence, he came across a beggar and gave him a dirham and the beggar prayed that God would grant him a long life. So by the blessing of his charity, I was commanded to delay my task." Similar to this is the story of the man who did such harm to his neighbors that Moses prayed to God against him. But in the morning [the man] set out a loaf of bread to give in charity and when a viper came down [from his ceiling] and ate some of the bread it fell dead upon the man's stack of firewood...[33]

And those who believe in God and His messengers, they are the utterly veracious and the martyrs [are] with their Lord; they have their reward and their light; while as for those who disbelieve and deny Our revelations, they are owners of Hellfire.

The utterly veracious (*al-ṣiddīqūn*) can mean "those who most fervently affirm the truth" or else "those who are themselves utterly honest and sincere," this latter being [more likely from the standpoint of grammar]... *And* they too are *the martyrs* (*al-shuhadā'*) *with their Lord.* If this verse were taken literally, it would mean that anyone who believes in God and His messengers reaches the rank of the *ṣiddīqūn*, the saintly,[34] which is below that of the prophets but above that of God's chosen friends, and also reaches the rank of the martyrs. This, however, is not the case. The word "believe," then, must be understood to mean "with a special and complete faith," the faith of those who, from the moment the message was conveyed to them, never doubted the messengers and never hesitated, but rather *hastened* to faith and gave their lives for the sake of God.[35]

It has also been said that this verse means that anyone who believes in God and His messengers with absolute faith will be in the company of the saintly and the martyrs even if his state in Heaven is not equal to theirs. This is similar to what the words of God [elsewhere] state: *Whoever obeys God and the messenger, they are with those whom God has favored, of the Prophets and saints, the martyrs and righteous....* [4:69].

In other words, this phrase urges to faith using hyperbole, a form of speech common to the Arabs, who would say concerning one known for his generosity, "He is Ḥātim himself!"[36] In a like manner, the Messenger of God is reported to have said in a *ḥadīth* related by al-Barā' ibn 'Āzib, "The faithful of my community are martyrs,"[37] and Mujāhid said, "Every believer is among the saintly and martyrs."[38] [In another *ḥadīth*], the Prophet mentions seven other types of people, in particular, [whose deaths] are honored as martyrdom.[39] Do you not then see that someone slain in the way of God has also been singled out for honor uniquely his? [For this reason] have some commentators taken the word *al-shuhadā'* [in its most general sense]: "those who bear witness for the communities [of believers]."

For Ibn 'Abbās, Masrūq, and al-Ḍaḥḥāk, the phrase ends with the words *the utterly veracious*, and the words *the martyrs* begin a parenthetical phrase which declares that *With their Lord shall the martyrs have their reward and their light*. Abū Ḥayyān, who also favors this reading, says, "The simplest and clearest reading is that the word *martyrs* is the subject of a new phrase and what immediately follows it is its complement."

[For me, however,] the simplest reading is that this verse is to be read without a stop and to be understood as saying that every genuine believer is *ṣiddīq* and *shahīd*—that is, in their company—and that God's words *they have their reward and their light* mean that the recompense and light they have will be similar to what the saintly and martyrs shall have, even while they are not of the same rank....

Spiritual Allusion

For men and women who give their lives and their spirits to what is pleasing to God Most High—and "whatever is lost for the sake of

God is God's duty to replace" [40]—*and lend to God a goodly loan* by removing their hearts from the love of all else and keeping them in the Divine Presence, the lights and mysteries given them *will be multiplied... and theirs will be a generous reward,* this being direct perception of the Most Holy Essence. Such are *the utterly veracious ones* referred to by His words, *those who believe in God and His messengers, they are the utterly veracious*, who believe with a special faith. Speaking of them, al-Wartajibī said,

> These are the ones who perceive God by God and follow His Messenger through a particular kind of gnosis and love granted them by God's grace and honor because of their submission to His commandments and prohibitions. *Those are the utterly veracious ones*, the mines of sincerity, certainty, and affirmation of God's word after having directly perceived Him with the perception of the saintly, which is untainted by opposition from the lower self or the Devil. *They are the martyrs* for God, slain by the swords of His Love, cast into the Ocean of His Union, then revived by His beauty. They martyr their [own] existence by effacement in God, and by passing away from the world in God's Infinitude and Majesty. They are a folk who view the cares of creatures by the Light of God and bear witness both for them and upon them by the sincerity of their insight. They are God's trustees, those whom He has chosen for sanctity (*al-ṣiddīqiyya*), blessedness, friendship, and vicegerency.

Al-Qushayrī said,

> The saint (*al-ṣiddīq*) is the one who is the same inwardly and outwardly. It has also been said that he is the one who keeps [God's] commandments even in difficulty, does not resort to license, and has no need for interpretation.
>
> The martyrs (*al-shuhadā'*) are those who witness (*yushāhidūna*) with their hearts the homelands of union and retreat within their innermost souls into the domains of nearness. *Their light* is what God has taken from the lights of Divine Oneness and applied to their inner visions.[41]

20. *Know that the life of the world is only play, diversion, ornament, boasting among you, and rivalry in respect to wealth and children; as the likeness of vegetation after*

rain, whereof the growth is pleasing to the husbandman, but afterward it dries up and you see it turning yellow, then it becomes straw. And in the Hereafter there is grievous punishment, and [also] forgiveness from God and His good pleasure. And what is the life of the world except a matter of deception?

21. *Race one with another towards forgiveness from your Lord and a Garden whereof the breadth is as the breadth of the heavens and the earth prepared for those who believe in God and His messengers. Such is the bounty of God, which He bestows upon whom He will. And God is of Infinite Bounty.*

Commentary

Know that the life of the world is only play, diversion, ornament, boasting among you, and rivalry in respect of wealth and children; as the likeness of vegetation after rain, whereof the growth is pleasing to the husbandman, but afterward it dries up and you see it turning yellow, then it becomes straw...

...*The life of the world is* like the *play* of children, the *diversion* of adolescents, the *ornaments* of women, the *boasting* of equals *and rivalry*, by which is meant the bragging, of farmers about *wealth and children* ... In other words, it is the basest of matters from which no sane person would seek his support, let alone his inner peace. It is, in addition, fast fading, like the *vegetation after rain, whereof the growth is pleasing to the husbandman...*[42]*... but afterward... dries up.* After having seen it blossom and ripen, *you see it turn yellow.... Then it becomes straw,* dried and broken stalks. The state of the world and its ephemerality is thus likened to the plants that spring forth and grow strong after a rain, delighting the tiller (*kuffār*), the one who covers up grain in the earth (*kafara al-ḥabb fī al-arḍ*). [This word] may also be taken to mean of "those who dispute that the rain and vegetation by which they are given their provision are among God's blessings, until the crop is hit by a blight, turns yellow, and then into dry stubble."

This similitude, however, applies to those wholly taken up by this world and its pursuit, not to those who live in the world while obeying God, or who provide for their children yet maintain worship. Rather, it concerns those who have been given youth and strength, beauty in their appearance and forms, and are then overtaken by infirmities and senility, and finally death, so that all that they were is effaced, and all that they possessed goes to others. Al-Qushayrī said,

> The world itself is a lowly thing and the lowest thing therein is the one in pursuit of it, while the least mindful is the one who fights to possess it. What else is it except carrion? And surely anyone who runs after carrion is not of sane mind, and anyone who hordes it is truly lost. This blameworthy world is everything that distracts people from the Hereafter: whatever form it takes, it is [called] "the world" (*al-dunyā*).

And in the Hereafter there is grievous punishment, and [also] forgiveness from God and His good pleasure. And what is the life of the world except a matter of deception?

The *grievous punishment* is for anyone who has lived in opposition to God, *and* the *forgiveness from God and His good pleasure* for anyone who has turned to God and withdrawn from what is other than Him.

Thus, while the world is naught but the basest of things—play and vain chatter, ornaments, boasting, and rivalry to get more—the Hereafter contains things of the greatest import: grievous punishment, forgiveness, and the good pleasure of God, the One worthy of all praise. . . .

The life of this *world* for the one who relies upon it *is but a matter of deception*. It is something which appears beautiful on the outside but which conceals what is ugly within, like [a charlatan] who first tricks people and then cheats them. The world appears to those who pursue it as sweetness and infatuation, overtaking them little by little, until they become totally entangled in it and neglect all preparation for the Hereafter. Life passes from their hands in vanity, and the world continues to delude and betray them until it brings them bankrupt to the moment of their deaths. Dhū'l-Nūn said, "O you who aspire to God! Do not pursue this world, and if you must pursue it, do not love it. For while it contains provision for your journey, your destination and rest are elsewhere."

Race one with another towards forgiveness from your Lord and a Garden whereof the breadth is as the breadth of the heavens and the earth...

Even as God demeans this world, He esteems the Hereafter and urges His servants to hasten towards what is promised to them there by His words, *Race one with another.* That is, hasten as if in an arena, racing against others in the accomplishment of good, *towards forgiveness from your Lord and a Garden ...* as wide as the seven heavens and seven earths if they could be placed end to end... And if [its] breadth is described as this great, its length must be even greater, as is true for all things that have breadth and length. But such a description is only a way of making something accessible to the understanding of the Arabs, for Heaven is much vaster than all that. How could it be otherwise when a single believer therein will be given the extent of this world ten times over?[43]

[*A heaven*] *prepared for those who believe in God and His messengers. Such is the bounty of God, which He bestows upon whom He will. And God is of Infinite Bounty.*

[God's words] *prepared for those who believe* have been cited as [one of the] textual proofs that Heaven is created, while [His words] *which He bestows upon whom He will*, that is, upon the faithful, have been cited as proof that "No one shall enter Heaven by his deeds," even as the *ḥadīth* states.[44] *And God is of Infinite Bounty* and gives this limitless bounty to whomsoever He wishes.

Spiritual Allusion

A certain sage likened this world to seven things, saying:

> It is like salt water which can drown you but not quench your thirst, and which harms but does not benefit; like the shade cast by clouds which first deceives then disappoints; like the lightning flash which appears then vanishes in an instant and may cause great damage; like summer clouds that can bring harm but no benefit; like the wildflowers in spring which are lovely when they bloom but then quickly fade and wilt; like a dream in which you taste great joy but then awaken to find nothing; and like honey into which poison has been mixed which tastes sweet but then kills.

About this list, his grandson said, "I pondered upon these images for seventy years and then added one more to the list: the world is a like the *ghūl*[45] who destroys those who respond to her but leaves alone those who turn away." In Sidī 'Abd al-Raḥmān al-Lajā'ī's book, *Quṭb al-'Ārifīn*, he says,

The first step for those on the path to God is to be repulsed by this lower world which is the darkness of hearts, a veil hiding the radiance of the Unseen, and a barrier between the lover and the Beloved. To the measure that aspirants reject this world they are ready for the journey….When the world is lifted from their hearts and has no more value for them than the wing of a gnat, then have they placed their feet on the first step in the Way….

Al-Qushayrī says in his spiritual allusion from this verse:

> It signifies the stages of the lower self (*al-nafs*), the heart (*al-qalb*), the spirit (*al-rūḥ*), and the innermost soul (*al-sirr*). [First, there is] the *play* of the lower self which like a child incites [you] to games against the Revealed Law (*al-sharī'a*) and towards following [your lower nature]. [Then, there is] the *diversion* of the heart, which like a youth becomes preoccupied with asceticism, scrupulousness, living without means,[46] and keeping [his soul] bound to these practices. [Then, there is] the *ornament* of the mature soul beautified by its inner states and [its journey] though the stations of unveiling, contemplation, and vision. [Then, there is] the *boasting* of the elder spirit (*shaykh al-rūḥ*) about the fruits of theophanies and revelations. [Lastly, there is] the *increase*[47] of the innermost soul in effacement from its human nature and subsistence in union in the Ineffable Ipseity of God (*Lāhūwiyyatihi*).[48]

The verse *Race one with another* …[to the end of this section] is encouragement to aspire towards God, to make haste in the path that leads to Him, and compete even as in the race. Thus, said the poet:

> The Race! the Race! In words and deeds!
> And beware of the lower self that can ruin the runner!

It is related that Abū Khālid al-Qayrawānī, who excelled in physical acts of devotion, once saw horses racing. Two of them pulled into the lead, then one of the two pulled ahead of the other, but the latter made such efforts that it regained its lead and won. At that, Abū Khālid burst through the spectators until he got to the winning horse and began kissing it, saying, "May God bless you! You endured and you won!" Whereupon he fell senseless to the ground. [About this verse], al-Wartajibī said:

> God is calling those who aspire to His forgiveness with haste and those who long for His beauty with longing. Both are included in this discourse, because both fell into the oceans of sin when they did not know God as He should be truly known. By His Mercy, He is calling them all to cleanse themselves of their illusions by coming to truly know Him.

That is, He is calling them to purify themselves by way of gnosis, but this is something that does not, in fact, happen.[49] And God Most High knows better.

22. *No affliction comes to pass in the earth or in yourselves but that it is in a Book before We bring it into being—that is surely easy for God—*
23. *That you do not grieve over what has escaped you, nor exult over what you have been given, and God does not love all prideful boasters,*
24. *Who hoard up wealth and who enjoin upon the people greed. And whosoever turns away, still God is the Wealthy, the Praiseworthy. ...*

Commentary

...No affliction comes to pass in the earth, such as drought, or the loss of crops and fruits, *or in yourselves*, such as a passing illness, a chronic malady, or the death of a child,[50] *but that it is* written *in a Book*, which is the Guarded Tablet, *before We bring it into being* by creating either the persons [afflicted] or the afflictions themselves. And to establish this in the Guarded Tablet *is surely* as *easy for God* in His Power as the blink of an eye. Just as afflictions are written, so too are the sources of joy and [Divine] gifts, to which His words *that you do not grieve* [*...or exalt*] refer. Thus, God Most High says, 'We tell you this that you may not be saddened to excess *over* something in the world that *has escaped you, nor exult* with the exultation of a *prideful boaster* over *what you have been given* of this world and its comforts, or of health and well-being.' Whoever truly knows that

everything is destined —that what has been destined to pass him by will pass him by without doubt and what has been destined to come to him will come without doubt—will not grieve or rejoice to excess about either of the two situations.

In addition to this, any affliction that someone undergoes raises him in spiritual degree and purifies him of some of his wrongs, even as a *ḥadīth* in the authentic collection of Muslim states, "The Messenger of God (may God bless him) said, 'There is no illness or fatigue, no sickness or sadness, and not even a worrisome care that afflicts a Muslim without its expiating some of the wrongs he has committed.'"[51] He also said (may God bless him) "How marvelous is the believer when confronted by God's decrees. If God decrees for him ease, he is content with it, and that is good for him, and if He decrees for him some hardship and he is content with it, that is good for him."[52] Also: "There is no Muslim who suffers so much as a thorn or anything greater except that a higher spiritual rank is written for him and one of his wrongs effaced."[53]

True, there is no one who does not rejoice if some bounty comes his way and no one who does not feel sadness if some hardship befalls him. This is a part of human nature. Thus, when 'Umar, may God be pleased with him, received the spoils of battle or some other wealth, he would say, "O God, we cannot help but rejoice in what You have given us."[54] But happiness should be expressed by gratitude, and sadness by patience. If sadness turns into grief so intense that it overwhelms patience, then it is a fault, and if happiness turns into exuberance so intense that one forgets to be grateful, then it too is a fault. This latter situation, in fact, may lead to pride: someone who is exuberant over his portion of the world and who places great value upon it is prone to boasting and pride, and *God does not love all prideful boasters.* [These words also imply] that excessive happiness is worse than excessive sorrow.

Those who hoard up wealth and who enjoin upon the people greed. And whosoever turns away, still God—He is the Wealthy, the Praiseworthy.

These words explain who the *prideful boasters* are.... They mean that *God does not love those who* rejoice excessively when given wealth or other worldly gain, for it then becomes so precious to them that they try to horde it and they encourage others to do the same, so that miserliness and hording increase. But even if there are those who *turn away* by refusing [to give charity] or by refusing to follow [God's] commandments, including this one which prohibits excessive happiness or sadness, *still God, He is the Wealthy* (*al-Ghanī*). It is not God who is in need of charity. [And He is] *the Praiseworthy* (*al-Ḥamīd*). Even if there are those who neither praise nor thank Him by giving in charity from the bounties they have received, this does not harm the Praiseworthiness of His Essence in the least.

This [verse thus] contains both an exhortation to give in charity and a declaration that to do so is for the good of the giver....

Spiritual Allusion

[The afflictions which] *come to pass in the earth* of the human nature are such things as being overcome by one's lower self or inclining towards its share of this world, and [those which come to pass] *within yourselves* are maladies of the heart such as conceit, ostentation, pride, envy, and other such vices, or maladies of the soul, such as self-satisfaction with having achieved such-and-such a spiritual rank, or with having been granted miracles or intuitions. [All these are] *in* the *Book* of God's Eternal Knowledge and Immutable Decree. Those for whom the winds of Destiny are favorable will be inspired towards the journey in spite of themselves, while those for whom they are contrary will be turned back or halted. But in either case, the return to God is an obligation of servanthood (*'ubudiyya*) and correct comportment. 'This We have done' so *you do not grieve over what has escaped you*—and surely anyone whose servanthood has been deepened and strengthened [by a loss] has really lost nothing at all—and also, that you *not exult over* something that is passing quickly away. Al-Qushayrī said of this:

> Such is the attribute of those who have been liberated from enslavement to their lower souls, for the true measure of spiritual travelers is in how they react to events. Those who are unchanged by what is disliked, abhorred, or loved are complete; those who are unchanged by what is hurtful—who neither rejoice over what is nor grieve over what is not—are mentors of their age. Such was the way of the Companions (may God be pleased with them) about whom Ka'b bin Zuhayr said:
>
> They rejoice not if their spears, in battle, find their marks
> Nor does grief overcome them if others' do the same

Al-Qushayrī then says, "If you wish to really know a man, seek him out at a time when he is undergoing some condition sent [from God]. [Great] shifts in mood are among the signs that the selfish nature is still present, regardless of the situation."

Al-Wartajibī relates that al-Wāsiṭī said: "The gnostics are effaced in the existence of the One Known. If they have reached [this] station, the goals of happiness or sadness no longer remain, even as God Most High says, *So that you do not grieve....*"

This is also what the *Ḥikam* refers to in the words, "The sadness that hearts experience is because of their lack of perception and vision of the Divine."[55] Or as Ibn al-Fāriḍ said in speaking of the Wine of gnosis:

> And if it but enter a man's mind,
> Gladness shall dwell with him and grief depart.

As God said through inspiration to [the Prophet] David (upon whom be peace), "Say to the saintly (*al-ṣiddiqīn*), 'Let your joy be in Me, and in My Remembrance seek My blessings.'"

Al-Ghazālī cites this verse as proof that material provision does not increase with supplication nor decrease if it is lacking. If such were the case [he reasons], then extreme sadness or happiness about material loss or gain would be justified, for [it would mean that] the loss had come about because someone had failed to supplicate God or was lax in doing so, or that the gain had come about because of someone's abundant supplication. [In addition, al-Ghazālī mentions what] the Prophet said to a beggar [who hesitated to accept a date]: "What ails you? If you do not take it, still it will come to you."[56] He then cites textual evidence that reward and punishment, although also predestined, may nonetheless be increased by supplication and decreased by its lack. He concludes that there is a distinction between what has been predestined in an absolute, immutable way, unconditionally and irrespective of human actions—this being material provision and lifespan—and what has been predestined to have a causal relation to human actions— this being reward and punishment in the Hereafter.

Concerning this distinction, there are various opinions, but in reality, it is a question of perspective. For the one who looks upon the world of Divine Wisdom (*al-Ḥikma*), which is the world governed by the Revealed Law, both [material provision and reward and punishment in the Hereafter] are connected to human actions.

If one turns towards the world of cause and effect and decreases in reverent fear (*al-taqwā*), then material provision comes by means of action.[57] If, on the other hand, one withdraws from the realm of cause and effect and attains the station of reverent fear, then material provision comes independent of action, for *whoever reveres God, God will make... a way out* [65:2]. That is, if someone reveres God and withdraws from the workaday world to worship [Him], God will take over his actions.

For the one who looks upon the World of the Divine Power (*al-qudra*), however—and this is the realm of the Supreme Truth—all actions are God's actions, without intermediary, and *He is not asked about what He does, but they are asked* [21:23].

This [perspective] also applies to spiritual provision, which is that God establishes you in devotion and grants you certitude, upon which reward and punishment are based. If you perceive the world of Divine Wisdom, you will see that spiritual sustenance arises from your practice and effort, the reason, in fact, that the Revealed Law was sent. But if you perceive the world of Divine Power, not only are practice and the effects of that practice effaced, but also the servant himself and his very existence. So mediate upon this.

About the verse, *God does not love all prideful boasters,* al-Qushayrī said, "Boasting arises from what remains of the lower self, while pride arises from the mind's illusion that there is something in which to take pride." *[They are the ones] who hoard* both the material and spiritual provision that has been given them, and if they are greedy for this provision, it signifies that because it pleases them, they is attached to them. Those, however, who attain a vision of the True Giver and the One from Whom all provision comes will not be greedy for anything. God makes them independent of all else. *And whosoever turns away* from this, *still God is the Wealthy,* and needs neither him or nor the entire creation, and He is *the Praiseworthy* before it ever existed. And God Most high knows better.

25. *We verily sent Our messengers with clear proofs, and revealed with them the Scripture and the Balance, in order that humanity may observe right measure; and We revealed iron. In it is mighty power and [many] uses for mankind, and that God may know the one who helps Him and His messengers, though unseen. Lo! God is Strong, Almighty.*

26. *And We verily sent Noah and Abraham And We placed prophethood and scripture among their progeny. And among them are those who are guided, but many of them are corrupt.*
27. *Then We caused Our messengers to follow in their footsteps; and We caused Jesus, son of Mary, to follow, and gave him the Gospel, and placed compassion and mercy in the hearts of those who followed him. But monasticism they invented—We did not ordain it for them—only to seek God's pleasure. And they did not observe it with right observance. So We give those of them who believe their reward, but many of them are corrupt.*

Commentary

We verily sent Our messengers with clear proofs, and revealed with them the Scripture and the Balance, in order that humanity may observe right measure; and We revealed iron. In it is mighty power and [many] uses for mankind, and that God may know the one who helps Him and His messengers, though unseen.

'*We sent Our* human messengers with miracles and proofs' or '*We sent* angels to the prophets and then the prophets to [their] peoples.' This latter reading is supported by the words which follow, *and We revealed with them the Scripture* which signifies all the scriptural revelations which are revealed by way of the angels…

And [We revealed] the Scale, which signifies the Religious Law (*al-sharī'a*). Here it is called *the Scale* inasmuch as it is the standard by which to weigh what is salutary and good against what is profligate and evil, [revealed] *in order that humanity may observe right measure*, which in the context means justice (*al-'adl*).[58] It has also been said, however, that by *Scale* is meant an actual physical scale, for it has been related that [the angel] Gabriel descended to [the Prophet] Noah (upon whom be peace) holding a scale and said to him, "Command your people to weigh with this."

And We revealed iron. In this verse, the verb, *anzalnā* may be taken in the literal sense of *We sent down* following the saying of Ibn 'Abbās, "Adam descended (*nazala*) from heaven with five tools of iron: the anvil, the tongs, the mallet, the hammer, and the needle." [It may also be understood in the sense that] God sends down the rain which tunnels through the veins of the earth creating the mines from which iron is brought forth, and thus did He both *send down* and *reveal* iron. It has also been said that by "iron" is meant "weapons."

As a whole, the verse means 'We have sent messengers with revealed scripture so that those who follow them willingly might find salvation, and have revealed iron by which those who oppose them might be battled and returned to justice.'

In it is mighty power by which enemies are kept at bay or battled *and [many] uses for mankind*, meaning the indispensible tools with which humans produce [what they need]. *And that God may know* outwardly *the one who helps Him and His messengers* with sword and spear and other such weapons striving against the foes of religion.

[This they do] *though [God is] unseen*, hidden from those who are of the station of belief in the unseen. *Lo! God is Strong,* and by His strength repels those who attack His community. And He is *Almighty*, and by His Might aids those who aid His religion and gives them fortitude in the throes of battle.

Concerning the relationship between the three things mentioned in this verse, al-Nasafī said:

> ...*The Scripture* contains the canon of revealed law and the constitution of religious rule enjoining *justice and excellence*, and forbidding tyranny and lewdness. *The Scale* signifies all the tools placed on earth with which human beings may achieve this in their dealings, and from *Iron*, which contains *mighty power*, is fashioned the sword for anyone who would revolt against what is just and withdraw his hand from the social pact.

And We verily sent Noah and Abraham and We placed prophethood and scripture among their progeny. And among them are those who are guided, but many of them are corrupt.

Only Noah and Abraham (may peace be upon them) are mentioned here since they are the fathers of all the prophets. *And We placed prophethood*, that is, revelation, *and scripture*, which signifies all the revealed books, or according to Ibn 'Abbās, all written language...*among their progeny. And among* that progeny or among those to whom the Scripture was sent *are those who are guided* to God, the Truth. *But many of them are corrupt*, having left the path of the righteous.

Then We caused Our messengers to follow in their footsteps; and We caused Jesus, son of Mary, to follow, and gave him the Gospel and placed compassion and mercy in the hearts of those who followed him.

Then We caused Our messengers to follow in the *footsteps* of Noah and Abraham and other prophets of the past or messengers of their day. *And We caused Jesus, son of Mary, to follow*, having sent messenger after messenger until the advent of Jesus,[59] *and gave him the Gospel...*[60] *And We placed in the hearts of those who followed him*, who are the Christians,[61] *compassion and mercy*, love, leniency, and kindness towards their brethren, qualities which are evident among the Christians, although not among the Jews. The first to follow Jesus were his disciples and one faction from among the Jews, while the remaining factions rejected him. Christians are thus the spiritual descendents of the disciples and the quality of mercy remains among them [to this day]....

But monasticism they invented—We did not ordain it for them—only to seek God's pleasure. And they did not observe it with right observance. So We give those of them who believe their reward, but many of them are corrupt.

...The word *rahbāniyya* (monasticism) signifies worship and withdrawal from people and is derived from the word *al-rahbān*, "one who fears"... It originated as a practice after the ascension of Jesus (upon whom be peace) when tyrannical kings rose up against the faithful and battled them three times, slaying a great number. The few that remained feared they would be compelled to leave their religion. So to save their faith and their lives they retreated to monasteries built on mountain peaks....

[But God] *did not ordain* monasticism as a religious obligation upon them. Rather, it was something they imposed upon themselves as a vow in order *to seek God's pleasure....But they did not observe* this vow the way it should have been observed, for their vow was a promise made to God, and a promise made to God should not be infringed upon in the least.

These words may also be understood to mean that they did not keep the vow as it should have been kept because when the Prophet appeared, they did not believe in him. This explanation is supported by the verse which follows: *Then We gave those* of the Christians *who believed* with sound belief—which includes belief in the Prophet Muḥammad (upon whom be peace)—*their* own special *reward. But many of them are corrupt*, having transgressed the limits that the followers [of Jesus] should observe, and having rejected God and His Messenger.

Spiritual Allusion

In every age, there are brought forth *messengers* calling to God. These are His gnostic saints who are the successors of the Prophets. They come *with proofs* of their sanctity which are *clear* to anyone whom Divine Providence has endowed with understanding. And *He revealed with them the Scripture*, an allusion to spiritual insights, *and the Balance,* which is the spiritual method appropriate to the time and by which an aspirant's progress is measured, so that to each might be given the appropriate litanies, practices, and states. [This is in order] *that people might maintain* in themselves *right measure* and neither go to extremes [in their practices] nor fall short.

We revealed iron, which alludes to the Divine Attraction (*al-jadhb*) present in the hearts of the gnostics. *In it there is power* so *mighty* that it may take away one's reason, and in it as well are *[many] uses for mankind*, for it is the light by which the saint walks among humans and by which the hearts of aspirants are drawn to God. In fact, anyone devoid of this attraction will remain outward and spiritual training will be to no avail.

God has chosen His friends to receive this light in order *that He may know the one who helps* His religion and the *sunna* of *His messengers, though* the Divine Will itself is *unseen*. And so even as they strive for the religion, they will always look towards what God is bringing to pass and what has already [been written] in the Divine Decree, for they are in the station of direct perception.

Lo! God is Strong, and gives strength to the hearts of those who seek Him. *And* He is *Mighty*, and honors those who strive to support the faith.

And We verily sent Noah and Abraham. These two messengers are singled out because Noah epitomizes strength and rigor, while Abraham epitomizes leniency and forbearance. And so it is with the saints of every age: there are those who tend towards rigor and those who tend towards gentleness. If God Most High wishes that a particular Path spread far and wide, He places therein both these opposites—saints who manifest rigor and saints who manifest gentleness—in order that there be equilibrium in creation. For if there is only the rigorous, creation is burnt up or drowned, as happened in the time of Noah, and if there is only the gentle, tepidity sets in, as happened in the time of Abraham, which is why his community was so small. When, however, both aspects were combined in the time of Moses (upon whom be peace)—for Moses himself epitomized rigor, while his brother, Aaron epitomized gentleness—the followers multiply.

As for the Muhammadan community, it has been made great by the fact that both these qualities have always been found in it. Thus, while the Prophet (upon whom be peace) was a person of gentleness and forbearance, there was 'Umar and his ministers who were rigorous and firm in God's religion. Then the Prophet was succeeded by Abū Bakr who was the opposite of 'Umar (may God be pleased with him) and when 'Umar came into power, there was 'Alī who was his opposite. In any group where both these opposites are present, the followers abound. So Glory be the One Who is the Best of Planners, the Infinitely Wise, and the Joiner of Opposites.

The words of God, *and We placed compassion and mercy in the hearts of those who followed him,* describe the aspirants and seekers of God, while the *monasticism* of this community is the mosques and *zāwiyas*, even as a *ḥadīth* states.[62] It is not for the gnostics [of this community] to live alone in the mountains or the wilderness. Rather, they should mix with people and guide them. Thus al-Wartajibī said concerning this verse:

> Here God Most High is describing the people of the *sunna* and the people of innovation (*bid'a*). The people of *sunna* are the people of mercy and clemency, while the people of innovation are those who follow monastic practices which they themselves have originated. God characterizes the hearts of those who hold fast to the way of His prophets as being full of love and compassion..., this love being from God's love itself, and this mercy being from God's mercy upon them when He chose them in eternity. They are the successors of the prophets and they are the mainstays of this religious community.
>
> Those, however, who in their zeal stop eating meat, who sit for "the Forty" in *zāwiyas* and so miss both the prayer in congregation and the Friday assembly expecting to win approval and praise from the generality are like those who

innovated monasticism for themselves. They are not upon the straight path but are following instead their own demons who have misled them in their religion and have made rooms and ornamentation fair-seeming to their hearts. *We did not ordain it for them—only to seek God's pleasure*, and God's pleasure is in following the religious law and the path of the Messenger (upon whom be peace and blessings).

His mention [above] of "the Forty" refers to the practice of those devotees who vow to make a spiritual retreat of forty days and nights and who, during that time, attend neither the prayers in the mosque nor the Friday prayer in assembly. [Concerning his judgement of some of them, however], as another has said, if someone is affirmed to be just and good, then it is better to remain silent about him and his practice.[63]

28. *O you who believe! Be mindful of your duty to God and believe in His Messenger. He will give you twofold of His mercy and will make for you a light wherein you shall walk, and will forgive you. And God is Forgiving, Merciful.*
29. *That the People of the Scripture may know that they do not control any of God's Grace and that Grace is in God's hand to give to whomsoever He will. And God is Possessor of Infinite Grace.*

Commentary

O you who believe! Be mindful of your duty to God and believe in His Messenger. He will give you twofold of His mercy and will make for you a light wherein you shall walk, and will forgive you. And God is Forgiving, Merciful.

O you who believe in the messengers who went before, *Be mindful of your duty to God* and fear Him *and believe in His Messenger,* Muḥammad (may God bless him and grant him peace) who is mentioned in your Scripture.[64] [*God*] *will give you twofold... of His mercy* for your having believed in [this] Messenger and in the messengers that went before him. This does not mean, however, that the earlier revealed laws remain valid following the advent of the Prophet. Their Laws were valid [for their times], but were then abrogated. It means, rather, that [a Christian or Jew] who comes to believe in our Prophet will be given a two-fold reward...as recompense for the difficulty of leaving behind what is familiar and customary. *And [God] will make for you a light wherein you shall walk* on the Day of Reckoning, *and their light will hasten before them...,*[65] *and He will forgive you* for your [past] disbelief and sins. *And God is Forgiving, Merciful.*

That these verses are addressing the People of the Book is supported by a *ḥadīth* in which the Messenger of God said [that among those given a two-fold reward] "is a man from the People of the Book who believed in his prophet and believed in me...."[66]

It has also been said, however, that these verses are addressed to the believers [of Islam] themselves and mean *O you who believe! Be mindful of your duty to God* concerning what He has prohibited for you, and keep to your faith, and *He will give you twofold of His mercy....*This explanation is supported by a *ḥadīth* in the two authentic collections:

> The parable [of you and] the people of the Book before you is that of a man who employed some laborers to work until the night for one *qirāṭ* each.[67] The Jews worked until midday and grew weary. Then the Christians worked till the *'aṣr* prayer and grew weary. Then you worked until nightfall and got the wages of the other two. And when it is asked, "How is it that they worked less but got the greater wage?" God says, "Have I dealt with you unjustly?" To which they answer, "No." Then God says, "Such is My Grace which I bestow upon whomever I wish."[68]

It has also been said that when the verse [concerning the People of the Book] *twice shall they be given their reward, for that they have persevered* [28:52-54] was revealed, the People of the Book who had come to believe [in Islam] grew boastful towards the Companions of the Prophet. Then, when this verse *O you who believe...*was revealed containing this promise to the faithful, the Jews became envious. Then the verse, *That the People of the Scripture may know that they do not control any of God's Grace...* was revealed, meaning that God has given this two-fold reward to the Muslims in order that the People of the Book might know that they do not own God's Grace, nor is it something which is under their control, nor can they choose whom they wish to receive it. *And* also, in order that they might know that *Grace is in God's hand.* It belongs to Him and is under His control *to give to whomsoever He will* from among His devotees. *And God is Possessor of Tremendous Grace*, grace which is limitless and infinite....

Spiritual Allusion

These [last] verses allude to a person who is descended from a pious and righteous family, honored for its religious learning or some other high rank, to whom genuine spiritual instruction appears from a source other than his own lineage. If he bows his head in acceptance and affirms these special qualities in other than his own lineage, then twice over will he be given recompense, and great will be his rank in the station of sanctity. For the locus of sainthood moves [from one folk to another] *in order that the people* who had previously been granted this special grace *may know* it *is in God's hand to give to whomsoever He will. And God is Possessor of Infinite Grace.*

He is the One by Whose Accord all things are accomplished, and there is no strength nor power but through God, the Sublime and All-Mighty.

May God bless our beloved master Muḥammad,
and his family and companions
and grant them peace.

Notes on the Chapter of Iron

1. The Supreme or Greatest Name of God is referred to in numerous *ḥadīth* which identify it with several different Divine Names or devotional formulae. According to Shawkānī, the 13th/19th century author of *Tuḥfatu al-Dhākirīn*, there are nearly forty different views among the scholars as to what exactly the Supreme Name of God is. (Shawkānī, p. 52).

2. In the present verse, the verb *sabbaḥa* is actually in the past although it carries the sense of an on-going action. The other examples are *yusabbiḥu* [62:1], *sabbiḥ* [87:1], and *subḥāna* [17:1].

3. A *ḥadīth* states, "Slowness (*al-ta'annī*) is from God and haste (*al-'ajala*) from the devil." Bayhaqī, *Shu'ab al-īmān*, 4197.

4. This is the third principal meaning of the root SBḤ.

5. We have used the word "sphere" to translate *falak* which literally means "orbit." The cosmological model al-Qushayrī describes is a series of spheres, one contained within the other, with the Essence being the "outermost" and the physical universe the "innermost."

6. *Al-āthār*, literally, "the traces" or "imprints," that is, manifestations of God's Names and Attributes in the physical world.

7. *K. al-Ḥikam*, 249, which continues: "He reveals the perfection of His Essence to those who have attraction; then He turns them back to the contemplation of His Qualities; then He turns them back to dependence on His Names; and then He turns them back to the contemplation of His created things."

8. See note 90.

9. A reference to the *ḥadīth qudsī*, "Majesty is My cloak, Glory, My loincloth. One who would try to take either of them from Me, him I shall cast into Hell." Abū Dāwud, *Libās*, 3567; Ibn Mājah, *Zuhd*; 4164; Aḥmad, *Musnad*, 7078, 8539, 8991.

10. *K. al-Ḥikam*, 139.

11. See p. 39 n. 18.

12. That is, the manner in which God is *with* (*ma'a*) you, or, according to a number of other Quranic verses, *with* those who are patient, those who are pious, and those who have faith.

13. He is paraphrasing *K. al-Ḥikam*, 34.

14. This paraphrases [3:7].

15. Ibn 'Ajība notes that the subject of the clause "that he may bring you forth" may be understood as referring either to God or to His Messenger.

16. Muslim, *Faḍā'il al-Ṣaḥābah*, 4611; Abū Dāwūd, *Sunna*, 4039; Aḥmad, *Musnad*, 10657.

17. Bukhārī, *Zakāt*, 1337; Muslim, *Zakāt*, 1716.

18. "[It is] a bridge stretched over the gulf of Hell, sharper than a sword and thinner than a hair. Whosoever has in the world kept upright

upon the Straight Path (*al-ṣirāṭ al-mustaqīm*) shall bear lightly upon the Traverse (*ṣirāṭ*) of the Afterlife, and will be saved. But whosoever deviates from uprightness in this world, and weighs down upon his back with burdens, and disobeys his Lord, shall slip upon taking his first step on the Traverse, and shall go to perdition." Al-Ghazālī, *The Remembrance of Death and the Afterlife*, p. 206.

19. "The substitutes (*al-budalā'*) are thirty men whose hearts are like the heart of [the Prophet] Abraham, upon whom be peace. Each time one of them dies, God substitutes another in his place." In another version, "The substitutes are forty men. Twenty-two of them in Shām (Syria) and eighteen in 'Irāq. Whenever one of them dies, God substitutes another in his place. And when the Judgment Day is to come, all of them will die." Al-Ḥakīm al-Tirmidhī, *Nawādir al-uṣūl,* 1:261. Other narrations mention other numbers.

20. *But those who keep their duty to their Lord, for them are made chambers above which are chambers, beneath which rivers flow. [It is] God's promise, and God never breaks His promise.* [39:20]

21. Being given the record of deeds in the right hand and behind the back is mentioned in the Qur'ān in [84:7-12] and in the left hand in [69:19-25].

22. Both are derived from the same root, NẒR.

23. As opposed to the hypocrites, whose disbelief is hidden.

24. Tirmidhī, *Tafsīr*, 3052; Ṭabarānī, *al-Kabīr*, 7369; *al-Awsaṭ*, 3382, 8067; Bayhaqī, *Shu'ab al-īmān*, 7369. Its complete wording is, "Beware of the believer's insight (*firāsah*), for verily he sees by the Light of God."

25. For examples of Ibn 'Ajība's own "break with the customary," see the Introduction. "Neglect of the outward," in this context means no longer being concerned with how one appears to people, this being the result of this break.

26. Muslim, *Tafsīr*, 5352.

27. Ḥākim, *Tafsīr*, 3746. By "thirteenth year" he means thirteen years after the revelation of the Qur'ān began.

28. By "inspirations" in this context is meant insights and interior states, both joyful and sad, that are sent by God.

29. He is quoting [2:101].

30. This vignette is cited in numerous commentaries including Ṭabarī, ibn Kathīr, and Suyūṭī and the words in parentheses are added from these narrations for the sake of comprehension. The most complete versions begin as quoted above, then continue, "When they presented him with the book [they had written] and asked, 'Do you believe in this?' he patted his chest and said, 'I believe in this! Why would I not believe in this!' meaning the [book of God] in the horn hanging from his neck. So they left him alone....But when he died, they found the horn still hanging around his

neck and said, 'Do you not see that when he said, "I believe in this!" he meant this book?' Then the Children of Israel split into around seventy factions, and the best of them all were the people of the Horn."

31. In the first there is a doubling of the consonant *ṣād*. Both words are derived from the same root, ṢDQ.

32. He is referring to a *ḥadīth* found in Bayhaqī, *Shu'ab al-īmān*, 2663.

33. Here Ibn 'Ajība refers the reader to his commentary on [13:39]. The complete verse is *God effaces what He wills and maintains what He wills and with Him is the Mother of the Book.* Commenting on this, Ibn 'Ajība quotes the words of a supplication that Ibn Mas'ūd and 'Umar used to make: "O God! If You have written us in the list of the wretched [in Hell], erase us therefrom and write us in the list of the blessed [in Heaven], for verily You efface what You will and You maintain what You will." The meaning of their supplication, Ibn 'Ajība explains, is "If You have manifested our damnation, erase it and manifest our salvation…" He then cites Ibn 'Atiyya's explanation that *the Mother of the Book* is what contains God's irreversible decrees and these include that there be matters which may be changed, effaced, or maintained.

34. The word *ṣiddīq* is close in meaning to the Hebrew term *tzaddik.* Both carry the sense of someone who has attained sanctity by way of righteousness, whose being is permeated by sincerity, and whose outward actions perfectly reflect his or her inward state. In the context of the commentary, the *ṣiddīq* has "acquired sanctity." The feminine form, *ṣiddīqa*, is used to describe Mary, the mother of Jesus, in [5:75].

35. Ibn 'Ajība speaks more about the meaning of *ṣiddīq* in the Spiritual Allusion to follow.

36. Ḥātim Ṭayy is a legendary figure known by the pre-Islamic Arabs as the paragon of generosity.

37. Cited by Ṭabarī in his *tafsīr* on this verse. The commentaries of Ibn Kathīr, Ibn 'Aṭiyya, and Tha'labī also mention this *ḥadīth*.

38. A saying quoted in *Tafsīr Baghwī.*

39. He is referring to a well-known *ḥadīth* in the *Muwaṭṭa'* of Imām Mālik, *Janā'iz*, 493.

40. This is a saying of the Sufis and appears in various forms as early as al-Qushayrī, always in the sense that whatever is given up or lost for the sake of God will be restored in an even greater and more blessed form.

41. Literally, "the *koḥl* with which God has painted their vision taken from the Lights of Oneness."

42. Ibn 'Ajība points out that the word used, *kuffār*, defined as "farmer," comes from the verb *kafara*, which means "to cover something up," just as a farmer covers up seeds with soil. This is the same word used to

denote one who disbelieves (*kāfir*), literally, "one who covers himself up (from God's grace)." The root KFR also yields the verb "to expiate a sin."

43. He is referring to a *ḥadīth* found in the Bukhārī, *Tawḥīd*, 6957, Muslim, *Īmān*, 272, and elsewhere. The version in Muslim states: "The Messenger of God said, 'I know the last of the people of the Fire to leave it and the last of the people of Heaven to enter it will be a man who leaves the Fire crawling. Then God, be He blessed and exalted, will say to him, "Go and enter Heaven." He will go to it but it will appear to him as if it were full. So he will return to his Lord and say, "O Lord, I found it full." Then God [will repeat what He said before and the man will again find it as if it were full]. Then God will say to him, "Go and enter Heaven and therein you shall have like unto the world ten times."...And the man will say, "Are You mocking me or laughing at me, and You are the Sovereign?" And at this we saw the Messenger of God laugh until his molars showed and say, "And he will be the lowest in rank of the people of Heaven!"'"

44. By which he means the *ḥadīth*, "Not one of you shall enter Heaven by his deeds." And they asked, "Not even you, O Messenger of God?" He answered, "Not even me unless my Lord enfolds me in His Mercy and Forgiveness." Bukhārī, *Riqāq*, 5986; Aḥmad, *Musnad*, 7176, 10205, 14700. Ibn 'Ajība's reference to textual proofs here concerns more specifically responses to the Mu'tazilī beliefs that neither Heaven nor Hell have yet been created and that people will enter Heaven solely because of their faith and good deeds.

45. A particular female jinn.

46. *Al-tawakkul*, literally, "trust and depence upon God." In the context, however, it means surviving without working of a living.

47. The term *takāthiru* as it appears in this verse is usually translated "rivalry;" Al-Qushayrī, however, is using it in a more literal sense of "increase" in this allusion.

48. Ibn 'Ajība adds here, "[Al-Qushayrī's allusion is correct] except that he has put mention of the soul (*al-sirr*) before mention of the spirit (*al-rūḥ*) and the opposite order is what is generally acknowledged...."

49. In the *Ṭarīqa Shādhiliyya* of Ibn 'Ajība's time, a rigorous process of purification and "slaying of the lower self" (*al-mujāhada*) came first, then the stage of contemplation and meditation (*al-mushāhada*). See Introduction, p. xiii.

50. Ibn 'Ajība was writing this commentary close to the time several of his children succumbed to the plague. See Introduction, page xv.

51. Muslim, *Birr*, 4670, which reads "believer" (*al-mu'min*) rather than "Muslim."

52. The better-known version of this *ḥadīth*, "The situation of the believer is truly amazing: everything is good for him, and this cannot be said

except of the believer. If comfort and ease come to him, he is grateful, and that is good for him; and if hardship befalls him, he is patient, and that is good for him." Muslim, *Zuhd*, 5318; Aḥmad, *Musnad*, 18171, 18175, 22798.

53. Aḥmad, *Musnad*, 23028.

54. Bukhārī, *Riqāq*, 5960. The complete quotation attributed to 'Umar ibn al-Khaṭṭāb, is "O God, we cannot help but be happy with what You have made beautiful for us. O God, I ask You that I might spend it rightly."

55. *K. al-Ḥikam*, 224.

56. Bayhaqī, *Shu'ab al-īmān*, 1194; Ibn Ḥibbān, *Zakat*, 3309.

57. That is, the work by which one earns a living.

58. See the commentary on *Sūrat al-Raḥmān*, p. 9.

59. Ibn 'Ajība notes that the verb *qafayna*, here translated as *We caused to follow up*, comes from *al-qafā'*, literally, the nape of the neck or the back of the head. It thus expresses the idea of someone coming right behind someone else.

60. Ibn 'Ajība notes that *al-injīl*, the word by which the Qur'ān refers to the revelation sent to Jesus (upon whom be peace) is not Arabic and may also be pronounced *al-anjīl*. It is closely related to the Greek and Latin term *evangel*.

61. The word used in Arabic, *al-Naṣāra*, means literally "the Nazarenes."

62. There are a number of *ḥadīth* which prohibit monasticism in Islam, the most common of which is "The monasticism of my community is striving in the way of God (*jihād fī sabīli Llāh*)." In the reference above, Ibn 'Ajība probably means a *ḥadīth* which appears in Abū Nu'aym, *Ma'rifat al-Ṣaḥāba*, 4391, which reads, "The monasticism of my community is sitting in mosques awaiting the prayer, and making the greater and lesser pilgrimages."

63. Ibn 'Ajība is taking exception here to al-Wartajibī's criticism.

64. This is according to [61:6]. *And when Jesus son of Mary said: O Children of Israel! Lo! I am the messenger of God unto you, confirming that which was [revealed] before me in the Torah, and bringing good tidings of a messenger who comes after me, whose name is the Praised One.* In Arabic the Praised One, Aḥmad, is a variation of the name Muḥammad. As early as *Tafsīr al-Rāzī* (see Introduction), there have been Muslim commentators who have cited the words of Jesus reported in the Gospel of John concerning "the Comforter or Consoler" (Greek: *Parakletos*) such as "Nevertheless, I tell you the truth; it is expedient for you that I go away: for if I go not away, the Comforter will not come unto you; but if I depart, I will send him unto you," [John 16:7–8] as proof that even in the scripture of the Christians as it now exists, Jesus speaks of the advent of the Prophet Muḥammad.

65. He is quoting verse 12 of this *sūra*.

66. Bukhārī, *Nikaḥ*, 4693.

67. A *qirāṭ* is defined as one sixteenth of a dirham.

68. Bukhārī, *Ijāra*, 2107; *al-Anbiyā'*, 3200; *Faḍl al-Qur'ān*, 4633; Muslim, *al-Amthāl*, 2797.

Biographical Index

Persons Cited in the Body of the Commentary Excluding Prophets

Terms used in these entries: *Ṣaḥābī* (pl. *Ṣaḥāba*) = a Companion of the Prophet; *Tābi'ī* (pl. *Tābi'īn*) = "A follower" = someone belonging to the generation following the *Ṣaḥābah* who had met one of them; *mufassir* = exegete of the Qur'ān; *muḥaddith* = collector or narrator of *ḥadīth; qāḍī* = judge.

ABŪ AL-'ĀLIYYA, Rufay'u Mihrān al-Riyāḥī al-Baṣrī (d. 90/708) p. 75. *Tābi'ī*, described as imām, reciter and preserver (*ḥāfiẓ*) of the Qur'ān. He grew up as an adopted child, was still a youth during the final years of the Prophet's life, and entered Islam during the Caliphate of Abū Bakr, whom he met. He is reported to have said, "Learn the Qur'ān five verses at a time and it will stay with you, for thus did Gabriel deliver it."

ABŪ BAKR AL-ṢIDDĪQ ibn Abī Quhāfa al-Taymī (d. 13/634) pp. 103, 123. Among the greatest of the *Ṣaḥāba* and the first of the Rightly Guided Caliphs. He was a successful cloth merchant in Mecca. When he heard during one of his journeys that Muḥammad had proclaimed his prophecy, Abū Bakr became the fourth person to enter Islam and the first not of the Prophet's family. In the years that followed, he used his wealth for the manumission of slaves. He was also the only person to accompany the Prophet on his Emigration to Medina and is referred to in 9:40, ...*When they two were in the cave, when he [the Prophet] said to his companion [Abū Bakr]: Grieve not. God is surely with us. Then God caused His peace to descend upon him and supported him with hosts you cannot see.*

Abu Bakr became the Prophet's closest advisor, and after his death became the first caliph. Upon assuming this role, he is reported to have said to the people, "I have been made your leader, though I am not the best of you. If I do what is right, help me. If I err, set me straight (*in aḥsantu, fa'īnūnī, wa in asa'tu, fa qawwamūnī*)." His reign lasted just over two years before he succumbed to an illness. His tomb is next to that of the Prophet and 'Umar ibn al-Khaṭṭab in Medina.

ABŪ ḤANĪFA al-Nu'mān ibn al-Thābit al-Taymī (80-150/699-767) pp. 33, 70. *Tābi'ī* and founder of the *Ḥanafī* school (*madhhab*) of jurisprudence, one of the four main schools (along with *Malikī*, *Ḥanbalī*, and *Shafi'ī*) in Sunni Islam. He was born and raised in Kūfā. In his youth, he worked as a silk merchant while pursuing religious studies. Imām Mālik said of him, "He was generous of nature, beautiful in both speech and appearance, strong of voice. When he spoke [of religious matters], he did so with complete fluency and his words were a medicine." He is also recognized as the first scholar to systematize *fiqh*.

ABŪ AL-ḤASAN AL-MANṢŪR p. 67. An unidentified Sufi.

ABŪ ḤAYYĀN, Muḥammad ibn Yūsuf ibn 'Alī ibn Ḥayyān al-Gharnāṭī (654-745/1256-1344) p. 108. *Mufassir* and among greatest authorities on the Arabic language of his day. He was born near Granada, moved to Malaga, and continued his travels until reaching Cairo where he stayed, eventually losing his sight, until his death. He is best-known for his eight volume Quranic commentary *al-Baḥr al-muḥīṭ*. (He is other than Abū al-Ḥayyān al-Tawḥīdī, the Mu'tazilite philosopher).

ABŪ KHĀLID al-Qayrawānī (*See* AL-QAYRAWĀNĪ)

ABŪ MŪSĀ AL-ASH'ARĪ (d. 42/662) p. 33. *Ṣaḥābī*. During the life of the Prophet, he was appointed to govern parts of Yemen. During the caliphate of 'Umar, he was made governor of Baṣra, and during that of 'Uthmān, he governed Kūfā. He fought in the battle of Ṣiffīn on the side of 'Alī and was asked to negotiate peace. After this, however, he distanced himself from both factions.

Abū Mūsā was known for the beauty of his voice in recitation of the Qur'ān, and in a *ḥadīth* which appears in the *Musnad* of Imām Aḥmad and elsewhere, the Prophet is reported to have said, "Abū Mūsā has been given the chanting voice of the family of Dāwūd (David)."

ABŪ NAṢR AL-ḤAMDĀNĪ, Abū 'Abd al-Raḥmān (d. 464/1072) p. 98. Known as Ibn Sāwī. He was a Sufi Shaykh who followed the path of the *malāmatiyya*.

ABŪ SA'ĪD AL-KHARRĀZ, Aḥmad ibn 'Īsā. (d. 277/890) p. 91. Among the Baghdad Sufis. He was a companion of Dhu'l-Nūn al-Miṣrī and others. Among his sayings, "Anything esoteric which is in contradiction to the exoteric is false," and "The saying 'No!' is not in the nature of a believer, for when he regards the aspects of generosity that exist between him and his Lord, he is embarrassed to say 'No' to anyone."

ABŪ AL-SA'ŪD al-'Umādī, Muḥammad ibn Muḥammad al-Muṣṭafā (898-982/1493-1574) p. 19. *Mufassir*, poet, and Ḥanafī scholar. He was born in Istanbul, in Turkey and became a leading scholar in Arabic, Persian and Turkish. His Quranic commentary, *Irshād al-'aqli al-salīm ilā mazāyā al-Kitāb al-Karīm*, is still studied. He is buried near the resting place of Abū Ayyūb al-Anṣāri in Istanbul.

ABŪ 'UBAYD, al-Qāsim ibn Sallām al-Harawī al-Azdī al-Khazā'ī (157-224/774-838) p. 34. Scholar and *muḥaddith* from the generation following the *Tābi'īn*. He was born and studied in Herāt then journeyed to Baghdād where he served as Qāḍī for eighteen years. He then moved to Egypt where he taught his books, including works on *ḥadīth*, Quranic commentary, and language, after which he made the Pilgrimage. He died and is buried in Mecca.

AḤMAD IBN ḤANBAL (164-241/780-855) p. 70. A great *muḥaddith* and founder of the Ḥanbalī school, one of the four main schools (*madhāhib*) of Sunni jurisprudence and the one followed today in the Arabian peninsula and Gulf countries. He traveled extensively in search of *ḥadīth*, of which he is said to have committed over three hundred thousand to memory, these being the ones recorded in his monumental collection, *al-Musnad*. His tomb is in the city of his birth, Baghdād.

AḤMAD IBN MUBĀRAK, al-Lamṭī al-Sijilmāsī (d. 1090-1156/1679-1743) p. 92. Mālikī scholar and Sufi. He was born in Sijilmasa but went to Fes as a boy to study and stayed there until his death. He is best-known as the author of *al-Ibrīz fī kalām Sīdī 'Abd al-'Azīz al-Debbāgh* but also wrote a treatise on the Quranic verse *And He is with you wheresoever you are* [57:4] to which Ibn 'Ajība refers.

'Ā'ISHA bint Abī Bakr (d. 58/678) p. 34. She was the third and most beloved wife of the Prophet and it is in the place that was once her room that he was buried. At one point during her life as wife of the Prophet, Ā'isha was suspected of marital infidelity by certain of the people and verses 11-16 of *Sūrat al-Nūr* (24) are believed to have been revealed to reprove such suspicion. In 656, after the death of 'Uthmān, she became involved in the revolt of Ṭalḥa and al-Zubayr against the supporters of 'Alī and the army which fought for her was defeated in a battle near Baṣra. This event became known as the Battle of the Camel, referring to the camel on which she herself was carried. Following this, she retired to Medina where she spent the remaining twenty-two years of her life. Besides her status as the Prophet's beloved wife, she is recognized as one of the greatest authorities in Islam and the primary narrator of scores of *ḥadīth*.

AL-AKHFASH, Sa'īd ibn Mas'ada, Abū al-Ḥasan (d. ca 225/839) p. 15. He was one of three Islamic scholars referred to by this nickname (which means "the weak-sighted one") and distinguished from the other two by the addition of "the middle one" (*al-awsaṭ*). Originally from Balkh, he was a student of Sibawayh, one of the first to systematize Arabic grammar, although older than his teacher. Among his authored works is a commentary on the Qur'ān, and a major work on grammar, *al-Awsaṭ fī al-naḥu* .

'AMR IBN ḤAZM ibn Zayd ibn Lawdhān al-Anṣārī (d. 53/673) p. 70. *Ṣaḥābī* whom the Prophet made governor of Yemen. During this period, the Prophet sent 'Amr a long letter, later included in the *ḥadīth* collections of Nasā'ī and Abū Dāwūd, in which he spoke of rules relating to devotional practices as well as other subjects.

AL-'AMRĀNĪ, 'Alī ibn 'Abd al-Raḥmān ibn Muḥammad (d. 1193/1779) p. 36. Sufi shaykh. He became known in Morocco as Sidi 'Alī al-Jamal ("The Camel") because of an incident that happened in his youth when he lifted a young camel out of a public road in Fes. He was the spiritual master of Mulay al-'Arabī al-Darqāwī, who was in turn the master of Ibn 'Ajība's shaykh, Muḥammad al-Buzīdī. Sidi 'Alī authored one work, a collection of insights on the Way called *Naṣīḥa al-Murīd fī ṭarīq ahli al-sulūk wa al-tajrīd* (*see* bibliography). Another Moroccan Sufi master, Sidī 'Abd al-Wāḥid al-Debbāgh, said concerning him, "No one really knows Sidī 'Alī al-Jamal except Sidī 'Alī al-Jamal!"

ANAS IBN MĀLIK ibn al-Naḍr (d. ca. 91/709) p. 29. One of the most famous of the *Ṣaḥābah*. Presented to the Prophet by his mother at the age of ten as a servant, Anas would become one of the foremost narrators of *ḥadīth*. He once told Thābit al-Banānī, "This is a hair from the head of the Prophet. He told me to place it under my tongue," and then did so. (Years later, upon his death) when he was being prepared for burial, it was still under his tongue.

'AQĪL al-Maghribī p. 68. An unidentified Sufi.

AL-BAJĀ'Ī, 'Abd al-Raḥmān ibn Yūsuf ibn 'Abd al-Raḥmān Abū al-Qāsim (d. ca. 599/1202) p. 113. Sufi from among the scholars of Bejaya (in present-day Algeria). He authored several works among which is *Quṭb al-'ārifīn wa maqāmāt al-abrār wa al-aṣfiyā wa al-ṣiddīqīn* which is cited by Ibn 'Ajība several times in his commentary (who refers to him as al-Lajā'ī).

AL-BAQLĪ, Ruzbihān ibn Abī al-Naṣr al-Faswī al-Shīrāzī al-Gāzrūnī (d. 606/1209) pp. 30, 68, 87, 92, 101, 109, 117, 123. Sufi, scholar in *ḥadīth* and *fiqh*, and author of an esoteric commentary on the Qur'ān, *'Arā'is al-bayān fī ḥaqā'iq al-Qur'ān* from which Ibn 'Ajība quotes extensively throughout *al-Baḥr al-Madīd*, mistakenly referring to its author as "al-Wartajibī," possibly the name of a scribe who copied the manuscripts of this *tafsīr* that were available in Morocco in Ibn 'Ajība's time. Only parts of this *tafsīr* still exist.

AL-BARĀ' IBN 'ĀZIB ibn al-Ḥarith al-Khazrajī (d. 17/690) p. 108. *Ṣaḥābī*. He entered Islam at a young age and fought beside the Prophet in fifteen battles. In the year 24/645, during the caliphate of 'Uthmān, he was made governor of Rayy (in Persia). He eventually retired to Kūfā and there he died. He figures in the narrative chain of numerous *ḥadīth* in the collections of Muslim and Bukhārī.

AL-BŪZĪDĪ, Muḥammad ibn Aḥmad al-Slimānī al-Ghomāri (d. 1229/1813) p. 4. Sufi shaykh. He was born and raised in the village of Benslimān, in the Ghomāra region of Morocco near Tetouan. After some years of spiritual journeying around Morocco, he met and became of the disciple of Mulay al-'Arabī al-Darqāwī (see below) and was eventually put in direct charge of Ibn 'Ajība's training in the path. During his life, Mulay al-'Arabī designated al-Būzīdī as his successor, but the latter's death pre-dated his shaykh's by ten years. His tomb is in Tijīsas, Ghomara, not far from Tetouan.

AL-ḌAḤḤAK, ibn Mazāḥim al-Balkhī al-Khorasāni (d. 212/827) p. 108. Considered a *Tābi'ī*. He was born and died in Khorasān and is known as a *muḥaddith,* particularly in Quranic exegesis. It is also said that he lived in both Balkh and Samarqand and at times taught as many as three thousand children whom he would pass among on a donkey.

AL-DARQĀWĪ, Abū 'Abd Allāh Muḥammmad al-'Arabi (1173-1238/1760-1823) pp. 4, 67. Sufi shaykh. Founder of the *Ṭarīqah al-Shādhiliyya al-Darqāwiyya* which is still widely followed in Morocco. He is also the author of a collection of letters pertaining to the spiritual path which have been translated partially into English and in their entirety into French (see bibliography). His tomb and original *zāwiya* are in the Bani Zarwal region of the Rif Mountains in northern Morocco.

DHU'L-NŪN al-Miṣrī, Thawbān (d. 245/860) p. 111. Born in Upper Egypt, he is one of the most renowned of the early Sufis and reputedly the first to systematize the *maqāmāt*, the stations of the spiritual journey. His tomb is in Cairo.

AL-FĀSĪ, 'Abd al-Raḥmān Abū Zayd (972-1036/1564-1626) pp. 72, 79. Scholar and Sufi. He was born in Qaṣr al-Kabīr in northern Morocco and studied in Fes with some of the greatest scholars of his day including Yaḥya Sirāj and Abū al-'Abbās al-Mansūr. He authored several useful works, among them marginal annotations (*ḥāshiyyāt*) to the *ḥadīth* collection of al-Bukhārī, the Quranic commentary of Jalāllayn, *Dalā'il al-Khayrāt*, and *al-Ḥizb al-Kabīr* of Imām al-Shādhilī. He is included in the chains of transmission (*silsilāt*) of the *Ṭarīqat al-Shādhiliyya* from the sixteenth century on.

AL-FUḌAYL IBN 'IYĀD (d. 187/803) p. 103. One of the early Sufis. As a youth he had been a thief and is said to have repented while he was climbing a wall in order to rob a house and heard someone reciting the verse *Is it not time for the hearts of the faithful to grow humble at the Remembrance of God...?* He became, thereafter, one of the greatest of the early Sufis, studying *ḥadīth* with Abū Ḥanīfa.

AL-GHAZĀLI, Abū Ḥāmīd Muḥammad ibn Muḥammad (449-504/1058-1111) pp. 72, 117. Sufi, scholar, prolific author, known as *Ḥujjat al-islām* ("The proof of Islam"). He was born and died in Ṭūs, in Khorasān. After an illustrious career as teacher and lecturer, he renounced his position at the age of around forty and took up the life of a wandering dervish. The fruits of both his scholarship and efforts in the spiritual path form the basis of his most famous work, *Iḥyā 'ulūm al-dīn*, "The Revival of the Religious Sciences." His works are said to have influenced St. Thomas Aquinas and numerous other western philosophers.

AL-ḤASAN, al-Baṣrī (d. 110/728-9) pp. 10, 28, 30, 63, 98. *Tābi'ī* and also considered one of the earliest Sufis. He was born in Medina the son of a slave who had been freed by Zayd ibn Thābit, the scribe of the Prophet. After taking part in the conquest of eastern Iran, he moved to Baṣra, where he spent the remainder of his life teaching to great multitudes. His tomb is found in that city.

AL-ḤUSAYN ibn al-Faḍl (*see* IBN AL-FAḌL)

IBN 'ABBĀS, 'Abd Allāh (d. 68/687) pp. 28, 33, 64, 71, 86, 103, 108, 119, 120. One of the best-known of the *Ṣaḥābah*, Ibn 'Abbās was the son of the Prophet's paternal uncle but born just three years before the migration from Mecca to Medina. It is recounted in the main *hadīth* collections that the Prophet prayed that God would "give him understanding in religion and teach him the explanation of the Book," following which the boy became blessed with an amazing memory. After the death of the Prophet, he spent much of his life collecting *ḥadīth* and commentary on the Qur'ān. He fought alongside 'Alī at Ṣiffīn, and died at Ṭā'if.

IBN 'AṬĀ', Abū Muḥammad 'Abd al-Wahhāb al-Khaffāf (d. 204/819) p. 70. *Muḥaddith*, *mufassir*. He was one of the learned of Baṣra and figures in the transmission of numerous *ḥadīth* and is cited as a reference in nearly all the major Quranic commentaries. He is the author of a *ḥadīth* collection and *tafsir* no longer extant and *Kashf al-Ẓunūn* also attributes to him a treatise on fasting.

IBN 'AṬĀ' ALLĀH, Tāj al-Dīn Abū al-Faḍl al-Iskandarī (d. 708/1308) p. 2. Sufi and one of the greatest Mālikī scholars of his day in Egypt. He became the spiritual disciple of Abū al-'Abbās al-Mursī, the successor of Abū al-Ḥasan al-Shādhilī, and eventually Shaykh of the Ṭarīqa Shādhiliyya in Egypt. He is the author of *Kitāb al-Ḥikam*, The Book of Aphorisms, a compendium of Sufic wisdom which has been the object of numerous commentaries. Other of his main works include *Laṭā'if al-minan*, on the life of his shaykh, and *Tanwīr fī isqat al-tadbīr*, both of which have been published in English (*see* bibliography).

IBN 'AṬIYYA, 'Abd al-Ḥaqq ibn Ghālib al-Muhāribī (481-542/1088-1148) pp. 14, 33, 47, 89, 105. Scholar, *mufassir*, poet, and head of the religious judges (*al-quḍā'*) of Mariyya, Ibn 'Aṭiyya was born in or near Granada. He is best known for his Quranic commentary, *al-Muharrar al-wajīz fī tafsīr al-Kitāb al-'Azīz* (see bibliography) which is said to have been the favorite commentary of Shaykh Abū al-'Abbās al-Mursī.

IBN 'AYĪNA, Sufyān ibn Mīmūn ibn al-Hilālī al-Kūfī (107-198/725-814) p. 19. *Muḥaddith* of the Sacred Precinct of Mecca. He was born in Kūfā, lived most of his life in Mecca, and eventually returned to Kūfā where he died. He was a trusted preserver (of *ḥadīth*) and so vast in religious knowledge that Imām al-Shāfi'ī said, "Were it not for Mālik and Sufyān, the knowledge of the Hijāz would vanish." It is recorded that he made the pilgrimage seventy times. His main works are *al-Jāmi'* in *ḥadīth* and a no longer extant *tafsīr*.

IBN AL-FAḌL, al-Ḥusayn ibn 'Umayr al-Bajallī (178-282/794-895) p. 20. *Mufassir*. He was born in Kūfā and became proficient in Quranic exegesis. He then migrated to Nisapūr where he spent the remaining sixty-five years of his life teaching. He is reputed to have prayed six hundred raka'at during each day and night.

IBN AL-FĀRIḌ, 'Umar ibn 'Alī (576-632/1181-1235) pp. 55, 93, 117. The renown Egyptian Sufi poet known as *sulṭān al-'āshiqīn* "The sultan of the lovers" of God. His father gained the name *al-Fāriḍ* as a religious judge who specialized in rulings in inheritance cases (*al-furūḍ*). 'Umar grew up in Cairo and studied traditional knowledge, then turned towards the Sufi path. A visionary experience led him to Mecca where he spent a considerable length of time in a valley not far from the city where much of his poetry was written, it is said, in an ecstatic state. After 15 years in the Hijāz, he returned to Egypt where he gained considerable fame as well as numerous detractors.

IBN ḤAJAR, Abū al-Faḍl al-Asqalānī (773-852/1372-1449) p. 76. Scholar, historian and *muḥaddith*. Ibn Ḥajar was born in Cairo and there he did his early studies. It is said that he was already leading the *tarawīḥ* prayers in Ramaḍan at the age of 12. Still young, he was appointed to the position of *qāḍī* and authored more than fifty works. Of these, the best known are *Fatḥ al-Bāri,* his monumental commentary on *Ṣaḥīḥ al-Bukhārī,* and *al-Iṣābah fī tamyīz asmā'i al-ṣaḥāba*, a comprehensive biographical dictionary of the Companions. His tomb is in Cairo.

IBN AL-ḤASHĀ, Abū Ja'far Aḥmad ibn Muḥammad ibn al-Ḥashā (d. ?) p. 14. He was a 7th/13th century Moroccan scholar and physician known for a now-rare work, *Mufīd al-'ulūm wa mubīd al-humūm*, which is a lexicon of scientific terminology found in Razi's *Kitāb al-Ṭibb al-Manṣūri* (*The Book of Medicine*, dedicated to the Samanid prince Abu Ṣāliḥ al-Manṣur ibn Ishāq, governor of Rayy).

IBN 'IYĀD, al-Fuḍayl (see AL-FUḌAYL)

IBN JUZAYY, Abū 'Abdallāh Muḥammad ibn Muḥammad ibn Aḥmad Ibn Juzayy al-Kalbī (693-741/1294-140) pp. 32, 69. *Mufassir* and renowned Mālikī scholar of Granada. Among his best-known works is his Quranic commentary, *Tas'hīl fī 'ulūm al-tanzīl.*

IBN MAS'ŪD, 'Abd Allāh al-Hudhalī (d. 32/653) pp. 47, 79, 98, 103, 104. One of the greatest of the *Ṣaḥāba*, Ibn Mas'ūd is said to have been either the third or the sixth convert to Islam. He was particularly well-versed in the recitation and interpretation of the Qur'ān, an expert in matters of law, and the transmitter of scores of important *ḥadīth.*

IBN RUSHD, Muḥammad ibn Aḥmad Abū al-Walīd (450-520/1058-1126) p. 71. Principle *qāḍī* of Cordoba and among the greatest of its Malikī scholars of his day. He is the grandfather of the philosopher known by this same name (d. 595/1198). Among Abū al-Walīd's best known work is his *Muqaddimāt* in *shari'a* law. He was born and died in Cordoba.

IBN ṬĀHIR, 'Abd Allāh Abū al-'Abbās (182-230/798-844) p. 20. He was the ruler of Khorasān for the last twenty or so years of his life and became well-known for his generosity, nobility, and love of knowledge. He is buried in Nisapūr.

JA'FAR AL-ṢĀDIQ, ibn 'Alī ibn al-Ḥusayn al-Basṭ (80-148/699-65) p. 30. One of the most illustrious and learned of the *Tābi'īn*, he was born and died in Medina where he taught and transmitted *ḥadīth* to both Abū Ḥanīfa and Imām Mālik. He came to called *al-Ṣādiq*, the Honest One, for the fact that he was never known to have told a lie. He is considered by Shī'i Muslims as the sixth of the twelve Imāms.

JĀBIR ibn 'Abd Allāh al-Khazrajī al-Anṣārī (d. 68-78/687/8-697/8) p. 35. *Ṣaḥābī*, and notably one of the six of the Khazrajī clan who made the first pledge to welcome the Prophet to Medina. He figures in the narrative chain of many *ḥadīth*, and participated in nineteen of the military expeditions of the Prophet.

AL-JANWĪ, Abū ʻAbd Allāh Muḥammad ibn al-Ḥasan (1135-1200/1701-1785) p. 92. He was among the great scholars and ascetics of Tetouan in his time and the best-known of Ibn ʻAjība's teachers, with whom he studied *tafsīr*, *ḥadīth*, and several works of *taṣawwuf*, notably al-Qushayrī's *Risāla*.

KAʻB IBN ZUHAYR ibn Abī Salmā (d. 26/645) p. 116. He was a famous Jāhilī poet when Islam appeared who initially opposed the new religion but eventually embraced it after meeting the Prophet Muḥammad. His *Dīwān* is still read.

AL-KHALĪL ibn Aḥmad al-Farāhīdī al-Azdī (100-ca 170/718-ca 791) p. 34. He was born into a Bedouin tribe in Oman and at an early age went to Baṣra to study Islamic sciences, grammar, and poetry. He is the reputed author of *Kitāb al-ʻAyn*, the first dictionary of the Arabic language. In addition, he is considered the first to systematize Arabic poetic meter and was the principle teacher of the other great Baṣra grammarian, Sībawayh. His tomb is in that city.

AL-KUWĀSHĪ, Abū al-ʻAbbās al-Mawṣilī (d. 590-682/1193-1283) p. 70. *Mufassir*, born in Kawāsha, a citadel near Mosul in Northern Iraq. He is the author of two Quranic commentaries, *al-Ṣaghīr* and *al-Kabīr*, the latter also referred to as *al-Tabṣira*.

AL-LAJĀ'Ī, ʻAbd al-Raḥmān (*see* AL-BAJĀ'Ī)

AL-MAḤALLĪ, Jalāl al-Dīn al-Maḥallī (791-864/1389-1459) p. 52. *Mufassir* and one of the two authors of the widely read Quranic commentary known as *Tafsīr Jalālayn* ("The Commentary by the Two Named Jalāl"). Al-Maḥallī began his commentary starting with *Sūrat al-Kahf* (18) and reached the end of the Qur'ān before he died. The work was then completed by Jalāl al-Dīn al-Suyūṭī (849-911/1445-1505).

MĀLIK, ibn Anas al-Aṣbaḥī (d. 179/795) pp. 69, 70. The founder of one of the four main schools (*madhāhib*) of Islamic law in Sunni Islam. Born into a family of *ḥadīth* narrators, he studied the recitation of the Qur'ān with Nāfiʻ and heard *ḥadīth* from al-Ẓuhrī and Ibn al-Munkadir. He taught al-Shāfiʻī, al-Thawrī and Ibn al-Mubārak.

His book, *al-Muwaṭṭa'*, is the earliest surviving work of Muslim law, and places great emphasis on the actual practice of Islam in Medina in Imām Mālik's time.

MASRŪQ ibn al-Ajd'a (d. 63/683) pp. 48, 108. A *Tābi'ī* who figures as a transmitter of numerous *ḥadīth*, Masrūq was originally from Yemen but came to Medina in the days of the caliphate of Abū Bakr.

MUJĀHID, ibn Jabr al-Makkī (d. 104/722-3) pp. 8, 27. A *Tābi'ī* known chiefly as being one of the earliest commentators of the Qur'ān. It is said that he read his *tafsīr* to Ibn 'Abbās thirty times to verify its accuracy. The existing work attributed to him in *Kashf al-Ẓunūn*, however, is more likely a compilation of his exegesis made by others.

AL-MU'ĀFIRĪ (*see* QĀḌĪ ABU BAKR)

AL-MUQĀTIL ibn Sulaymān al-Azdī (d. 150/767/8) pp. 99, 105. A theologian and *mufassir* from Balkh who taught principally in Baghdad.

AL-NASAFĪ, 'Umar ibn Muḥammad ibn Aḥmad Abū Ḥafṣ al-Samarqandī al-Ḥanafī (461-537/1068-1142) pp. 2, 20, 35, 79, 87, 120. *Mufassir*. He was born in Nasaf (a town near Samarqand) and died in Samarqand. He is best-known for his Quranic commentary, *al-Tafsīr fī al-tafsīr*, but is said to have authored more than 100 other works on subjects ranging from Ḥanafī jurisprudence, *ḥadīth*, and poetry, to a biographical index of the scholars of Samarqand.

QĀḌĪ ABŪ BAKR, Muḥammad ibn 'Abd Allāh ibn al-'Arabī al-Mu'āfirī (468-543/1076-1148) p. 72. *Mufassir*, *muḥaddith*, and one of the greatest of the Malikī scholars of Andalusia. He was born in Seville and while still young traveled to the east with his father where he met and studied with the scholars of the day including al-Ghazālī, who was still teaching at the Madrasa Niẓamiyya in Baghdad. After his return to Seville, Ibn al-'Arabī (whose name can be distinguished from the famous Sufi, Ibn 'Arabī by the presence of the article *al-*) authored numerous works, among which is his *Aḥkām al-Qur'ān*, a compendium of rules governing belief and action arranged by order of the *sūras*, as well as commentaries on *al-Muwaṭṭa*, and on al-Tirmidhī's *Sunan*. He died near Fes returning from an extended stay in Marrakesh where he had gone with a delegation from Seville to pledge fealty to the Almohad leader Ibn Tumert.

QATĀDA ibn Di'āma (71-117/680-726) pp. 22, 49. A *Tābi'ī* who lived and died in Baṣra and was a companion of al-Ḥasan al-Baṣrī. About him, Imām Aḥmad ibn Ḥanbal said, "Qatāda is the greatest of the Baṣrī people in memorization." He was also an authority on *ḥadīth*, Arabic, and the histories and lineages of the Arabs.

AL-QAYRAWĀNĪ, Aḥmad ibn Ibrāhīm ibn Abī Khālid (d. 369/980) p. 113. Physician and historian, from the people of al-Qayrawān (Kairouan, in modern-day Tunisia). He authored numerous works in medicine, herbal cures, psychology, and even child rearing.

AL-QUSHAYRĪ, 'Abd al-Karīm ibn Hawāzin ibn 'Abd al-Mālik ibn Ṭalḥa, al-Nisapūrī (376-465/986-1072) pp. 12, 14, 16, 17, 23, 24, 26, 29, 30, 31, 34, 49, 63, 67, 73, 90, 91, 92, 97, 101, 106, 109, 111, 113, 116, 117, 118. Sufi, scholar, *mufassir*, known as the Master of Khurasān of his age. He lived his whole life in Nisapūr and died there. His best known works are his treatise on Ṣufism, *al-Risāla*, which has been published a number of times in Arabic, and his Quranic commentary, *Laṭā'if al-ishāra*, also published in more than one edition, from which Ibn 'Ajība quotes numerous times throughout this work, both in his commentary and spiritual allusions.

SA'D AL-DĪN, Mas'ūd ibn 'Amr ibn 'Abd Allāh al-Taftāzānī (712-793/1312-1390) p. 2. Theologian of the Maturīdī school. He was born in Taftāzān (in Khorasān), lived and taught for a time in Sarakhs (located in the northeast of present-day Iran), but was then exiled by Tamerlane to Samarqand where he died. His best-known work is a commentary on al-Nasafī's *'Aqa'ida*. He also wrote a commentary on the forty *ḥadīth* of Nawawī.

SAHL ibn 'Abd Allāh (see al-Tustarī)

AL-SAḤNŪN, 'Abd al-Salām ibn Sa'īd ibn Ḥabīb (160-240/777-854) p. 2. *Qāḍī* and *faqih*. He was born in al-Qayrawān (Kairouan, in modern-day Tunisia) and after completing his studies, was appointed *qāḍī* in 234, a post which he retained until his death. He is best known for his work on Mālikī fiqh, *al-Mudawwana*. He is buried in the city of his birth, Kairouan.

AL-ṢAQALLĪ, Aḥmad ibn Idrīs (d. 1171) p. 92. Sufi, and the representative (*muqaddam*) of Shaykh Abū al-Ḥasan al-Tādilī in Fes.

AL-SHĀDHILĪ, 'Alī ibn 'Abd Allāh Abu al-Ḥasan (591-656/1195-1258) p. 24. The founder of the Sufic order which bears his name. He was born in the Ghomāra region of Morocco near Chefchaouen and studied in Fes. After a discipleship with Mulay 'Abd al-Salām ibn Mashīsh atop Jebel 'Alam in the Rif Mountains of Morocco, he took his spiritual teachings first to Tunisia and then Egypt, where he spent the rest of his life. He died en route to one of the several pilgrimages he made during his life and was buried on the old pilgrims' route, near the Red Sea.

AL-SHĀFI'Ī, Muḥammad ibn Idrīs al-Qurashī (d. 204/820) p. 70. Founder of one of the four main schools (*madhāhib*) of Sunni jurisprudence. He was born in Gaza around the year 150 (ca. 767), the same year in which Imām Abū Ḥanīfa died. At the age of two, he was taken by his widowed mother to Mecca where he spent most of his younger years. It is said that he had memorized the Qur'ān by the age of seven and was proficient in the varieties of its recitation and its commentary by the age of thirteen. By around the age of twenty he was living in Medina where he had became the student of Malik ibn Anas, many of whose opinions in fiqh he would later adopt. Much of his life after this was spent in traveling—to Yemen, Egypt, Iraq, Syria, and Persia—ever in search of knowledge. He died in Cairo where his tomb is a highly venerated place of devotion.

AL-SUDDĪ, Ismā'īl ibn 'Abd al-Raḥmān (d 128/745) pp. 27, 30. *Tābi'ī*, *mufassir*, al-Suddī was originally from the Hijāz, but lived in Kūfa most of his life and was among the major transmitters of Quranic commentary from ibn Mas'ūd and Ibn 'Abbās. His grandson Muḥammad ibn Marwān is also known as a *mufassir*, but is considered less reliable. The two are sometimes distinguished as "*al-Suddī al-kabīr*" and "*al-ṣaghīr*."

AL-ṬARṬŪSHĪ, Muḥammad ibn al-Walīd al-Qurshī al-Fihrī, known as Abū Randaqa (421-520/1059-1126) p. 15. Mālikī scholar, historian, and ascetic. Born in the city of Tortosa, he is said to have traveled to the East in 476, accomplished the pilgrimage, visited Iraq, Egypt, Palestine, and Lebanon, and then lived for a time in Syria and Alexandria where he remained teaching until his death. His best-known work is probably *Sirāj al-Mulūk*, a historical compendium described as a collection on 'the lives of the Prophets, narratives of the saints, admonitions of the scholars, wisdom of the sages, and gems from the caliphs.' He was the author of a treatise opposing Imām al-Ghazālī's *Ihyā 'ulūm al-Dīn* and a treatise on goodness towards parents.

AL-TĀWUDĪ, Muḥammad ibn al-Ṭālib ibn 'Alī ibn Sūdah al-Fāsī (1111-1209/1700-1795) p. 19. He was a Mālikī scholar and teacher, one of the leading masters of Fes, who became widely known after his journey to Egypt and the Hijāz. Among his works are commentaries on Bukhārī, Muslim, and Abū Dāwūd, and a commentary on Nawawī's collection of forty *ḥadīth*. He also wrote two biographical collections, *al-Fahrasat al-ṣughrā*, on the lives of his own teachers, and *al-Fahrasat al-kubrā*, on students and others.

AL-ṬAYYIBĪ, al-Ḥusayn bin Muḥammad bin 'Abd Allāh Sharaf al-Dīn (d. 743/1342) pp. 62, 88. He was the author of a commentary on the *tafsīr al-Kashāf* by al-Zamakhsharī (d. 538/1144).

AL-THA'LABĪ, Abū Isḥāq (d. 427/1035) p. 52. *Mufassir*. He was one of the people of Nisapūr and the author of *al-Kashf wa al-bayān fī tafsīr al-Qur'ān*, one of Ibn 'Ajība's primary references, as well as al-*'Arā'is fī qiṣaṣ al-anbiyā'* on the lives of the prophets.

AL-TUSTARĪ, Sahl ibn 'Abd Allāh (200-283/815-896) pp. 68, 101. One of the early Sufis. He was born in Tustar, in Khorasān. For a time, he was one of al-Ḥallāj's teachers and this latter accompanied him to Baṣra where he spent most of his life. Al-Tustarī's doctrine, however, was probably better represented by his student Ibn Sālim (d. 909/296) founder of the Sālimiyya school to which Abū Ṭālib al-Mekkī, the author of *Qut al-Qulūb*, belonged. A mystical commentary on parts of the Qur'ān is attributed to al-Tustarī.

'UMAR IBN AL-KHAṬṬĀB (r. 13-23/634-44) pp. 34, 115, 123. The second of the Rightly Guided Caliphs. At first an enemy of the Prophet's mission, he became one of its staunchest defenders. His conversion is said to have taken place after his own sister had embraced the new religion. Rushing to her house to confront her, he found her with a scroll (*ṣaḥīfa*) on which was written a *sūra* of the Qur'ān which, according to some versions, was *Ṭā Hā*, and others *al-Ḥadīd*. After consenting to wash, 'Umar began to read the page. According to the version in Bayhaqī, *Dalā'il al-Nubūwa*, 'Umar said, "I opened the scroll, and there upon it was *In the Name of God, the All-Merciful, the Compassionate*. When I read these Names of God, I became so seized with awe that I cast the scroll away from me. When I regained my composure, I went back to reading and found the words, *All that is in the heaven and earth glorifies God* [57:1], and again, when I read the Name of God, I became overwhelmed with awe. I again regained composure and read on until I came to the words, *Believe in God and His Messenger* [57:7] and upon reading them, I said, 'I testify that there is no god but God and I testify that Muḥammad is God's servant and messenger.'" Following this, 'Umar went straight to the Prophet and declared his Islam.

As caliph he was universally respected for his integrity and uncompromising devotion to the faith.

UMAYYA IBN ABĪ AL-ṢALT (d. 05/626) p. 56. A well-known Jāhilī poet who wrote largely about subjects related to the Next World. He was born in Ṭā'if, spent part of his life in Damascus studying ancient books and returned to Ṭā'if upon hearing about the advent of Islam. It is said that he met the Prophet Muḥammad in Mecca but did not become a Muslim.

AL-'UTBĪ, Muḥammad ibn Aḥmad ibn 'Abd al-'Azīz ibn Abī 'Utba al-Qurṭubī (d. 254/869) p. 57. He was an Andalusian scholar and the author of *al-Mustakhraja al-'utbiyya 'alā al-Muwaṭṭa'* a work based on Mālik's *al-Muwaṭṭa'* but containing many reputedly obscure *ḥadīth* and points of fiqh.

'UTHMĀN IBN 'AFFĀN, ibn Abī al-'Abbās ibn Umayya (r. 23-35/644-56) p. 47, 79. The third of the Rightly Guided Caliphs. He had been a wealthy merchant who became a Muslim before the Emigration. He eventually became known as "Dhū al-Nūrayn"—"the man of the two lights"—because he married two of the prophet's daughters: first Ruqayya, and then, after her death, Umm Kulthūm. During the later years of his caliphate he was accused of nepotism, a charge which led to his murder by a group of dissidents from Egypt, who besieged his house, it is said, for forty-nine days, and then stormed it and stabbed him to death while he was reading the Qur'ān.

AL-WAGHLĪSĪ, Abū Zayd 'Abd al-Raḥmān (d. 786/1384) p. 8. One of the principle scholars of the Mālikī rite in North Africa and Andalusia. He died in 786 /1384 in Bejāya (in modern day Algeria)

AL-WARTAJĪBĪ (*see* AL-BAQLĪ)

AL-WĀSIṬĪ , Muḥammad ibn Mūsā (d. 331/942) p. 117. One of the greatest of the early Sufis, and foremost of the followers of Junayd. He was born in Farghāna (in present-day Uzbekistan) and journeyed to Khorasān where he spent the remainder of his life. Sha'arānī said of him, "No one has spoken as he has about the principles of Sufism." Among his sayings: "We are tried by living in an age in which there is neither the manners (*adab*) of Islam, nor the virtues of the Jāhiliyya, nor the dreams of the chivalrous," and "Beware of delighting in the gift (*al-'aṭā'*), for it is a veil for the people of purity (*al-ṣafā'*)."

ZARRŪQ, Aḥmad ibn Aḥmad ibn Muḥammad ibn 'Īsā al-Barnusī Abū al-'Abbās (846-899/1442-1493) p. 3. Scholar, *muḥaddith*, and Sufi, called *zarrūq* because of his blue eyes. A Berber born in Morocco, Zarrūq journeyed east as a young man, and after studying in Egypt and Medina, returned to Morocco to become one of the best-known shaykhs of the Shādhiliyya during the Merinid period. He was a prolific writer, leaving among other works, a commentary on the *Ḥikam* of Ibn 'Aṭā' Allāh, and a widely read treatise of the Principles of Sufism (*Qawā'id al-taṣawwuf*). Although he spend several years spreading the teachings of the Shādhiliyya in Fes, in 886/1481, he settled in Masurata, near present-day Tripoli, where he spent the remaining twelve years of his life and where he is buried.

AL-ZUJĀJ, Abū Isḥāq (241-311/855-923) p. 53. *Mufassir* and grammarian. He was born and died in Baghdād. His books *I'rāb al-Qur'ān*, in three volumes, and *Khalq al-insān* have been published.

Index of Quranic Verses Cited

Other than those of the three chapters commented upon

18:104 *Those whose effort goes astray in the life of the world, and yet they reckon that they do good work.* 26
20:5 *The Most Merciful assumed the Throne.* 11
20:102 *On that day, the Trumpet shall be blown and We shall gather the sinful together blue-eyed* . 43 n. 64
21:23 *He is not asked about what He does, but they are asked.* 118
23:99 *...And behind them is a barrier (*barzakh*) until the day when they are raised.* 84 n. 65
23:14 *Then We caused it to grow into another creation.* 65
25:56 *Then God assumed the Throne of the All-Merciful.* 11
25:60 *When it is said to them, 'Prostrate to the All-Merciful (*al-Raḥmān*),' they say, 'What is* al-Raḥmān*?'* 37 n. 1
26:90 *And the gardens shall be brought near to the righteous.* 24
28:52 *Twice shall they be given their reward, for that they have persevered.* 125
30:44 *And those who do right make comfort for themselves.* 77
36:11 [Adam was created] *from sticky clay.* 13
36:35 *They and their spouses shall be in shade, reclining upon couches.* 57
39:18 *And the Trumpet is blown, and all who are in the heavens and the earth swoon away, save him whom God wills. Then it is blown a second time, and behold them standing waiting!* 80 n. 3
39:20 *But those who keep their duty to their Lord, for them are made chambers above which are chambers, beneath which rivers flow...* 128 n. 20
39:22 *He is upon a light from his Lord.* 101
39:23 *God has revealed the fairest of discourse: a book (containing) that which is repeated and which has inner resemblance.* 4 n. 3
40:32 *Verily I fear for you the Day when there will be mutual calling, a Day when you will turn back.* 41 n. 54
41:30 *Verily, those who say, 'Our Lord is God' and then remain upright—to them do the angels descend.* 77
42:52 *You would not have know what the Book is nor faith.* 67
43:71 [In that Garden] *is all that souls desire and brings delight to the eyes.* 28
47:15 *Therein are rivers of water unpolluted, and rivers of milk whereof the flavor never changes...* 43 n. 71

Index of *Ḥadīth* Cited

Both in the text of the commentary and notes

...A people who will come after you. They will find a book between two covers. 54

Among [God's] tasks is to forgive sins, to dispel sorrows, to raise up one people and bring low another. 19

[Among those given a two-fold reward] is a man from the People of the Book who believed in his prophet and believed in me. 125

An angel comes into where the embryo has formed in the womb, 41 n. 50

An hour spent by a scholar reclining upon his pallet reflecting upon his knowledge is better than seventy years of physical acts of worship by a devotee. 46 n. 98

Be steady and abundant in (the supplication), 'O You Who are endowed with Majesty and Generosity (*yā Dha al-jalāli wa al-ikrām*). 16

Both are from my community. 52

[Charity] wards off seventy different kinds of harm and evil. 107

Do not wish for death, for verily the terror of the vantage point is mighty. 4 n. 8

Do you know what these two gardens are? They are two orchards within two orchards. 27

Do you know what your Lord says? He says, 'Is the reward for one whom I have graced with monotheism other than heaven?' 30

Every night, during the last third of the night, our Lord, be He blessed and exalted, descends to the heaven of this earth. 82 n. 45

Every verse has an outer aspect and an inner, a limit and a vantage point. 3

For anyone who says 'Glory be to God, Praise be to God, There is no god but God, and God is greater,' a thousand trees are planted in Heaven. 29

For everything there is a bride (*'arūs*), and the bride of the Qur'ān is *Sūrat al-Raḥman.* 37 n. 1

God be He Blessed says, 'Majesty is My cloak, Glory, My loincloth. One who would try to take either of them from Me, him I shall cast into hell.' 127 n. 9

God be He Blessed says, 'The Heavens and earth have not the strength to bear Me and are too narrow to contain me, but the

The parable [of you and] the people of the Book before [you] is that of a man who employed some laborers to work until the night for one qirāṭ each. 125
The pen has dried… 19
The servants of Heaven are the children of the unbelievers. 53
The substitutes [*al-budalā'*] are thirty men whose hearts are like the heart of [the Prophet] Abraham, upon whom be peace. 128 n. 19
The word "womb" is taken from God's Name *al-Raḥmān*. 37 n. 1
This fire of yours which men kindle contains but a seventieth of the heat of Hell. 65
Verily God apportioned His mercy into one hundred portions. 11
What ails you? If you do not take it, still it will come to you. 117
When the stars are mentioned, desist. 71
Why do I see you silent? Truly the Jinn are better than you in their response! 35
Your prayer has been answered. 16
Zamzam will never fail nor will its water grow scarce. 53

General Index

Including topics, images, proper names of people (apart from those mentioned in Biographical Index above), places, and books.

A, ‘A

Abraham, the Prophet, 120-123, 128 n. 19
Abū Dāwūd al-Iṣbahānī, 83 n. 51
Adam, the Prophet, 8, 13, 14, 49, 64, 119
‘adl. See justice
afflictions, 114, 117
afrād (solitary saints), 99
‘ālam al-ashbāḥ (world of forms), 102
al-Ān (a river in Hell), 43 n. 65
Amorite (language), 75
angels, 9, 16, 18, 19, 25, 45 n. 90; encircling of, on the Day of Judgment, 21; Noble Scribes, 83 n. 45
Angel of Death, 107
Arabs, 34, 65, 71, 108, 112
‘āfār and *markh* trees, 65
āthār (formal manifestation), 90
Attraction, Divine (*jadhb*), 67, 122

B

Balance, 9, 10, 12, 118, 119, 122. *See also* scale.
banana tree, 57
baqā (Everlastingness), 78. *See also* Subsistence, Station of
baraka (blessing), 35
barzakh, 74, 84 n. 65. *See also* isthmus
basṭ (expansive state), 23
bid‘a (innovation) , 123
blueness of eyes, 43 n. 64
Bride of the Qur’ān, 37 n. 1
Bridge, the (*al-Ṣiraṭ*), 98, 99, 127 n. 18
Budūr al-Sāfirah, al- (by Jalāl al-Dīn al-Suyūtī), 22
butter as a symbol of the Supreme Truth, 51

C

calendar, Roman and Gregorian, 40 n. 32
charity, 34, 94-97, 106, 107, 116
Christians, 121

K, L

karāmāt (miraculous deeds), 31
khush'u (humble submission), 104
Kitāb al-Ḥikam (by ibn 'Aṭā'illāh), 11, 42 n. 59, 43 n. 62, 67, 72, 90, 91, 117, 127 n. 7
knowledge, formal, 1, 17, 36, 37, 39 n. 23, 41 n. 45, 46 n. 96, 58, 72, 89, 96, 105
Kūfā, 53
Kuffār, 110, 129 n. 42
Lāhūwiyyah (the Divine Ipseity), 113
Laṭā'if al-minan (by ibn 'Aṭā'illāh), 2, 82 n. 33
al-Lawḥ al-maḥfūẓ. *See* Guarded Tablet
light crossing the Bridge, 99; in the grave, 77; of attraction, 122; of faith, 39 n. 24, 95; of gnosis, 51, 61; of God, 93, 101, 109, 128 n. 24; of Oneness, 12, 109, 129 n. 41; of the heart, 17; of the natural reason 12, 15.
Lote-Tree of the Furthest Boundary, 76. *See also* Heaven
lower self, the (*al-nafs*), 17, 23, 25, 51, 67, 97, 109, 113, 118, 130 n. 49; maladies of, 116

M

Medina, 103, 45 n. 89
ma'iyya. *See* "withness"
Malakūt (realm of angels and spirits), 17, 39 n. 26, 76
markh and *'afār* trees, 65, 82 n. 38
martyrs (*al-shuhadā'*), 75, 76, 77, 85 n. 66, 99, 106, 107, 108, 109
Mary, the mother of Jesus, 119, 121, 129 n. 34
Mecca, 37 n. 1, 40 n. 36, 60, 80 n. 11, 95, 96, 103
Mediterranean Sea, 15, 40 n. 35, 40 n. 36
meditation, 17, 24, 31, 36, 37, 76, 89, 96, 130 n. 49
Mercy (*al-raḥma*), Divine, Essential and Attributive, 11; entering Heaven by, 53, 112; in the hearts of Christians, 121; descent of, 68
mimosa. *See* lote-tree
monasticism, 119, 121, 123, 124, 131 n. 62
moon, size of, 8, 38 n. 7; light, 51, 72; of faith, 17; of Oneness, 11, 39 n. 24
Morocco, 15
Moses, the Prophet, 20, 24, 105, 107, 123
Mother of the Book, 20, 129 n. 33
Mount Uḥud, 96

Mursī, Abū al-'Abbās, 39 n. 27
Mu'tazilites, 39 n. 27
Muḥammad, the Prophet (by his proper name), 8, 52, 75, 78, 79, 83 n. 45, 95, 99, 124, 131 n. 64
mudhākarāt (spiritual discourse), 55
mujtahid (one able to interpret the Revealed Law), 12
murāqaba (vigilance or watching over the soul), 44 n. 79
muqallid (follower of tradition), 12
muqarrabūn. *See* Ones Brought Near
mushāhada (vision, perception, consciousness, meditative practices), 44 n. 79, 79, 130 n. 49
muṭṭala'u (vantage point), 3
al-Muwaṭṭa (by Imām Mālik), 70

N

nafs. *See* lower soul
Nawādir al-uṣūl (by Ḥākim al-Tirmidhī) 33, 44 n. 76, 52, 77
Nazarenes. *See* Christians
Night of Ascension, 49, 85 n. 67
Night of Power, 83 n. 45
Noah, the Prophet, 119, 120, 122, 123

O

oath, 33
Ocean of esoteric truths, 17; of the Divine Essence, 89, 92; of the *Jabarūt*, 12; of Unicity, 31
oceans of sins, 114
oil, 22, 24, 84 n. 54
Ones Brought Near (*al-muqarrabūn*), 33, 35, 37, 47, 50, 51, 54, 55, 73-76, 78, 80 n. 12. *See also* "the Foremost"

P

Parakletos (=the Comforter), 131 n. 64
patience, 115
pearl(s), 13, 15, 17, 29, 40 n. 39, 53, 55
Persian Sea, 15
Place of Gathering, 21, 22, 60
Place of Standing, 22, 100
pomegranate, 32, 33, 36, 45 n. 88
poverty, protection from, 47
prayer, canonic (*al-ṣalāt*), 50, 123
pride, 87, 114, 115, 116, 118

Q

qabḍ. *See* contraction
qalb. *See* heart
Qānūn fī al-ṭibb (by Ibn Sīna), 82 n. 35
Qur'ān, blessing of, 7, 11, 71; is remembrance, 104; noble and generous, 69; portions of, 83 n. 45; teaching, 5, 6, 9; touching, 69, 70, 72, 83 n. 48
qaswah. *See* heart, hardness of
qudra. *See* Wisdom and Power
Qūt al-qulūb (by Abū Ṭālib al-Mekkī), 79
Quṭb al-'Ārifīn (by 'Abd al-Raḥmān al-Lajā'ī), 113

R

race, striving as if in, 50, 80 n. 10, 112, 113
raḥa (rest and serenity), 74
al-Raḥīm (God's Name), 10
al-Raḥmān (God's Name) 7, 8 10, 11, 37 n. 1
al-Raḥmāniya (All-Mercifulness), 11
rain, as a sign, 64; likened to the remembrance of God, 105
rawḥ (rest), 74
rayḥān (sweet-smelling herb, nourishment), 13, 38 n. 13, 75, 77
Reckoning. *See* Day of Judgment
Red Sea of the Essence, 17
remembrance of God. *See* God, remembrance
reproduction, human, 62, 63, 82 n. 35
Revealed Law (*al-sharī'a*), 9, 17, 31, 43 n. 63, 55, 113, 117, 118, 119
Rīf Mountains, 15
Rigor, divine, 11, 17, 90, 103

S, Ṣ

Sabbath, 19
Sābiqūn. *See* Foremost
saintly (*ṣiddiqūn*), 76, 107, 108, 109, 117
Ṣalāt. See prayer, canonic
scale, 9, 119, 120. *See also* balance
seas, the two, 13, 15, 17
Sebta, 15
self-direction and choice (*al-tadbīr wa'l-iktiyār*), 23, 26, 61, 82 n. 33
seven, *ḥadīth* of the, 22, 42 n. 56
Shām (Syria) 46 n. 94, 128 n. 19
sharī'a. See Revealed Law

Bibliography

Works in Arabic

'Abd al-Bāqī, Muḥammad Fu'ad. *Al-Mu'jamu al-mufahrasu li alfāẓi al-Qur'ān al-Karīm*. Dār al-Ḥadith, Cairo, 1994

Adnarwī, Aḥmad al-. *Ṭabaqāt al-Mufassirīn*. Maktabat al-'Ulūm wa'l-Ḥikam, Madina, 1997

Bayhaqī, Imām Abū Bakr Aḥmad ibn al-Ḥusayn, al-. *Dalā'il al-Nubūwa*. Dār al-Kutub al-'Ilmiyyah, Beirut, 1405/1984.

———. *Shu'ab al-īmān*. Dār al-Kutub al-'Ilmiyyah, Beirut, 1410/1990.

Darqāwī, Mulay al- 'Arabī, al-. *Majmū'a rasā'il*. Ed. Muḥammad Bassām Bārūd, Cultural Foundation Publications, Abu Dhabi, 1999.

Daylamī, Abū Shujā' Shīrawayh bin Shīrawayh, al-. *Al-Firdaws bi athūr al-khiṭāb* Dār al-Kutub al-'Ilmiyyah, Beirut, 1986.

Dhahabī, Abū 'Abd Allāh Shams al-Dīn al-. *Tadhkira al-ḥuffāẓ*. Dār al Kutub al-'Ilmiyya, Beirut, 1419/1998.

Ghazālī, Abū Hamīd Muḥammad ibn Muḥammad, al- . *Iḥyā' 'ulūm al-dīn*. Dar al-Fikr, Beirut, 1414/1994.

Ibn 'Abbād, Abū 'Abd Allāh Maḥammad ibn Ibrāhīm. *Gayth al-mawāhib al-'aliyya fī sharḥ al-ḥikam al-'aṭā'iyya*. Ed. 'Abd al-Ḥalīm Maḥmūd, Cairo, 1970.

———. *Rasā'il al-Kubrā*. Ed. Kenneth Honerkamp. Dar el-Machreq, Beyrouth. 2005.

Ibn Abī Usaybia'. *'Uyūn al-anbiyā' fī ṭabaqāt al-ṭubbā'*. Dār al-Kutub al-'Ilmiyya, Beirut, 1419/1998

Ibn 'Ajība, Aḥmad. *Al-Baḥr al-Madīd fī tafsīr al-Qur'ān al-Majīd*. Cairo, 1999-2001

———. *Kitāb sharḥ ṣalāt al-quṭb ibn Mashīsh*. Ed. 'Abd al-Salām al-'Umrānī, Dar al-Rashād, Casablanca, 1999.

———. *Mi'rāj al-tashawwuf ilā haqā'iq al-taṣawwūf*. Muṭab'a al-Marīnī, Tetouan, 1982.

Ibn 'Aṭā Allāh, Abū al-Faḍl Aḥmad ibn Muḥammad. *Kitāb al-ḥikam*, (lithograph), Morocco, undated.

———. *Laṭā'if al-minan*. Dār al-Ma'ārif, Cairo, 1992.

———. *Al-Tanwīr fī isqāt al-tadbīr*. 'Alam al-Fikr, Cairo, 1998.

Ibn 'Aṭiyya, Abū Muḥammad 'Abd al-Ḥaqq ibn Ghālib. *Al-Muḥarrar al-wajīz fī tafsīr al-kitāb al-'azīz*. Fes. 1977-1989

Ibn al-Athīr, Muḥyī al-Dīn Abū al-Sa'ādāt al-Mubārak ibn Muḥammad al-Jazrī. *Al-Nihāya fī gharīb al-ḥadīth wa'l-athar*. Dār al-Fikr, Beirut, 1997.

Ibn Hishām, 'Abd al-Mālik. *Al-sīra al-nabawiyya*. Dār al-Kutub al-'Ilmiyyah, Beirut.

Ibn 'Iyyād. *Kitāb al-mafākhir al- 'aliyya*. Cairo 1355/1937.

Ibn Kathīr, 'Imād al-Dīn Abū'l-Fidā'i Ismā'īl. *Ṣifat al-Jannat*. Ed. Ayman ibn 'Arif al-Dimashqī, Mu'assasat al-Kutub al-Thaqāfa Beirut, 1414/1993.

———. *Tafsīr al-Qur'ān*. Ed. Ḥusayn ibn Ibrāhīm Zahrān, Dār al-Fikr, Beirut, 1408/1988.

Ibn Khallikān, Shams al-Dīn Abū'l-'Abbās al-Barmakī. *Wafāyāt al-a'yān fī abnā'i abnā'i al-zamān*. Dar al-Thaqāfa, Oman, 1968.

Ibn Qayyim al-Jawziyya, Muḥammad ibn Abī Bakr. *Miftaḥ dār al-sa'āda*. Ed. Ḥassān Abd al-Mannān al-Tībī & 'Aṣam Fāris al-Hurstānī, Dār al-Jīl, Beirut, 1414/1994.

———. *Zād al-Ma'ād fī hadyī khayri al-'ibād*. Ed. Shu'ayb and 'Abd al-Qādir al-Arna'ūt. Kuwait: Maktabah al-Manār al-Islāmiyah, 1412/1992.

Ibn Qunfudh, Abū al-'Abbās Aḥmad ibn al-Ḥusayn al-Qasanṭīnī. *Uns al-faqir wa 'izz al-ḥaqīr fī ta'rīf bi al-shaykh Abī Madyan al-Ghawth wa aṣ'ḥābihi*. Dar al-Muqṭim, 2002.

Ibn al-Ṣabbāgh, Muḥammad ibn al-Qāsim al-Ḥimyarī . *Durrat al-asrār wa tuḥfat al-abrār*. Tunis, 1304/1886-7.

Iṣfahānī, Abū Nu'aym, al-. *Ḥilyat al-awliyā' wa ṭabaqāt al-aṣfiyā'*. Dār al-Kutub al-'Ilmiyya, Beirut, 1997.

Kittānī, Muḥammad ibn Ja'far al-. *Salwat al-anfās wa muḥādithat al-akyās*. Dār al-Thaqāfa, Casablanca, 2004.

Makhlūf, Muḥammad ibn Muḥammad. *Shajarat al-nūr al-zakiyya fī abaqāt al-Mālikiyya*, Dār al-Fikr, Beirut.

Makkī, Abū Ṭālib, *Qūt al-qulūb*, Dār al-Ṣādar, Beirut, 1307.

Mundhirī, al-Ḥāfiẓ Zakiyya al-Dīn 'Abd al-'Aẓīm, al-. *al-Targhīb wa'l-tarhīb min al-ḥadīth al-sharīf.* Dār al-Fikr, Beirut, 1993.

Nawawī, Muḥyi al-Dīn Abū Zakariyya ibn Sharaf, al-. *Al-Adhkār*. Al-Maktabat al-Thaqāfiyah, Beirut, undated.

Ṣāwī, Aḥmad al-. *Ḥāshiya 'alā tafsīr Jalālayn*. Dār al-Kutub al-'Ilmiyya, Beirut, 2006.

Shawkānī, Aḥmad, al-. *Tuḥfat al-dhākirīn*. Dār al-Kutub al-'Ilmiyya.

Beirut.

Ṣuyūṭī, Jalāl al-Dīn, al-. *al-Itqān fī 'ulūm al-Qur'ān*. Al-Maktaba al-tawfiqiyya, Cairo.

Ṣuyūṭī, Jalāl al-Dīn, al-. *Ṭabaqāt al-mufassirīn.* Maktaba wahba, Cairo, 1396.

Ṭabarānī, Sulaymān ibn Aḥmad ibn Ayyūb ibn Mutayr al-Lahkmī al-. *al-Mu'jam al-awsāṭ*. Maktaba al-Ma'ārif, Riyāḍ, 1985.

Ḥākim al-Tirmidhī, al-. *Nawādir al-uṣūl fī aḥādīth al-Rasūl*. Ed. 'Abd al-Raḥmān 'Umayr, Dār al-Jīl, Beirut, 1412/1992.

Ziriklī, Khayr al-Dīn, al-. *al-A'lām*, 11th edition. Dar al-'Ilm li'l-Malāyin, Beirut, 1995.

Works in English and French

Abūl Quasem, Muhammad (see *Ghazali* below).

'Alawī, Mustapha. *Sagesse céleste* (trans. of *al-Mawādd al-ghaythiyya an-nāshi'a 'an al-ḥikam al-ghawthiyya* by Chabry, M., La Caravane, Paris, 2007.

Darqāwī, Mulay al-'Arabī. *Lettres sur la Voie spirituelle (du) Shaykh al-'Arabī, al-Darqāwī*. Trans. Chabry, M. Librarie al-Ghazali, Paris, 2003.

Ghazālī, Abū Hamīd Muḥammad ibn Muḥammad, al-. *The Book of Remembrance of Death and the Afterlife*. Trans. T.J. Winter, Islamic Texts Society, London, 1989.

———. *The Recitation and Interpretation of the Qur'an*. (Book 8 of *Iḥyā 'ulūm al-dīn*). Trans. Abūl Quasem, Muhammad. University of Malaysia Press, Kuala Lumpur, 1972.

Haddad, Imam 'Abdallah Ibn 'Alawi al-. *Gifts for the Seeker*. Trans. Mostafa al-Badawi. Fons Vitae, Louisville, 2003.

Heer, Nicolas & Honerkamp, Kenneth (translators). *Three Early Sufi Texts*. Fons Vitae, Louisville, 2003.

Ibn 'Ajība, Aḥmad . *(Fahrasa) The Autobiography of a Moroccan Soufi*. Trans. from the Arabic by Jean-Louis Michon and from the French by David Steight. Fons Vitae, Louisville, 1999.

Ibn 'Aṭā Allāh, Abū al-Faḍl Aḥmad ibn Muḥammad. *The Book of Wisdom*. Trans. Victor Danner. Classics of Western Spirituality, New York, 1978.

———. *Laṭā'if al-minan*. Trans. Nancy Roberts. Fons Vitae, Louisville, 2005.

Ibn Qayyim al-Jawziyya, Muḥammad ibn Abī Bakr. *Medicine of the Prophet*. Trans. Penelope Johnstone. Islamic Texts Society, London, 1998.

Jackson, James Grey. *An Account of the Empire of Marocco*. London, 1811.

Nwyia, Paul. *Ibn 'Aṭā Allāh et la naissance de la confrérie sāḍilite*. Dar al-Machreq, Beirut, 1990.

Penelope Johnstone (see above *Ibn Qayyim al-Jawziyya*)

Lings, Martin. *Muhammad—his life based on the earliest sources*. Islamic Texts Society, London, 1983.

Lings, Martin & Safadi, Yasin Hamid. *The Qur'ān*. World of Islam Publishing Company, London, 1976.

Pickthall, Marmaduke (translator). *The Meaning of the Glorious Koran*. Allen & Unwin, London, 1976.

Roberts, Nancy (see above *Ibn 'Aṭā Allāh*)

Shimmel, Annemarie. *Mystical Dimensions of Islam*. University of North Carolina Press, North Carolina, 1975.

Winter, T.J. (see above *Ghazālī*).

Software and On-Line Resources.

Al-Muhaddith v. 11.20. Dar al-Hadith. Washington D.C.

Al-Maktabat al-Shāmila v. 2. distributed through http://wwww.waqfeya.net/shamela

Ibn Sina, Abū 'Alī al-Shaykh al-Ra'īs. *Kitāb al-Qānūn fī al-ṭibb* Rome, 1593, on line at http://ddc.aub edu.lb/projects/saab/avicenna/

Solstice Calculator, on line at http://stellafane.org/misc/equinox.html

The Hijacked Caravan, on line at http://www.ihsanic-intelligence.com/